BLOODY LIES

3-25-2015

To Judy!

Thanks for

reading!

Enjoy Bloody

Lies!

John M Ferak

BLOODY LIES

A CSI Scandal in the Heartland

JOHN FERAK
FOREWORD BY MAURICE POSSLEY

Black Squirrel Books™ 🐿️™

an imprint of The Kent State University Press

Kent, Ohio 44242   www.KentStateUniversityPress.com

BLACK SQUIRREL BOOKS™ 🐿™
Frisky, industrious black squirrels are a familiar sight on the
Kent State University campus and the inspiration for Black
Squirrel Books™, a trade imprint of The Kent State University Press
www.KentStateUniversityPress.com

Every effort has been made to obtain permission from persons interviewed
by the author who are quoted in this book.

Library of Congress Cataloging-in-Publication Data
Ferak, John, 1973–
Bloody lies : a CSI scandal in the heartland / John Ferak.
pages cm
Includes bibliographical references and index.
ISBN 978-1-60635-197-0 (pbk.) ∞
1. Murder—Nebraska—Case studies. 2. Criminal investigation—Nebraska—Case
studies. 3. Evidence fabrication—Nebraska—Case studies. 4. Judicial error—
Nebraska—Case studies. I. Title.
HV6533.N2F47 2014
364.152'3092—dc23
2013043208

18 17 16 15 14   5 4 3 2 1

To my wife, Andrea

CONTENTS

Foreword *by Maurice Possley* ix

Acknowledgments xiii

1 Easter Massacres 1

2 Legend 12

3 Suspect 14

4 Mystery Car 27

5 No Luck 35

6 Case Solved 44

7 Blood 55

8 Odd Find 62

9 Ring of Truth 66

10 Leopold and Loeb 72

11 Wisconsin 80

12 Diary 89

13 Conspiracy 98

14 Ransom Theory 107

15 Tipster 116

16 Freedom 124

17 Judgment 132

18 Finder 139

19 Deep Throat 147

20 Smell Test 153

21 Tarnished 159

22 Blunder 164

23 Underdog 170

24 Evidence 178

25 Phantom 185

26 Verdict 192

27 The Cop 203

Epilogue 214

Notes 222

Index 235

FOREWORD

Maurice Possley

For most citizens, it is counterintuitive, at the very least, that an innocent person who is not insane or subjected to torture or physical abuse would falsely confess to a crime. That is one of the reasons the issue of false confessions remains a vastly misunderstood or unappreciated issue in the American system of criminal justice.

As an investigative journalist at the *Chicago Tribune,* I, along with two other reporters, focused on this issue in a series of articles about false and coerced confessions in Cook County. One of the articles detailed the case of Daniel Taylor, who was arrested at age seventeen for a double murder. After hours of interrogation by Chicago police detectives, Taylor gave a confession that was transcribed by a court reporter. Only then did Taylor realize that he had been in jail at the time of the crime.

Did that prompt police to question whether the confession was false? It did not. Instead, the detectives set about undermining the jail records and producing false reports to buttress the confession. In 1995, Daniel was convicted by a jury that ultimately could not accept that he had confessed to a crime he did not commit.

The *Chicago Tribune* investigated the case in 2001 and found new evidence of his innocence, including a man who was in jail with him at the time of the crime. But prosecutors refused to acknowledge that Taylor's confession was false. It was not until the summer of 2013 that the state finally conceded Taylor was innocent and dismissed the case—more than twenty years after his arrest.

Sadly, Taylor's case is not an anomaly. As senior researcher at the National Registry of Exonerations, a joint project of Michigan Law School and Northwestern University's Center on Wrongful Convictions, I have become acutely aware of just how prolific the problem actually is. As of September 2013, the Registry listed more than 1,220 wrongful convictions in the United States since 1989. A total of 152 of these were the result of false confessions, and three out of every four involved homicides.

That is only part of the picture, however. Another eighty-seven exonerated defendants who did not falsely confess were implicated by false confessions from actual or potential codefendants. This adds up to a grim total of 239 innocent defendants convicted by false confessions—cases that account for about 20 percent of all known exonerations.

There are three basic types of false confessions that researchers identify: voluntary, internalized, and compliant.

A voluntary confession usually is given by someone who is mentally ill (for example, John Karr in the JonBenét Ramsey murder case), who is seeking publicity, or who is trying to cover up for the true guilty party. For example, in 1990 in Idaho, Laverne Pavlinac read about a murder and decided to implicate her boyfriend as a way of ending their relationship. She would end up implicating herself as well, and both she and her boyfriend were convicted of murder. Four years later, they were exonerated when the real killer confessed to the crime.

Secondarily, there are confessions made when individuals come to actually believe that they committed the crime; these are also known as internalized confessions. In 1998, after hours of intense questioning by police, fourteen-year-old Michael Crowe confessed to stabbing his twelve-year-old sister to death. The interrogation, which was recorded, shows a distraught Crowe at the soul-crushing moment when he came to believe that he actually killed his own sister but didn't remember doing so.

These are not the norm, however, in the realm of false confessions. The most common form of false confession occurs when a suspect, despite the knowledge that he or she is innocent, breaks down and tells the interrogators what the suspect believes they want to hear simply because he or she wants to end the interrogation. This may occur in as little as a few hours or after as long as two or three days of interrogation.

Suspects sometimes say they were physically abused, but typically the pressure is exerted psychologically through threats, cajoling, and promises. Calvin Ollins, a fourteen-year-old with an IQ of 70, confessed to taking part in an abduction, rape, and murder of a medical student in Chicago in 1986 because "The police told me that I was helping them solve the case and that if I signed the confession, they would let me go." Of course, the police didn't let Calvin go and instead used his conviction to send him to prison for life without parole before he was exonerated by DNA testing fifteen years later.

The power of a confession in the criminal justice system cannot be underestimated. Such is their sway on juries that confessions become the bedrock of convictions despite evidence that points to other suspects or that should eliminate the defendants who have falsely confessed. And once a defendant is convicted, legal opportunities to overturn the convictions are lessened significantly.

John Ferak's *Bloody Lies* provides an intimate look into the dark abyss of the criminal justice system where false confessions are spawned. Drawing upon extensive access to court records and numerous interviews, Ferak takes readers into a world that while seemingly counterintuitive, is nonetheless very real and pockmarked by corrupt and misguided police officers.

I first became acquainted with John when he was a reporter for the *Omaha World-Herald* and was covering the investigation of the 2006 murders of Wayne and Sharmon Stock of Murdock, Nebraska, and how their nephew, Matthew, confessed to their murders. His reporting exposed serious flaws and injustice in the case.

John's book presents readers with an in-depth look into an egregious—though, sadly, not atypical—example of how detectives put on blinders and wrestle a confession from a suspect they believe is guilty. One investigator put it this way to Matt Livers, a special education student: "I will go after the death penalty. I'll push and I'll push and I'll push and I will do everything I have to, to make sure you go down hard for this."

For readers intrigued by the workings of the criminal justice system as well as for those unfamiliar with it, *Bloody Lies* will take you on a journey that will provide new insights into the most disturbing problem of false confessions.

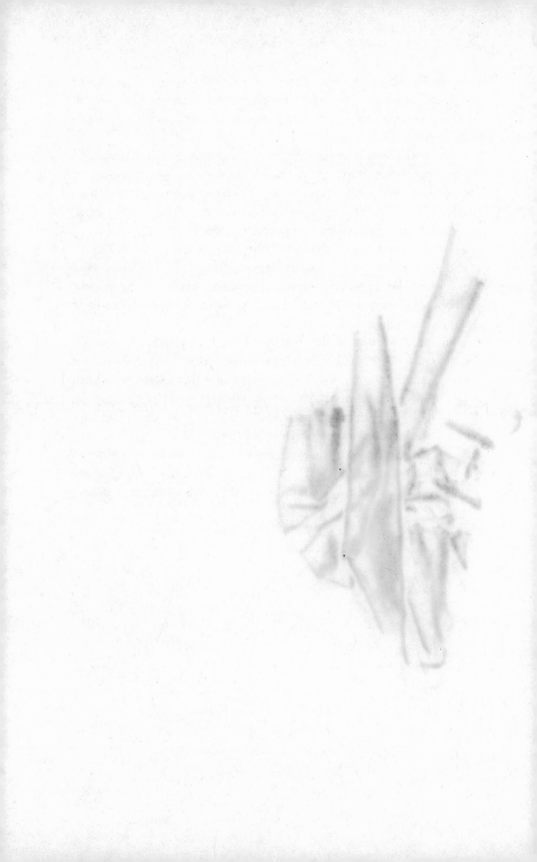

ACKNOWLEDGMENTS

It took more than three years to research, write, revise, and assemble the sad but very important story that became *Bloody Lies: A CSI Scandal in the Heartland.*

Various entities and several individuals deserve to be singled out for helping to make this book possible:

The *Omaha World-Herald* for the opportunity to report on the 2006 tragedies in Murdock and also allowing me considerable time to further investigate the many twists and turns in this remarkable case. All told, I produced more than one hundred noteworthy stories about the case from 2006 to 2012.

Bill Pfeffer, Omaha criminal defense attorney, for hounding me several years ago to write a book about the Murdock case.

Those who served as a tremendous resource over these past several years and greatly assisted in my investigative research efforts to accurately compile this book:

Jerry Soucie, Nebraska criminal defense attorney.

Steven A. Drizin, clinical professor of law at Northwestern University School of Law, associate director of Bluhm Legal Clinic, and director of the Center on Wrongful Convictions at Northwestern School of Law.

Locke E. Bowman, clinical professor of law at Northwestern University and director of the Roderick MacArthur Justice Center in Chicago.

Maren Chaloupka, the plaintiff's trial lawyer, in Scottsbluff, Nebraska.

Dr. Scott A. Bresler, assistant professor of clinical psychiatry at the University of Cincinnati, clinical director of the Risk Management Center in the Division of Forensic Psychiatry, and director of Inpatient Psychology at University Hospital.

Maurice Possley, Pulitzer Prize–winning journalist and author of *The Brown's Chicken Massacre,* for writing an excellent Foreword that gives true-crime readers more enlightenment and a deeper understanding regarding the police's role in causing false confessions.

Clarence Mock, Nebraska trial lawyer, for graciously providing access to volumes of court documents, transcripts, photos, and exhibits that were an essential part of the 2010 criminal prosecution of Dave Kofoed. Several photographs in this book that are credited as part of the author's collection were provided courtesy of Mock. Most of these photographs were taken by the Douglas County Sheriff's Office CSI unit and the Nebraska State Patrol.

Kent Sievers, Nebraska photojournalist, for his fantastic photo, which was used on the book cover.

Authors Mike Dauplaise, Jeffrey Koterba, Robert Kurson, Bill Lueders, Jim O'Shea, and Robert Sberna for their valuable insight and advice at various stages of this book-writing and publishing journey.

Bill Osinski, author of *Guilty by Popular Demand.* I can't thank him enough for his guidance and wisdom as I made last-minute revisions to my final manuscript and his positive recommendations of publishing with The Kent State University Press.

For making this book possible: The Kent State University Press: Acquisitions Editor Joyce Harrison, Director Will Underwood, Managing Editor Mary D. Young, Design and Production Manager Christine Brooks, Marketing Manager Susan Cash, Jason Gosnell, and the rest of their fine staff.

Sharon Cekada, Wisconsin photojournalist.

Valerie Ahwee for proofreading and editing this book.

The Eastern Illinois University Journalism Department and its student-run daily newspaper, the *Daily Eastern News,* where I first learned the motto, "Tell the truth and don't be afraid."

Graphic crime scene photographs

that appear on pages 5, 7, and 8

may be disturbing to some readers.

1

EASTER MASSACRES

It was Easter Sunday night, April 16, 2006, in a remote section of Cass County, Nebraska.

A visitor strolled up to Wayne and Sharmon Stock's impressive, tan, two-story farmhouse on a desolate stretch of gravel road. It was none other than Charlie, the friendly mixed-breed dog belonging to the Stocks' son Andy and his fiancée, Cassondra Alexander. The Stocks were only too happy to feed Charlie.

About 9:30 P.M., Wayne called his son about the wandering pet. Andy and Cassondra arrived around 10 P.M. to retrieve Charlie. The two young adults stayed for about fifteen minutes, sharing small talk about their trip earlier that day to visit Cassondra's parents and grandparents. The Stocks lived about two miles from the nearest town, Murdock, population 269. It's a vibrant little farming community nestled along Nebraska's two-lane Highway 1, sandwiched between Omaha and Lincoln. The Stocks' large extended family stretched out across a remote corner of southeastern Nebraska, a region dominated by cornstalks, combines, and cattle. Rolling hills, rich black soil, and soybean fields surrounded the Stock farm. Together, Andy and his father ran the Stock Hay Company. Wayne, age fifty-eight, ran his lucrative agriculture business from his farmhouse. He stored his company's financial records and sales receipts in his upstairs office.

That Easter Sunday night, Andy and Cassondra said goodbye to Wayne and Sharmon and headed home with their dog in tow. Andy lived right around the bend from them. Upon returning, Cassondra soon went to bed. Andy took a shower and then joined her ten minutes later. Charlie slept inside the couple's house, as always.

. . .

Sometime after 10:30 P.M., Wayne and Sharmon locked their doors and turned off their house lights. They put on their pajamas and prepared for a good night's rest after a very full day. Their Easter Sunday had begun with a morning worship service at the Ebenezer United Methodist Church in Murdock.[1] Then they had enjoyed an afternoon brunch with Wayne's elderly mother at her house, about a half-mile from the Stocks' farm. More than a dozen relatives attended the brunch, and the family gathering broke up at about 5 P.M. Back at their farm, Wayne and Sharmon hosted an Easter egg hunt around suppertime for their grandkids. Finding the colorful eggs had left the youngsters wide-eyed and beaming. Family meant so much to the Stocks. Their two oldest children, daughter Tammy and son Steve, both lived in the Lincoln area. Andy Stock, the youngest of the three siblings, was the only child to remain steadfast to his parents' farming operation. As Wayne and Andy farmed the land, Sharmon operated a popular cake-decorating business out of the farmhouse. The Stocks considered themselves truly blessed in so many ways.

Likewise, everyone in this part of rural Nebraska regarded the Stocks as pillars of their community—salt-of-the-earth types. The Stock name stood for honesty, integrity, and loyalty. Wayne and Sharmon had a strong commitment to family and a deep devotion to their Christian faith. Few people knew, however, that Wayne and Sharmon were millionaires. They never flaunted their wealth or discussed their personal financial affairs, even within the family.[2]

And so Wayne and Sharmon Stock's hectic and fulfilling Easter drew to a close. Their window shades were drawn. They closed their bedroom door, as always. The two empty-nesters rolled into bed together, barefoot and clad in their pajamas.

When they closed their eyes and pleasantly drifted off to sleep, they had no idea they had only hours left to live.

. . .

Sometime around midnight, a vehicle cruised along Nebraska Highway 1 and the two occupants inside scouted the country for houses off in the distance. Several houses dotting the rural landscape caught their eye, but these sites were bypassed for many reasons. Some of the properties had barking dogs roaming the front yard. Others had multiple cars in the driveway or illuminating house lights. All of these places appeared too risky to approach. Eventually, the two occupants passed along a county spur with a giant grain elevator towering over the landscape. Soon after passing this town, the two occupants veered off the two-lane asphalt road and turned onto a gravel road. Their vehicle rolled along 286th Street, kicking up gravel dust as its headlights illuminated the hilly terrain. The driver and passenger peered out into the night at the endless miles of farmland. Hardly anyone else was on the road at this late hour. Soon the pair of motorists headed in the direction of a solitary and darkened residence. This place with its tan-colored siding didn't have the tired, worn-out look like so many other farmhouses battered by years of neglect. In fact, this dwelling was quaint, cozy, and modern. An open porch with white trim wrapped around the front of the house. A two-story red-brick chimney was flanked by two upstairs windows. A boulder rested in the front yard next to the mailbox. The property had a towering cluster of pine trees, an antique windmill, and metal outbuildings. Because there were no vehicles in the driveway, the travelers were not entirely sure anyone was even home. The driver slowed and gracefully eased into a circular gravel driveway. The driver parked toward the back and turned off the lights.

The driver hurried to retrieve several ammunition rounds stored inside the vehicle. The passenger then loaded the red shells into the first of two shotguns. He turned off the safety, and carefully handed the loaded weapon back to his partner. He then repeated the process for his own weapon. A few minutes later, two shadowy figures emerged, careful not to make a sound. One person motioned for the other to follow. They crept toward the dark house, each brandishing a loaded shotgun. Upon approaching the house, the pair tried to gain access through a sliding door. They also tried the back door. But both doors were locked. Frustrated, they strode through the grass and meandered into the backyard. This time, they targeted a first-floor window near the large wooden deck. The two gently set down their shotguns. They reached into their pockets and put on some cloth garden gloves so they would not leave behind any fingerprints. The trespassers cut a hole through a window screen. They pried it off quickly and propped it up against the house. Slowly, the window was lifted open. One person hoisted the other through the opening. The intruder who emerged inside the laundry room then unlocked a back door to let the second person inside.

The interlopers tiptoed into the darkened kitchen of the tidy home. While in the downstairs kitchen, they heard loud snoring coming from an upstairs hallway. They also noticed an orange glow coming from the second-floor stairwell. Curious, they checked it out. Brandishing their loaded shotguns, they passed the darkened living room and reached the bottom of the split-level staircase with wood railings. They crept up the lime-green shag-carpeted stairs and stared down the carpeted hallway. The first door on their left was closed. A couple of other rooms and a bathroom lay ahead. The snoring was louder here.[3]

.   .   .

The two intruders whispered and plotted strategy. Then they went down the hallway and entered the bathroom, which had an illuminating night-light and doors leading to other rooms. As one person stood behind in the bathroom, the other poked his head into the next room and flipped on a light switch. But this wasn't another empty room. It was the Stocks' bedroom. The bright light appeared to stir the gray-haired man in pajamas. He began to wake up.

"What do I do?" shouted one intruder, panicking. "Do something!" yelled the other.

And so he did.

"Die motherfucker!" the shooter screamed.

A loud bang from the .12-gauge shotgun rang out. The deafening first shot missed the sleeping couple, but startled them awake. The Stocks were trapped, the sanctity of their master bedroom violated. Wayne Stock owned an assortment of hunting rifles and shotguns, but his weapons cache was locked away in his gun cabinet in his office across the hall. As Wayne tried to escape the bedroom, one of the armed intruders fired a second shotgun blast, striking his left knee and shattering his leg. The gray-haired farmer fell to the floor, entangled in the blankets and sheets from his bed. Wayne lunged at one of the invaders, and they struggled over the shotgun at the foot of the entrance into the master bedroom.

"Do something!" Wayne's attacker pleaded to his accomplice.[4]

The second invader aimed at Wayne's head and released the trigger. Wayne Stock collapsed, his lifeless body dropping to the floor. Sharmon screamed in horror. Now it was her turn to be slaughtered. She found herself pinned against the north wall on her side of the bed. Before she could place a distress call from the telephone at her bedside, one of the shooters briskly moved into the bedroom and leveled the shotgun up against her face. A deer slug blew out both of her eyeballs. Part of her jawbone and a row of teeth landed near the foot of her bed. Sharmon Stock tumbled to the floor with the telephone cord tangled about her body. Blood flowed from the large gaping hole in her

A high-caliber deer slug tore through Sharmon Stock's face as she frantically attempted to dial 911 for help. *(Author's collection)*

face, and it soaked through the carpet. Sharmon, age fifty-five, died wearing the pajama pants and sky-blue shirt she wore to bed.

Sharmon's killer quickly retreated from the slain couple's bedroom. As he stepped over her husband's body near the hallway, he paused. Even though his accomplice had presumably killed Wayne Stock, he wanted to make sure of it. He stuck the barrel of his shotgun up against the back of the farmer's head and fired off another round, just for kicks. Wayne Stock's brain spattered all over the hallway and into the other upstairs rooms. Now that both of the homeowners were clearly dead, the two assassins bolted down the staircase to flee. Sharmon Stock's killer made sure to disconnect the phone in the kitchen as he ran out of the house. But in their mad dash to flee, both of the killers carelessly left behind several noteworthy clues.

· · ·

Andy Stock, age twenty-seven, carried on the Stock family traits of righ-teousness, trustworthiness, and a strong work ethic. He helped his father operate the Stock Hay Company, a two-person, third-generation operation. Their small agriculture-based business produced alfalfa hay, brome grass, low-potassium grass, and wheat straw. Alfalfa provided nourishment for cattle at several area feedlots and for cows at other small milking dairies across the region.[5]

On the day after Easter, Andy awoke around 6:30 A.M. He put on blue jeans, a T-shirt, a flannel shirt, and brown work boots. Since it was crop-planting season, Andy knew he had a busy week ahead of him at his father's farm. That morning, he began his day by leaving his rural acreage and driving into Murdock to fill the gas tank of his fiancée Cassondra's car. He returned shortly. By 9 A.M., Andy headed to his parents' farm. He retraced the same route he made the previous evening when he and Cassondra fetched their mischievous wandering dog, Charlie.

When Andy arrived at the Stock farm, Monday's edition of the *Lincoln Journal Star* newspaper was still in the plastic delivery tube at the end of the driveway. Wayne Stock hadn't brewed coffee in his kitchen. Wayne's truck sat parked inside a Husker red-painted machine shed, as if it hadn't moved an inch that Monday morning. When Andy poked his head in the kitchen to say hello, he didn't see or hear anyone. Confused, Andy headed back outside to scour the large farm. He observed no sign of his father tinkering with the tractors, machinery, or heavy equipment.

Andy shuffled back toward the farmhouse for another look. Once inside, he opened the door leading to the garage. His mother's silver Buick LeSabre remained parked in its familiar spot. That, too, was puzzling. Andy knew his mother often went to visit her seriously ailing mother in the town of Elmwood, six miles up the road. Now his mother also seemed to have vanished.

Andy headed back inside the house to do more investigating. He yelled for his father. He called out for his mother. Echoes filled the empty house, which was eerily still. Andy tried to use his parents' telephone, but couldn't get a dial tone. He canvassed the living room, family room, kitchen, and laundry. Nothing appeared disturbed or in disarray. Andy's mother always kept the house immaculate and clean, and that's how it looked. Andy knew that his father spent considerable time in his upstairs office, handling and filing paperwork and bills for the Stock Hay Company. Perhaps his father had just hunkered down at the computer, too distracted to hear his son call

Andy Stock discovered his father Wayne Stock's body in the blood-spattered upstairs bedroom hallway on the morning of Monday, April 17, 2006. *(Author's collection)*

out his name. Andy headed upstairs to find out for himself. There at the top of the staircase, Andy saw his father's corpse, facedown in a puddle of blood.

Wayne Stock's brains were exposed, his head horribly disfigured. Andy observed fragments of brain matter scattered every which way possible in the narrow hallway. Pieces of flesh and blood were sprayed onto the white walls and into the adjacent bathroom. A pool of blood soaked the hallway's carpet, forming an ugly black liquid. Blood spatter shot across the hallway and splotched the carpet in Wayne's office several feet away, even staining some clothes hanging inside an open closet.

The shotgun slayings of Wayne and Sharmon Stock in peaceful rural Nebraska are regarded as among the most gruesome and sickening crime scenes, according to several longtime law enforcement officials who worked on the case. *(Author's collection)*

After discovering his father's murder, Andy raced back outside in a panic. He still did not know what happened to his mother. From his parents' gravel driveway, Andy flung open his truck, grabbed his cell phone, and pressed three digits. He was simultaneously grief-stricken and terrified by the scene in the second-story hallway of his childhood home.

The sheer horror of the crime scene traumatized Andy Stock. A year later, he told Cass County authorities, "Every night, I wake up covered in sweat with the image of my parents' deformed heads burned into my mind."[6]

At 9:11 A.M., an emergency dispatcher some thirty miles away in Plattsmouth answered Andy's 911 distress call. An ambulance was dispatched to the Murdock farmhouse, in reference to an apparent death scene. Road patrol deputies from the Cass County Sheriff's Office rushed toward the western end of the largely agrarian county, to the small-town disaster rapidly unfolding.

In the meantime, Andy Stock grew even more worried about his mother's welfare. He called his grandmother's house in Elmwood to break the shocking and horrible news, but relatives confirmed that Sharmon wasn't there. Andy hung up the phone. He waited in his driveway for emergency crews to arrive at the farm. He was terrified and all alone. Sometime later, an ambulance unit from Elmwood's volunteer fire and rescue arrived at the Stock farm. The gory scene was left undisturbed until Cass County Sheriff's deputies Virgil Poggemeyer and Chad Mayfield arrived to investigate. Upon inspecting the hallway, Poggemeyer noticed that the man's death did not appear to be a suicide because the weapon was missing. The two deputies performed a sweep of the farm property, including a machine shop and outbuildings, but failed to locate Wayne's wife.

After being apprised of the situation, Sheriff's Sgt. Sandy Weyers notified all on-duty patrol cruisers to race toward the crime scene near Murdock as fast as possible. She also summoned investigators, Earl D. Schenck Jr. and Rex Southwick, to join her. While Weyers, Schenck, and Southwick sped to the scene about thirty miles away, the two uniformed patrol deputies already at the scene meticulously canvassed the interior of the farmhouse. Room after room showed no sign that an invader had rifled through drawers, desks, or the couple's belongings. Whoever killed the Stocks didn't seem interested in their valuables or prized possessions. After all, a wad of cash remained neatly tucked inside Wayne's wallet in his office directly across the hallway from his dead body. His gold-colored wristwatch was also out in plain view. The jewelry box on Sharmon's bedroom dresser looked untouched as well. Her ticking wristwatch, which was on top of her jewelry, was just where she had left it. Upstairs, however, the deputies discovered two ammunition rounds near Wayne Stock's body. Poggemeyer concluded that Wayne had been dead for several hours. His right arm, folded under his body, had turned gray and his toes were purple. Finally, Poggemeyer entered the couple's master bedroom. His gaze swept the room and his eyes focused on the tan carpeting. He spotted an arm.

Sharmon Stock's body was concealed between her bedside and the north wall. The telephone cord stretched across her body made it obvious that she died trying to summon help. Both victims were clad in pajamas and barefoot, making it obvious that they were killed during their sleep.[7] At 10:07 A.M.,

This unmarked Cass County Sheriff's vehicle nearly destroyed the marijuana pipe containing the DNA residue of Wayne and Sharmon Stock's killers. Luckily, authorities recovered the drug pipe on the murdered couple's gravel driveway. Evidence marker B was a bloodstained flashlight also dropped by the fleeing killers. *(Author's collection)*

Sergeant Weyers and the two male investigators, also not well-versed in pro-cessing violent crime scenes, arrived at the farmhouse. That morning, a small silver LED flashlight turned up in the grass near the house. The flashlight bore what appeared to be fresh bloodstains. Then, not far away, investigators caught a very lucky break. In fact, it was a miracle that one of the most im-portant clues was not crushed and forever destroyed. A Cass County Sheriff's investigator had pulled his unmarked car directly into the crime scene. His tires came within a matter of inches of crushing the metal marijuana pipe discovered in the Stocks' gravel driveway near the front door. Luckily, the clue was spared. Obviously the red-and-silver dope pipe did not belong to the homicide victims or their son Andy or the volunteer rescue squad at the scene. Investigators bagged it for DNA testing.

So far, the local law enforcement agency had gotten off to a great start. Ammunition shells left behind indicated that Wayne and Sharmon had been killed with a .12-gauge shotgun. The flashlight signified the killings occurred at night, and the shooter wanted to catch the couple off-guard. The pipe sug-gested the killer or killers were high. All these clues were helpful. Nonethe-less, the local cops had their work cut out for them. Sergeant Weyers ordered Schenck and Southwick—a former county sheriff in Fairbury, Nebraska—to hunt for the murder weapon. Both investigators roamed the murder house for several minutes. They checked the kitchen, sunroom, living room, and hallways. They went back upstairs. They inspected the bedrooms, office, and bathroom. They returned back outside empty-handed.

The murder weapon remained at large, as did the killers.

The Cass County Sheriff's Office realized it had a terrible situation on its hands. It needed a crime scene expert—and fast.

2

LEGEND

Back at the Cass County Law Enforcement Center in downtown Plattsmouth, a seasoned sheriff's lieutenant scrambled to call David Wayne Kofoed, who was thirty miles away in northwest Omaha.

By 2006, Kofoed was a larger-than-life figure in Nebraska's law enforcement community even though he did not carry a badge or possess a firearm. Kofoed, age forty-nine, served as commander of the Douglas County Sheriff's Office crime lab. Kofoed joined the county agency in late 1999 after a successful but not spectacular ten-year stint as a criminalist for the Omaha Police Department. Nobody in Omaha was more devoted to forensics than Kofoed, not by a long shot. Work became his mission and obsession in life. His dedication and attention to detail set him apart from his less ambitious peers. He mastered his craft involving fingerprints, alternative light sources, blood patterns, hair samples, and clothing fibers. He became skilled at digital photography. He drew remarkable diagrams depicting crime scenes. Above all, he was meticulous, thorough, and a classic workaholic. Usually Kofoed worked seventy to eighty hours a week, carefully piecing together evidence to rid the world of evil. "Dave is like a dog on a bone when it comes to his work," said Mike Stone, the Omaha crime lab manager, now retired. "You can't tell him to go home. You have to blast him out of there."[1]

Kofoed agreed. "When you get involved in a case, you want to see it through to the end."

Although being commander of the county crime lab was his dream job, Kofoed recognized his new job had obvious drawbacks. His former employer, the Omaha Police Department, typically averaged at least thirty murders per year, plus dozens more nonfatal shootings. Douglas County, the so-called other crime lab within Omaha, rarely handled more than a couple of murder cases a year. Most of the county's territory consisted of quiet suburban subdivisions on the fringe of metropolitan Omaha. Some local politicians bemoaned that the county did not even need a crime lab, given that the county barely had any violence to justify a dozen employees and twenty-four-hour coverage.

Kofoed and his boss, Sheriff Tim Dunning, had no intentions of closing down. They had their sights set on expansion.

To drum up more work for his agency, Kofoed marketed his agency's help at minimal costs to smaller agencies across Nebraska and in southwestern Iowa. Kofoed guaranteed lightning-fast turnaround time for processing forensic evidence tests, unlike the Nebraska State Patrol's crime lab in Lincoln, which offered its services at no cost to other law enforcement agencies but had a reputation for lengthy backlog. Kofoed quickly developed a list of repeat customers. As many as forty-five law enforcement agencies started summoning the Douglas County forensic services unit on a frequent basis.

A shrewd self-promoter, Kofoed stopped calling his employees "evidence technicians." They became known as crime scene investigators, or the more sexy term, CSIs. Kofoed's charm and ability to market himself and his agency were his greatest assets. Rarely a month passed without a softball human-interest feature involving Kofoed or one of his favorite employees hamming it up for the Omaha TV cameras. Sometimes Kofoed showed off a new gadget that detected the presence of invisible blood. Other times, Kofoed boasted about his crime lab's role in solving an area crime. The barrage of constant positive press through Omaha's television, radio, and newspaper stories gave Kofoed instant credibility across the tight-knit Nebraska and Iowa law enforcement community. As a result, when small-town Nebraska police departments and sheriff's offices had a rare violent crime on their hands, they didn't waste much time trying to figure out what to do.

Without a doubt, Kofoed's press clippings mirrored his legendary accomplishments. He usually found pivotal evidence, often in the most unusual places. Largely thanks to Kofoed, many of Nebraska's most evil killers ended up right where they belonged—in prison for life or on death row.[2]

As soon as Kofoed heard about the bloody farmhouse, the crime lab commander dropped everything. He notified a couple of his top CSIs to load up the forensic equipment at once. The situation sounded bleak. Neighboring Cass County Sheriff's investigators needed serious help.

There was no time to spare.

3

SUSPECT

The Douglas County mobile crime lab van kicked up dust as it sped along the gravel roads past miles and miles of farmland, an hour from Omaha.

Finally, they came upon a very tidy country farm, a most unusual setting for the CSI team. "You're talking about a farmhouse in the middle of nothing," remarked Douglas County criminalist Don Veys.[1]

The Douglas County CSI team had been told that two people were killed, and the crime scene was extremely bloody.

"It was a very brutal crime scene," Kofoed recalled. "One of the worst I ever seen."[2]

The bodies unnerved Kofoed. Wayne Stock lay facedown in his hallway, fatally shot in the back of his head. He had crawled out of his bedroom after suffering the initial gunshot to his knee. Wayne and Sharmon Stock were the last people the residents of Cass County ever suspected would be victims of foul play, especially in the horrific manner they died.

"What really bothers me is these two people were just sleeping in bed," Kofoed said. "He was shot in the head, clearly an execution. The female victim was holding a phone in her hand, and she had been shot in the eye at close range."

Kofoed encountered a chaotic scene when he arrived at Murdock.

Roughly twenty law enforcement officials from Cass County and the Nebraska State Patrol had already trampled through the two-story, blood-soaked farmhouse by the time Kofoed's metropolitan CSI unit got busy and down to work. This greatly perturbed Kofoed because several of the initial responders walked through the farmhouse without wearing any protective gear to prevent contaminating the crime scene.

Wayne Stock farmed more than a thousand acres in western Cass County, a scenic stretch of Nebraska countryside between metropolitan Omaha and Lincoln. *(Author's collection)*

That first afternoon, Kofoed took charge of the crime scene. He gave any necessary crime scene tours for the coroners or those needing to remove the two bodies upstairs. Kofoed's CSI partner, Don Veys, took hundreds of photos of the farmhouse, moving from room to room to document the site. Forensic scientist CL Retelsdorf videotaped the perimeter of the farmstead. Bloodstain analyst Michelle Steele helped Kofoed process the handful of live and spent red shotgun shells left near the bodies and on the carpeted staircase. Also upstairs, the Douglas County CSIs made a startling observation. They realized there were two different shooters who killed the gray-haired male victim. The blood spatter on the walls left behind a perfect silhouette of a person. "The one who was in the hallway was actually sprayed with a considerable amount of blood, probably from head to toe," Veys concluded.[3]

Outside, the CSIs saw a detached window screen resting against the back of the house. The laundry room window was partially open. All the other

Crime-scene tape stretches across the front yard at the southeastern Nebraska farmhouse of Wayne Stock, fifty-eight, and wife Sharmon, fifty-five. The Stocks, who lived near the tiny town of Murdock, were slain as two intruders barged into their master bedroom in the early hours of April 17, 2006. *(Author's collection)*

windows on the Stocks' two-story house were closed shut that cool April morning. Veys suspected the intruders had cut a hole through the screen to gain entry through the back window, so he snapped numerous photos of the open window, including close-ups of the tampered screen. But the small-town investigators from Cass County had their own opinions too. The open window didn't fit their theory. "We were told, and I don't remember exactly who told me, or who told us, that the window wasn't involved," Veys would later testify. "But it was obvious it was about the only thing on the entire property that was out of place, so it was not dismissed."[4]

And besides, the local cops sensed the killer was not a stranger or transient. They suspected a murderer, seething with rage, simply walked in through

This is the backyard window where the killers gained entry. The intruders pried off the screen, lifted open the window, and crawled through the laundry room. Shockingly, Cass County Sheriff's investigators immediately dismissed the detached screen as unimportant. Investigators wrongly assumed that the killers walked in through the front door. *(Author's collection)*

the front door and right back out. After all, the interior front door was found wide open. The rest of the house appeared as neat as a pin. Both victims had suffered gruesome shotgun wounds at point-blank range.

Veys had never encountered deer slugs used in a slaying during his thirty-five-year career of working literally thousands of death scenes. "This was just, boom, boom, boom, boom, boom, and done," Veys said.[5] "It didn't appear random at all."

That first afternoon, Kofoed cleared the other agencies out of the house. He began the delicate and meticulous process of preserving and analyzing the evidence. Thanks to Kofoed's presence, the Cass County Sheriff's Office felt the crime scene was in excellent hands. The Douglas County mobile crime lab unit stayed at the farmhouse for three straight days gathering up helpful clues to give the detectives some solid leads.

The Cass County Sheriff's Office, with special assistance from the Nebraska State Patrol, oversaw the double murder investigation. The bloody bedroom left the police fairly certain that the victims had died for a reason. This seemed like an assassination, pure and simple. Somebody had revenge in mind.

Investigators quickly ruled out robbery or burglary as the motive because room after room at the Stock farmhouse was left immaculate and undisturbed by their killers. *(Author's collection)*

Authorities recovered several high-caliber shotgun ammunition rounds near the bodies of Nebraska farmers Wayne and Sharmon Stock. *(Author's collection)*

"At first glance, this appeared very personal. The type of killing that had been done did not resemble robbery," Veys agreed.[6] "The house had not been ransacked. Someone came in and went directly to the bedroom and killed them. Why would they go to this particular farmhouse? The only farmhouse that didn't have a dog."

.   .   .

Cass County Sheriff's Sgt. Sandy Weyers grew up around the village of Eagle, Nebraska, a town of one thousand people less than twenty miles from the Nebraska capital of Lincoln. She had socialized in the past with the brothers and sisters of victim Sharmon Drake Stock.[7] The Drakes were one of the largest families in western Cass County. In fact, Sharmon came from a family of more than a dozen siblings. Wayne Stock, on the other hand, had only a sister, Barbara Livers. One of Sharmon's brothers, Kirk Drake, got a call from one of his sisters on that tragic Monday, April 17, 2006. "Kirk, you need to get out to Sharmon and Wayne's as soon as you can. They've been murdered," he remembered her saying.[8]

Since he lived nearby, Kirk sped out to the Stocks' large farm operation along 286th Street, about a mile from the nearest paved road. As he came up the hill, he saw several police cars parked near the front entrance. Yellow crime scene tape stretched across the entire front yard, taped to the Stocks' mailbox at the end of their driveway. "I'll never forget that as long as I live," he said.[9] Kirk Drake had an empty feeling, a hopeless feeling. No one could believe it: Wayne and Sharmon Stock were murder victims.

As the first day of the investigation wore on, Sergeant Weyers headed up the road to Elmwood to interview Sharmon's grieving siblings. Weyers was a husky, no-nonsense cop. She had sandy-colored shoulder-length hair and a deep voice. She was respected and admired within the Cass County law enforcement community. She absolutely wanted to do her best to make the victims' families whole again. Wayne and Sharmon were widely popular, and two of the most genuine people in the region of southeastern Nebraska. The Stocks had farmed the land for generations in Cass County. Everyone knew they ran the Stock Hay Co., a thriving and successful hay-baling business. Wayne and Sharmon were devout Christians, very active in their church in Murdock. Sharmon had worked for nearly twenty years as a small-school substitute teacher. Then she became locally famous for her popular cake-decorating business. She made cakes for weddings, graduations, retirements, and anniversaries. Everyone loved her cakes. As for Wayne, he owned more than a thousand acres of farmland and also several rental properties. When he wasn't busy driving a combine to bale hay, he regularly pitched in to help the other area farmers at harvest time, just because he enjoyed helping other people.[10]

Above all, Wayne and Sharmon's family was their pride and joy. They fished together, hunted together, and held frequent family cookouts. The holidays were extremely special, and sometimes Wayne dressed up as the local Santa Claus. Days before her slaying, Sharmon made all of her grandchildren personal Easter baskets, each one individually decorated.

"They touched so many lives," said daughter Tammy Vance.[11]

"They were so genuine," said Kirk Drake, Sharmon's brother. "You got what you saw. They enjoyed the farm life."[12]

The families of Wayne and Sharmon put their faith in their friends and neighbors who worked as public servants for the Cass County Sheriff's Office. But practically everyone in the agency was inexperienced at investigating a homicide because murder did not happen very often here. Cass County typically went five or ten years at a time—perhaps longer—without a single murder case. That afternoon, most of the Cass County Sheriff's investigators were already busy following up other tasks, but not Investigator Earl Schenck Jr. He just milled about the farmhouse, Weyers noticed.[13]

Schenck (pronounced Skank) was put in charge of solving the high-profile double murder investigation by Weyers and Lt. Larry "Ike" Burke. Schenck, at a towering six foot three, was around forty and had graying sandy blond hair. Like his boss, Weyers, he also had no prior experience leading a murder investigation.

His only experience in a homicide investigation involved assisting in an unsuccessful landfill search for Brendan Gonzalez's body, the missing four-year-old boy from Plattsmouth who was killed by his father Ivan Henk, back in 2003. Schenck was an interesting character—the Johnny Cash of Nebraska law enforcement with police blood in his veins. He was lawman by day and country musician by night. He came from one of the most recognized law enforcement families in all of Nebraska. Earl's late grandfather, Dan, was the Howard County sheriff for many years in St. Paul. His father, Earl Schenck Sr., retired from the Nebraska State Patrol and later became the Keith County sheriff in Ogallala, a small city in the beautiful Sandhills of western Nebraska. Earl's twin uncles, Jerry and Harold, also served as Nebraska State Patrol officers and were stationed together in Grand Island. Another uncle, Dan, also retired from the State Patrol.[14]

Earl Jr. got his start at the Ogallala Police Department and later joined the Merrick County Sheriff's Department. By 2000, Schenck moved clear across the state and joined the Cass County Sheriff's Office, twenty miles south of Omaha. First, he was a uniformed deputy in road patrol. Then he got promoted to investigator. Schenck became familiar with the names and faces of local youth who got into mischief and also caused his own share of problems based on his job performance.[15]

. . .

In September 2004, Weyers found Schenck's patrol car parked at his home near Plattsmouth when he claimed to be conducting a criminal investigation in Lincoln. When she called him again to ask where he was, Schenck assured Weyers that he had driven his patrol car to Lincoln to conduct a criminal investigation. Schenck was given a one-day suspension for skipping work without permission, placed on probation for six months with monthly evaluations by Weyers, and ordered to attend counseling.

On April 17, 2005, Cass County Sheriff Bill Brueggemann, Cass County attorney Nathan Cox, and Schenck received a complaint letter from the parents of a young man who had committed suicide. The parents reported that Schenck took the card the young man had left them in order to compare the handwriting with the suicide note left in the truck. Then Schenck never returned the card. The parents wrote: "Your apparent lack of compassion and follow through during this extremely difficult time for our family is very disconcerting."

In November 2005, Schenck left a loaded shotgun in an unsecured location following a firearms training exercise and no one noticed it for a week. Finally, another Cass County Sheriff's employee discovered the loaded shotgun. Schenck received a one-day suspension for that incident.

Also prior to the Stock murders, Schenck was suspended for three days without pay and placed on three months' probation after an incident at a high school in rural Cass County, where he worked in his spare time as the high school's wrestling coach. Schenck left a note in one of his wrestler's lockers that read: "If you touch my food again, I will put a bullet in your fat melon head. Love, Coach Schenck." After the school investigated the matter, Schenck resigned as the wrestling coach.

When he wasn't working his day job at the Cass County Sheriff's Office, Schenck wore an oversized gold belt buckle, light blue jeans, a flannel shirt, and a white cowboy hat. He threw an acoustic guitar over his shoulder. His fans knew him as "Duke," the singing Nebraska Sandhills cowboy who chased his dream of becoming a popular country musician. Schenck was seventeen when he first began performing country music in the Nebraska Sandhills. By age forty, Duke was a regular performer at Nebraska bars, county fairs, and town festivals. He also took the stage in Colorado, Iowa, Kansas, and even Nashville, Tennessee. He wrote his own lyrics, and some of his country songs became very popular with his Indie fans, notably his song "Eye Catcher," about a young gullible cowboy who falls for a pretty lady in a sundress. She steals his heart and his money, but he still wants her anyway.[16]

The decision to appoint Schenck to supervise the high-profile double murder investigation, which was bound to draw enormous and intense statewide news media coverage, did not sit well with the local prosecutor. Nathan Cox, a rusty-haired, conservative Mormon in his early forties, groaned after learning the news. "Earl, at times, is a bit of a cowboy," Cox later testified in a sworn deposition. According to Cox, Schenck did his own criminal investigations and arrived at his own conclusions rather than checking all the related facts.[17] But Cox had no control over the appointment of the lead investigator for the Wayne and Sharmon Stock double homicides. Sergeant Weyers and Lieutenant Burke of the Cass County Sheriff's Office made that call, and Cox had to live with it.

So that first evening, Sergeant Weyers and Investigator Schenck traveled six miles up the road to the town of Elmwood, population seven hundred. The investigators expressed their deepest condolences as they gathered in the living room with several shaken and distraught brothers and sisters of Sharmon Stock, who were also looking for answers. The Drakes carried definite clout in the western Cass County region near the small towns of Alvo, Avoca, Eagle, Elmwood, Murdock, and Weeping Water. The family owned small businesses and was civic-minded. They wore their hometown pride on their sleeves. Now they were filled with rage and mostly disbelief. The Drakes urged the pair of local sheriff's investigators to focus on the couple's nephew as the obvious suspect. The family agreed: Matt Livers had the hatred and desire to kill. Matt had feuded with Wayne and Sharmon over his intentions to inherit his grandmother Lorene's house, the Drakes commented. Lorene Stock and her late husband Willard lived just around the bend from the crime scene. Matt had previously lived in the basement of his grandparents' place a few years earlier, but he was forced out after Wayne and Sharmon intervened. They determined that their nephew had become a freeloader and too much of a burden upon his elderly grandparents. Incidentally, Matt also spent Easter

Sunday at his grandmother's house, along with his parents and Wayne and Sharmon Stock. It marked the family's first Easter without Willard Stock, Matt's grandfather, who died the previous summer at age eighty-nine. The Drakes wondered if Matt had a heated exchange or fight with his uncle and aunt at the Easter brunch and then returned hours later to assassinate them in their sleep. Two of the Drakes claimed Sharmon was afraid of Matt Livers.[18] The two sheriff's investigators listened intently as Kirby Drake remembered how his sister Sharmon adamantly opposed Matt's desire to acquire his grandmother Lorene Stock's house. In fact, Sharmon once told her estranged nephew, "Over my dead body will you get that house," Kirby recounted.[19] The Drakes also speculated that Matt Livers dabbled in illicit drugs, even though they lacked any proof or firsthand knowledge. Schenck and Weyers told the family that a metal pipe used to smoke marijuana was found on the Stocks' gravel driveway.

It was late and dark by the time Schenck and Weyers thanked the family for their time and finished up the first day of interviews. But Schenck wasn't ready to call it a night. He teamed up with Bill Lambert, a Nebraska State Patrol investigator about the same age, and the two men drove to the residence of Lorene Stock, the mother of Wayne Stock and Barb Livers, Matt's mother. The elderly widow lived in a brick ranch house only a half mile from the murder scene. When they arrived, the lawmen were greeted by Barb. Schenck needed to interview her son, Matt, he advised. But Matt wasn't there. He had already headed home for Lincoln, she replied. Schenck insisted he needed to speak with Matt at once, so she gave him Matt's cell number. It was around 10:45 P.M. when Schenck made contact with the nephew of the murder victims. Matt, age twenty-eight, agreed to return to Murdock for a police interview. Matt, of course, was long regarded as the black sheep of the Stock family, and he knew that. At the time of the killings, Wayne and Sharmon's nephew really had not amounted to much. But unlike most people, he had severe mental limitations. During his schooling, he had been diagnosed as being borderline mentally challenged. As an adult, his intellectual capacity put him at below 99 percent of the adult population.[20] When Matt grew up in Murdock, members of his proud, prominent farm family tried to downplay his problems. His uncle Wayne also served on the Elmwood-Murdock school board, a largely rural K-12 district of about four hundred students. While in school, Matt often became the target of ridicule and teasing. Other students didn't understand his varying degrees of learning disabilities. He stuck out and had very few friends. At family gatherings, Matt did not really hang around and socialize with his more successful cousins, such as Wayne's sons, Andy and Steven, or their sister Tammy. The Stocks and the Drakes—Sharmon's family—considered Matt Livers odd and strange.

At the time of the slayings Matt rented a house in Lincoln with his fiancée, Sarah Schneider, and another friend of theirs, Susan Gill. A month before the murders, Matt lost his job as a private security guard at a large Lincoln corporation. Just days before the murders, Matt returned to Nebraska on a Greyhound bus after traveling to Texas to visit Ryan Paulding, his best friend.[21] Perhaps Matt killed his well-to-do uncle and aunt out of spite, a payback for not having the family's wealth, power, and prestige, the investigators thought.

. . .

Matt Livers hopped into the front seat of the unmarked police car idling in his grandmother's driveway, some fourteen hours after the bodies were found. Schenck got behind the wheel. Lambert positioned himself in the back seat. The three men went for a ride in the country before ending up at the Weeping Water Volunteer Fire Department for the interview. The investigators asked Matt to recall his activities on Easter. He remembered he had left his grandmother's place by 5 P.M. because he promised to babysit his fiancée's three-year-old son. She had to leave for her job as a hospital nurse. Matt maintained he remained at his house in Lincoln the entire night and never left to go anywhere. The investigators casually questioned him about his employment history. Matt admitted that almost every job he ever had ended with a layoff. Then, he boasted, he had just had an interview over the phone earlier in the day with a national trucking firm out of Wisconsin. He had been accepted into the company's driving training school, Matt said proudly. But Schenck wasn't interested in Matt's purported job leads. The small-town investigator asked who Matt thought might have killed his relatives. Matt shrugged. He called the murders unbelievable. "That's the funny thing, I do not know a single soul," he answered.[22] Matt had only good things to say about his murdered aunt and uncle, even though Matt's extended family mostly had only bad things to say about him during their earlier interview with Schenck and Weyers. "They did anything and everything for people," Matt said.

Their deaths left Matt shocked, and he even had goose bumps up and down his arms as he drove past their farmhouse on his way to the interview. The murders scared him, Matt admitted.

Schenck wasn't buying Matt's story.

He didn't think Matt appeared upset or distraught when talking about his dead uncle and aunt. He sensed that Matt presented a cheerful and carefree attitude. Plus, Matt's interview was a complete contradiction of the interview he and Weyers had just had with a half dozen respected brothers and sisters of Sharmon Stock. Matt denied having had any heated arguments or disagreements with his murdered relatives, except for one time when he was about thirteen, he remembered. He also denied having any arguments with Wayne or Sharmon about inheriting his grandmother's house. Matt did admit, however, that he and his fiancée Sarah hoped to acquire the house someday, but only after "Grandma is dead and long gone," as Matt put it bluntly.

Matt reasoned that all three of Wayne's grown kids had their own houses. Even Matt's only brother had his own house in Houston. Therefore, it made the most sense for him and Sarah to move into his grandmother's house, Matt explained to Schenck and Lambert. The two investigators chose not to ask Matt any deep, probing questions about the murders, at least not yet. Since the two cops were already briefed from Kofoed and the other Omaha CSIs about the apparent involvement of a second gunman, they asked Matt to name other people who had disagreements with his murdered uncle and aunt. He suggested his cousins William ("Will") and Nick Sampson. The Sampson brothers were in their twenties, but they were rambunctious teenagers growing up in Murdock. They used to ride noisy dirt bikes and all-terrain vehicles through Wayne Stock's farm fields. That made Wayne angry, Matt told the investigators. Schenck quickly remembered the Sampson brothers from his days as a road patrolman. He recalled how Nick Sampson had several run-ins and scrapes with the Sheriff's Office, including some infractions involving illegal drugs.

· · ·

Since it was well past midnight, the lead investigators were exhausted. They drove Matt back to his grandmother's house and let him go, since they had no grounds to arrest him for murder. However, they asked Matt if he was willing to furnish a DNA sample and fingerprints to compare with the crime scene evidence. Matt replied he was willing to do anything to help solve the case and identify the real culprits. Schenck and Lambert sensed they were already on right track. In nearly twenty years of Nebraska law enforcement, Schenck had never quite seen anything like what he had witnessed in the upstairs bedroom outside Murdock: Wayne Stock's disfigured head and a gaping hole that tore through Sharmon Stock's face.

Schenck wanted to make sure Wayne and Sharmon Stock received justice. The focus of his double murder investigation was obvious. Matt "appeared to be totally at ease with the deaths of two people he described as 'Great people,'" Schenck stated in his investigative report. "At this point in the investigation, Matt Livers is being developed as a possible suspect." Schenck suspected Matt killed his relatives to inherit his grandmother's house. "This statement seemed to be a touchy subject for Matt, who felt compelled to detail how every other family member has property and he does not," Schenck noted.

The first full day of the investigation came and went without any arrests. However, the fortunes of the Cass County Sheriff's Office were soon about to change thanks to a pair of well-intentioned tipsters. Investigators figured this hot tip into the county's 911 dispatch center marked their lucky break.

4

MYSTERY CAR

Within days of the slayings, an unexpected tip came into the Cass County Sheriff's Office. Justin Hergenrader and girlfriend Tamarra Jeffrey thought they spotted Wayne and Sharmon Stock's killer speeding away from the murders. The young couple had a rural newspaper delivery route for the *Lincoln Journal Star,* the capital city's newspaper. Typically, the couriers finished their route before the crack of dawn every morning. The Stocks were one of their regular customers. Sometime around 3:45 A.M., the pair was at the intersection of 286th Street and Bluff Road, a mile down the road from Wayne Stock's country farmhouse. Suddenly, Tamarra Jeffrey noticed something odd as she gazed out the passenger-side window of Justin's truck—a car parked near the rural cemetery, at such an unusual time. Because her boyfriend did not slow down, she could not tell if anyone was inside the car during her quick glance. A couple of minutes later, Justin Hergenrader came upon the two-story farmhouse of Wayne and Sharmon Stock. He stuffed the freshly printed Monday morning newspaper into the plastic red tube at the end of Wayne Stock's driveway and then drove through their circular gravel driveway. Hergenrader then proceeded south on 286th Street. As he drove past Callahan Cemetery, Justin got a better glimpse of the stationary car with its lights off. The suspicious car was parked in a grassy ditch outside the brick pillars surrounding the darkened and dreary cemetery. The car appeared empty. There was no sign of anyone. Justin's attention drifted back to the unlit stretch of road in front of him. He and his girlfriend continued with their usual newspaper deliveries for the next fifteen minutes.

Then, all of a sudden, the couple feared they had a brush with death.

. . .

Justin grew fidgety as he noticed beaming headlights in his rearview mirror. He had just pulled up to a rural acreage near the village of Eagle. This time, his girlfriend was in the best position to stuff the newspaper into the customer's box. With the car hurtling toward his Ford Ranger, Justin yelled for her to hurry up. They shrieked. They feared a rear-end collision with the maniac driver heading toward them. They closed their eyes and braced for an awful crash. Then, at the very last second, the speedy lead-foot motorist veered across the center line of the paved state highway. The mystery motorist glanced over his right shoulder and peered at their truck as he passed them, decelerating slightly. Then, in a flash, the driver floored the gas pedal and sped away, easily reaching seventy miles per hour. The car buzzed along the asphalt and headed straight toward the bright city skyline of Lincoln, another ten miles or so up the road. The time was now 4:15 A.M. Their brush with near death left Tamarra bewildered. The reckless motorist was driving the same car she observed at the rural cemetery, fifteen minutes earlier. Justin agreed, but the newspaper carriers did not call 911. After all, they had no inkling that

Within days of the murders, Cass County Sheriff Bill Brueggemann and his investigators converged upon a rural cemetery just down the road from the Stock farmhouse. At that time, investigators believed that whoever killed the farm couple had parked by the cemetery and walked to the Stock farmhouse to commit the shotgun slayings in premeditated fashion. *(Author's collection)*

a violent double murder had just transpired inside the Stock farmhouse. Finally, a day and a half later, after the Stocks' murder case became front-page news in the *Omaha World-Herald* and *Lincoln Journal Star,* the couple decided to contact local law enforcement. Sensing a break in the case, the Cass County Sheriff's Office rushed out to interview them at their residence in Greenwood, a farming community of six hundred along U.S. Highway 6, about fifteen minutes from the murders. Unfortunately for Sheriff's officials, Justin and his girlfriend struggled to give specifics and intimate details about their encounter with the mystery car. The best they could offer was a partial license plate and a vague, general description. Justin believed the midsize car was light brown or tan. It had four doors and looked at least five to ten years old, he estimated. The driver sported facial hair, perhaps a beard. Justin and Tamarra did not get a good look at the man's face or approximate age because of the total darkness. The newspaper carriers insisted that they did not see any passengers in the speeding car. This response frustrated law enforcement, who already knew that two shooters were involved, based on the human silhouette left near the top stairwell. The two eyewitnesses remembered the speeding car contained an O or zero as the first letter of its Nebraska license plates. This key detail effectively ruled out the car being from Cass County. (The alpha-numeric prefix for Cass County began with 20.) Justin suspected the driver was in a hurry. He and Tamarra didn't recall seeing anybody else on the roads as they distributed the newspapers early that Monday morning in a mostly remote rural area of western Cass County. "It's just us and the deer," Justin told the investigators. The encounter with the possible getaway driver wasn't the newspaper carriers' only strange observation during the early morning hours of Monday, April 17. The two spotted an orange glow-ing light coming from an upstairs bedroom as they brought the Stocks their final newspaper, between 3:45 and 3:55 A.M. The couriers had never seen any inside lights on during any of their previous early morning deliveries to Wayne Stock's farmhouse.[1] So who could it be? Would the mysterious car at the cemetery be identified?

·   ·   ·

Lead investigator Earl Schenck immediately suspected Matt Livers was behind the wheel. Matt had light brown hair, a goatee, and he lived in Lin-coln, the same direction the speeding car was headed. Back at the Sheriff's Office, Schenck accessed his law enforcement computers and automobile databases. He researched motor vehicle registrations involving Matt and his immediate family. Matt, though, did not own a brown or tan car. Matt had a red Pontiac Sunbird convertible and an older, gray Chevy Tahoe with a noisy muffler. Next, Schenck researched Matt's cousins, the Sampson brothers, Will and Nick. This time, Schenck sensed he uncovered a match. His limited research led to Will Sampson's tan, 1998 Ford Contour with four doors. This particular cousin also lived in Lincoln. At first blush, it seemed outrageous and far-fetched for Will's car to serve as the getaway vehicle. After all, the newspaper carriers insisted that a zero or O was the first numeral or letter in the Nebraska-issued license plate of the strange car. Will's Nebraska license plate began with P and was PHM 252.

Even though the license plate did not match the witnesses' description, Will's car still seemed the logical murder vehicle to the Cass County Sheriff's investigator for one chief reason.

Will had dropped off his car at an auto-detail shop in Lincoln shortly before sunrise, merely hours after the farmhouse slayings thirty miles away. The scheduling of a professional auto cleaning seemed just a little too convenient to overlook, so Will's tan Ford Contour became a top priority in the early stages of the double murder investigation. Around supper time, on April 19, the Nebraska State Patrol's Bill Lambert and Cass County's Earl Schenck showed up unannounced at Will Sampson's apartment. They notified Will that his name came up during their investigation of his relation to the victims' nephew, Matthew Livers. (The Sampson brothers were not directly related to the Stocks, but they grew up in Murdock and were first cousins with Livers, having the same grandparents.) Following the brief introduction, Will obliged their request for a sit-down recorded interview over at the Nebraska State Patrol office headquarters in Lincoln. Will figured it was in his best interest to cooperate. He never thought about asking for a lawyer. That evening, Will told the fact-gathering detectives that he had not seen his cousin Matt Livers since a large family gathering at Christmas, about four months prior. The two investigators quizzed Will about his own whereabouts on Easter. Will and his future wife, Alynn, visited her sister's family, also in Lincoln. Around 1 P.M., they ate lunch at a Ruby Tuesday's restaurant and stayed there about two hours before departing for their apartment. Will maintained they took a long afternoon nap and stayed home the rest of the night. Will and Alynn resided in a multi-level brick apartment building in Lincoln. Most apartment complex dwellers kept their cars parked in the paved stalls adjacent to their numbered buildings. Before the crack of dawn on Monday, Will's alarm clock sounded, and he got out of bed no later than 5 A.M., he said. Alynn was sound asleep, as usual. She didn't need to get up until 7. Will recalled he put on his work clothes and boots and left their apartment around 5:30.

   This was about fifteen minutes earlier than usual, he said. Around 5:45, Will arrived at a friend's house to give Joseph Hale a ride to work, as always. But this particular Monday was different. Hale directed Will to the Lincoln Auto Detail shop at 48th Street and Nebraska Highway 2. By 6 A.M., Will pulled into the detail shop and parked the car. Hale left $40 cash, plus the keys, inside the car. Will admitted he had never used the auto-detailing business previously. He just knew that Hale's brother worked there. Will told the suspicious investigators that he had his car detailed because Joseph Hale owed him a favor. It was meant to be a thank-you for giving Hale numerous rides to and from work every day for quite some time. After leaving the car behind, a fellow construction worker gave Will and Hale a lift to a nearby grocery store. From the grocery store, the young men climbed into the usual shuttle van that drove these construction workers to their work site assignments in Omaha. Will worked as a building framer, and his employer primarily handled construction jobs around metropolitan Lincoln and Omaha. That Monday evening, April 17, Will returned around 7:30 to pick up his car. The interior, including the vents and dashboard, was cleaned and vacuumed, but Will Sampson wasn't impressed by the detail job, he told both investigators.

· · ·

Will gave absolutely no indication his car served as the getaway vehicle.[2] In fact, when Will got up for work on Monday morning, he found his car in the same stall where he had parked it on Easter Sunday. He had not lent his car to anyone, he stressed. Will also flatly denied that his younger brother, Nick, borrowed his car. Besides, younger brother Nick owned a sleek black-colored truck with an extended cab. Nick lived about fifteen miles from Lincoln, in the small town of Palmyra. The Sampson brothers got together irregularly, Will admitted. Will last saw his brother about two weeks earlier, when Will was at the Bulldog Bar & Grill in downtown Murdock. Nick, age twenty-one, held a part-time job back at their hometown's one and only watering hole. As for the Stocks, Will told the police he knew Wayne and Sharmon as possible shirttail relatives through a marriage of sorts, but nothing more. He had never been inside their farmhouse. Will recalled he last saw them at Christmas, perhaps at the Methodist church service in Murdock. Will's mother and his sister still resided in Murdock. In a casual tone, Will described how he had a good relationship with the Stocks, but again, he only saw them around town, either at church or the Bulldog, perhaps once or twice a year. Will first learned about the tragedy on the local television stations. The killings stunned him. He termed them "Something unheard of in a small town." Will wasn't sure whether he needed to feel concerned for his own family's well-being. "It depends on the motive behind the murders," he said. Will was asked who he thought was responsible. After a long sigh, he shrugged. He simply could not think of anyone in his family who had a grudge or deep animosity against the Stocks. Someone may have killed them over a business dispute since the Stocks owned a prominent hay-baling business, he speculated. "If anything, they . . . are pretty wealthy for a small town," Will said. "I have no idea who would want to hurt Wayne or Sharmon." Lambert and Schenck asked Will if he smoked marijuana. (This time, they were careful not to reveal that a marijuana pipe was recovered outside the victims' house.) Will said he considered himself a recreational marijuana user. Back in 2006, he smoked pot once every couple of weeks inside his apartment. He typically smoked a joint, pipe, or bong. He had all the necessary instruments to smoke marijuana at his place, he admitted. As for weapons, Will confessed he did not own any firearms. During his years at Elmwood-Murdock High School, he shot trap and was pretty good, he quipped. But that was more than five years ago. Nowadays, he no longer owned a shotgun. Growing up, Will usually borrowed a shotgun from his grandfather, Kenneth Livers, who lived in Murdock. Will's grandfather was a military veteran who taught Will how to use a shotgun and how to reload the plastic shells. The cops honed in on the weapons arsenal angle because the Sampson brothers and Matt Livers shared the same grandfather, who had access to weapons and lots of ammunition. But the investigators made no inroads in getting Will to implicate Matt Livers as the killer. In fact, Will referred to Matt Livers as a "mama's boy growing up." Livers went out of his way to stay out of trouble, Will remembered. As a youth, Livers did not fit in particularly well with other kids in the Elmwood-Murdock school district, Will recalled. "Matt needed someone to hang around with, so he was with us," Will explained. As a teenager, "Matt was scared of smoking cigarettes, smoking pot, and underage drinking," Will noted. As an adult, Matt consumed beer every now and then, but he did not get rowdy or boisterous. According to Will, Matt didn't seem capable of killing his uncle and aunt. Matt was not the type to fly off the handle or carry a vendetta, Will suggested.

· · ·

Will's future wife was a respectable and highly intelligent young woman born in South Korea. She worked for an international adoption agency. She, too, was of little help to bolster the investigators' working theory that Will's car had served as the getaway vehicle in the Stock murders. Alynn High vehemently denied that Will lent out his car to anyone on Easter weekend. She insisted no one could have sneaked into their locked apartment and borrowed Will's set of keys for the car during the night. Will owned the only set of keys, and she never drove his car. "It is a gross and nasty car," she admitted. Alynn told the police how Will occasionally cleaned the car himself. But she agreed with the investigators' observation that the Monday morning auto detailing seemed a little strange. On the other hand, she was under the impression Will had given numerous rides to Joseph Hale while Hale remained under court probation because of a drunk-driving offense.

As for Will's whereabouts on Easter, Alynn assured the police he remained with her at all times inside their apartment. When she went to bed around midnight or 1 A.M., Will was already fast asleep. She scoffed at any notion that Will managed to sneak out of their bedroom in the middle of the night to facilitate the murders. Besides, she was a light sleeper. Even the smallest noises regularly woke her up. She remembered stirring when Will got up and left the apartment by 5:30 A.M. The investigators tried another tactic. They asked how Will took the news about the Stocks' deaths. Alynn remembered that upon learning the news, he called his mother in Murdock to inquire about the tragedy. He seemed shocked, but really hadn't talked much about the case over the past couple of days. She and Will definitely planned to attend the upcoming funeral, along with nearly everyone else in the communities of Murdock and Elmwood. She denied that Will was violent. His temper flared only when he got mad at himself, like when something in the apartment broke. Will had never been abusive or violent toward her. Whenever they got into an argument, he typically left the room rather than let the situation escalate, she told Lambert and Schenck. Overall, she considered Will easygoing and not the type to fight. When the interviews were finished, the two investigators focused again on Will's tan Ford Contour.

·   ·   ·

Naively, Will signed the legal paperwork to grant the Nebraska State Patrol permission to enter his apartment and to manually inspect his tan car as it related to the Stock homicides. His car would be towed to the Douglas County Sheriff's CSI lab in Omaha for chemical tests, he learned. If any of the crime lab's preliminary chemical tests resulted in a positive reaction for blood, Sampson's car would remain impounded indefinitely for more extensive chemical forensic tests, Investigator Lambert informed him. Will nodded in agreement. Around 10 P.M., Mike's 66 Towing Service in Lincoln arrived at Will's apartment complex with a flatbed truck. Will carefully drove his car up the lowered rear ramp just as the State Patrol instructed. Tow operator Gary Smith secured the car and pulled it onto the trailer. Then Will watched helplessly as his car headed off into the night for a sixty-mile journey bound for Omaha, guided by a Nebraska State Patrol police escort. In the meantime, Douglas County CSI director Dave Kofoed waited patiently for the car's arrival at his agency's secure impound garage. This was another of those moments when Kofoed put his love of job above everything else. Kofoed and two of his CSIs worked feverishly from midnight until 8 A.M. processing the car.

. . .

The results of their forensic examination caught Schenck and Lambert by surprise.

5

NO LUCK

Under Kofoed's careful watch and direct supervision, forensic scientist Christine Gabig cut out small pieces of floor carpeting and seats for further laboratory tests. She examined all of the obvious locations for blood, including the steering wheel, door handles, gas and brake pedals, gear shifts, and emergency brakes. The front seats, back seats, and ignition key area were also swabbed for the presence of blood. Another CSI, Mark Williams, took about eighty-five photographs showing the car's appearance. The trunk contained several cluttered toolboxes, but nothing extraordinary. The steering wheel cover, rubber brake pad, and floor mats were also removed for further analysis. The car contained a number of unknown stains on the passenger side of the floorboard, the driver's side door, and underneath the driver's floor mat. CSI Gabig sprayed various chemical agents in the hopes of finding human blood, and many parts of the car reacted to the chemical agent. Around 5 A.M., Nebraska State Patrol Investigator Bill Lambert rustled Will Sampson out of bed with a phone call. Some of the preliminary chemical tests were positive. Lambert didn't offer specifics, and Will didn't ask any questions. Because of the preliminary find, the Douglas County CSIs needed to impound his car for more extensive tests, Lambert advised.

· · ·

It turned out that the chemical tests on Will Sampson's vehicle did not contain the victims' blood. Given that Will Sampson worked in heavy construction, the chemical agent was probably reacting to iron contained in dirt instead of iron in blood, Kofoed advised the lead investigators.[1] Anyway, the following afternoon, Nebraska State Patrol Investigator Scott Haugaard drove to the

Douglas County CSI Chief Dave Kofoed, pictured behind the chain-link fence in the background at the right, prepares to supervise a forensic examination of this car, owned by Will Sampson, a cousin of prime suspect Matt Livers. Investigators suspected that Livers borrowed his cousin's car as his getaway vehicle. *(Author's collection)*

Lincoln Auto Detail shop and showed a color photograph of Will Sampson's tan Ford Contour car. At the business, employee Matt Hale, age twenty-seven, confirmed that he had just cleaned the car only a few days earlier. In fact, the car became the hot topic of conversation among the employees all morning, Matt Hale advised. The notion that the car might be involved in the high-profile Stock homicides freaked him out, Matt Hale told police. Matt Hale explained that he and another employee had cleaned the interior of the car. In an effort to cooperate with police, Hale agreed to surrender a pair of plastic bags filled with the vacuumed debris from Monday's detail job. One bag contained debris from the driver's side. The other bag contained material from the front passenger's side. The State Patrol hoped the vacuum debris would be their smoking gun, but Matt Hale was skeptical. He candidly told State Patrol Investigator Haugaard that he never saw any blood, shotgun shells, or human tissue inside the car as he vacuumed, washed the car, and cleaned the seats.[2] The bags of vacuum debris were also brought to the Douglas County crime lab in Omaha. Again, nothing of evidentiary value was found. The lead investigators were stunned and frustrated. But since

Schenck and Lambert had identified Will's car as an integral piece of the double murder mystery puzzle, it remained at the Douglas County Sheriff's Office impound lot in northwest Omaha.

. . .

Meanwhile, the lead investigators theorized that Matt Livers's struggles to hold down a steady job had snowballed into a nasty inheritance dispute that became his motive for murder. Cass County Sgt. Sandy Weyers and Lt. Larry "Ike" Burke made the thirty-five-mile drive to the town of Elmwood to check out the American Exchange Bank. A community of about 680 residents and shrinking, Elmwood resembled many small communities throughout Nebraska with a declining population. Several grain silos dotted the landscape, and the town leaned on agriculture to stay prosperous. The community had a gas station with a convenience store where local farmers gathered for hot coffee, a hotdog, or a slice of warm pizza. Entrance signs reminded highway travelers that Elmwood was the proud hometown of one of Nebraska's greatest early twentieth-century authors, Bess Streeter Aldrich (1881–1954), who was buried at the Elmwood Cemetery. Now a museum, the Aldrich House in Elmwood was on the National Register of Historic Places and drew occasional history buffs into town. At the town's bank, Sergeant Weyers and Lieutenant Burke opened the murder victims' safety deposit box with a key. The metal tube contained car titles, land abstracts, and copies of the combination to the floor safe in the Stocks' farmhouse. The investigators jotted down the safe's combination. Upon returning to the crime scene, the investigators opened the safe, but found nothing was taken. In fact, the Cass County investigators found it unusually odd that nothing appeared missing from the Stocks' farmhouse. Wayne's collection of assorted hunting rifles and shotguns all remained neatly intact. None of Sharmon Stock's jewelry was missing. Next, the lead investigators hoped the victims' legal will might shed light on the motive for their slayings. Perhaps Matt Livers was cut out of their will or stood to inherit some family property or wealth upon their deaths. The will had been drawn up in the 1980s. The document put Elmwood attorney Brian McHugh in charge of managing the Stocks' wealth and assets until their youngest son, Andy, turned thirty. Then assets would be divided evenly among the Stocks' three grown children, Steven, Tammy, and Andy.[3] However, the will never mentioned Matt Livers. It was plainly obvious that the victims' nephew never stood to benefit or inherit anything through the Stocks' untimely deaths.

. . .

On the fifth day of the murder investigation, the happy-go-lucky Livers agreed to cooperate further with investigators. Livers drove from Lincoln all the way to the Douglas County Sheriff's Office in Omaha to provide fingerprints and palm prints, along with hair and DNA samples. Livers also let CSI Josh Connolly take photographs of his hands, arms, and face to document any possible cuts and scratches. Livers offered no restraint or resistance in complying with the investigators' demands. In his mind, Livers was helping the investigators eliminate him from their list of potential murder suspects.[4] Later that day, the small-town rumor mill spread like wildfire. Gossip across Cass County speculated that Livers had been arrested in connection with the homicides, possibly on a drug charge. Although the rumor was totally false, it was so rampant it reached Livers. Naturally, he was deflated and angry, realizing his reputation had been shot to hell.

.   .   .

From the beginning, Cass County Sheriff's investigators targeted Matt Livers as the obvious killer of relatives Wayne and Sharmon Stock despite lacking any hard evidence or eyewitnesses placing Livers at the scene of the crime. *(Author's collection)*

Back in Lincoln, NSP Investigator Bill Lambert poked around at the Novartis Pharmaceutical plant along Interstate 80. Lambert delved into the prime suspect's unstable work history. At the facility, Silverhawk Security supervisor George Mackey explained that he had recently fired Livers because of integrity and temper-control issues. Livers lasted less than four months on the job. Livers had manned a command post at the entrance doors, monitored surveillance cameras, and performed foot patrol around the plant, which was a restricted area because it made pharmaceutical controlled substances. Mackey considered Livers a classic "know-it-all," a young guy who did not seem interested in learning more about the security profession from more veteran, experienced officers. Livers was often reprimanded for being too chatty, not listening, or failing to perform certain tasks. He often became defensive or angry. Once Mackey gave Livers a write-up for sleeping on the job. The company realized Livers was a liability and his bad attitude alienated coworkers. Ultimately, Livers was fired after he kicked a hole in a large wooden door out of frustration and then failed to take responsibility. However, the aftermath of Livers's firing was extremely bizarre, Mackey told the homicide investigator. When Livers returned to Novartis to bring back his old security uniforms, he began crying uncontrollably. "It's not like he worked there for the past twenty years," Mackey said, shaking his head.[5]

Lambert left the Novartis plant convinced that Livers possessed an explosive and violent temper.

· · ·

The memorial service for Wayne and Sharmon Stock would be held inside the high school gymnasium in Murdock to accommodate the large crowd wishing to pay its final respects. The Hammons Funeral Home handled the difficult arrangements for Wayne and Sharmon Stock. Hundreds of mourners converged upon the Ebenezer Methodist Church in Murdock for the Friday evening double wake. People were terribly sad. They waited in the long line for hours just to sign the memorial guestbook and offer their condolences to Wayne and Sharmon's grieving grown children. Outside the church hall, a team of NSP investigators conducted an undercover stakeout because the killer or killers were still at large. Four NSP lawmen sporting binoculars carefully panned the tree-lined neighborhood streets near the Methodist church for suspicious characters like Nick Sampson, whose older brother Will's car was already in police custody. Along with Matt Livers, Nick Sampson was being considered as the other prime suspect.

Wayne Stock and his wife Sharmon were two of Murdock's most well-liked and respected citizens. Their horrific murders inside the couple's bedroom in the early hours of April 17, 2006, terrified the region. *(Author's collection)*

It was already getting dark when NSP Investigator Scott Haugaard spotted Nick Sampson standing near a street corner outside the Ebenezer church. Nick Sampson wore blue jeans and a black leather jacket. The young man had bushy brown hair and piercings in both of his ears. Haugaard stepped out of his unmarked police cruiser and ordered Nick to furnish identification. Nick's hands trembled as he struggled to retrieve his identification from his back pocket. The investigator inquired why Nick was hanging around the street corner while everyone else was inside the church to pay their final respects to the Stocks. Nick answered that the church had asked him to guard the perimeter to keep the television news media away. The investigator noted that Nick's speech appeared choppy and he had trouble speaking. Nearby, Nick's longtime girlfriend, Lori Muskat, smoked several cigarettes as she watched the encounter. Haugaard also made her furnish identification. Finally, Haugaard returned their identification cards. They were not under arrest or in any trouble, he advised. He let them go about their business. Then, from the distance, the sharp-eyed investigator noticed that Nick continued to pace back and forth between the rear of the church and the street corner. It seemed that Nick continued to look in the general direction of where Haugaard had parked his unmarked cruiser. After the wake ended, all of the NSP investigators huddled. They agreed to conduct more surveillance of Nick Sampson. The NSP tailed Nick's black truck to a nearby house on Oak Street. Police officers watched Nick and his girlfriend Lori head inside.[6]

That same night, Nick placed a call to his first cousin Matt Livers, who was not at the wake. Nick sensed the police were aggressively pursuing both of them as the possible killers. Nick already knew his own brother's car had been seized as the possible getaway vehicle. The next day, a Saturday, Nick Sampson and Matt Livers mustered up the courage to show their faces at the Elmwood-Murdock High School. They didn't know it, but several undercover police officers were also positioned within the large crowd of mourners too, watching their every move like hawks.

. . .

April 22, 2006, marked one of the saddest events in the history of tiny Murdock, but nobody wanted to miss it.

More than one thousand mourners were packed inside the small school gymnasium. Everyone came to pay their last respects to one of the town's most beloved couples who died together in a senseless and unfathomable tragedy. Murdock had never experienced a murder in the town's entire one-hundred-year history. The gym floor was decorated with a sea of pretty flower bouquets from countless people across the region whose lives were forever touched by Wayne and Sharmon Stock. Family members and lifelong friends came from all over the country to attend the somber memorial service and give the Stocks a proper and fitting good-bye.

"That was a tough day," recalled Kirk Drake, Sharmon's brother. "Everyone was still wondering how-when-why it happened."[7]

In the hallways before the service, farmers, small-business owners, and schoolteachers shook their heads in utter disbelief. So many sad and sorrowful faces showed up for the memorial service that volunteers scrambled at the very last minute to set up about seventy extra metal folding chairs on the gym floor. The wooden bleachers couldn't accommodate any more people. People of all ages were in attendance—schoolchildren, the middle-aged, and the elderly. These were mostly community folks who had grown up with Wayne and Sharmon and had known them their entire lives. The couple had been married for more than thirty-seven years when their lives were brutally cut short. Wayne was born on the Fourth of July in 1947. He graduated from the old Murdock High School, then had faithfully served in the Nebraska National Guard and obtained a degree in building construction from Southeast Community College in Lincoln. Everybody knew him as a lifelong farmer, owner of Stock Hay Co., a devout and committed Christian who was a faithful member of Murdock's Ebenezer United Methodist Church. He had lived in Murdock his whole life.

Sharmon (Drake) Stock was three years younger, born on July 25, 1950. She graduated from the old Elmwood High School and married Wayne Stock on August 17, 1968. She had worked for many years as a school paraprofessional in the tiny neighboring town of Manley. Sharmon, too, liked to stay active and involved in her community. She was involved with the Methodist church and the Modern Murdock Extension Club, which was a neighborhood bridge club, a group of women who liked to play cards and chat.[8]

"Everybody loved them, and everybody knew them," remarked local farmer Jim Stock, a first cousin of Wayne Stock. "I don't think they had an enemy in the world."[9]

As the clock approached 10:30 A.M., the pianist began playing "Just a Closer Walk with Thee" and the emotional memorial service got underway. Only days earlier, Andy Stock, Steven Stock, and Tammy Vance all shared a lovely time with their parents at Easter. Andy was the last to see them alive, but not before he gave his mom and dad a hug on their back porch before he went home after retrieving his wandering dog, Charlie.

Now the three exceedingly bright and well-raised siblings in their twenties and thirties had to lean on each other for strength and comfort. Future birthday parties, graduations, holidays, or family vacations would not include their parents. Wayne and Sharmon would never see their grandchildren grow up. Andy, Steven, and Tammy would be forced to spend quiet and reflective time at their parents' grave sites in the local cemetery. Because of the murders, Andy inherited his father's profitable hay business, but many years sooner than he had ever imagined. The murders were an enormous cross to bear for eighty-year-old Lorene Stock. She had just lost her husband, Willard, the previous summer, but he had lived a long and productive life, passing away at age eighty-nine. Now Lorene had to endure the heartbreak of burying her only son and her loving daughter-in-law. Even the Methodist minister, Rev. Jon Wacker, became emotional at times during the difficult community memorial service. The clergyman had gotten to know Wayne and Sharmon personally during his time shepherding the church faithful in Murdock, and he liked them a lot. As he panned the standing-room only crowd in the small-town gymnasium, the minister knew that everyone felt anger, confusion, and grief. He knew the Stocks were the pillars of their community. Wayne and Sharmon never missed any of their own kids' school events and games. The couple emphasized the importance of being righteous and having a strong character. Murdock would never be the same without them. "The world went from being all right to being all wrong," Reverend Wacker told everyone.[10]

The Methodist minister choked up as he tried to share some of his most fond memories of Wayne and Sharmon. After he paused, he smiled. Reverend Wacker spoke about Wayne Stock, the devoted farmer who loved the land; Sharmon Stock, the teacher at heart, who collected antiques and loved spending time with children. Then he joked about Sharmon's card-playing club. He suggested the ladies never really played cards. "I never knew socialize was spelled 'G-A-B,'" Wacker said.

The crowd erupted in laughter. A sea of hands went up when the minister asked if anyone had enjoyed one of Sharmon's decorated cakes for a birthday, an anniversary, or a graduation party.

When the eulogy turned to the topic of anniversaries, the minister turned and politely asked the family, "Did Wayne really buy Sharmon a paddleboat for Mother's Day?"

There were more hearty laughs and some wide-eyed smiles from the mourners. "Isn't that a great memory?" Wacker continued. "That can't be taken away from you."

Of course, there was one face in the crowd at the memorial service that left relatives uneasy and uncomfortable—Matt Livers. It was no longer a secret that Wayne's estranged nephew was considered the prime suspect. And even though the Cass County Sheriff's Office had failed to uncover any eyewitnesses or physical evidence to tie him to the crime scene, Matt Livers was still being targeted as the obvious mastermind and late-night assassin. Why? Because several highly persuasive and influential members of the victims' family told their local cops it had to him.

6

CASE SOLVED

Tuesday, April 25, marked the eighth full day since the farmhouse murders, and both lead investigators had grown sick and tired of their lead suspect's prolonged denials of guilt.

That afternoon, Earl Schenck and Bill Lambert pulled into the concrete driveway of Matt Livers's house in Lincoln. The young man, who had no prior criminal history, not even a speeding ticket, willingly hopped into the backseat of Schenck's cruiser. Livers went on a sixty-mile drive to the Cass County Law Enforcement Center, not realizing, of course, that he was not coming back home. That afternoon in downtown Plattsmouth, the two armed investigators led the victims' nephew into the tiny windowless interrogation room. They closed the door behind them. At first, Schenck and Lambert tried the Mr. Nice Guy approach. At ease, Livers casually explained that he was awoken from a nap on his living room couch late that Monday morning by a phone call from his mother. Matt's fiancée answered the phone. "I heard Sarah say, 'Wayne and Sharmon are dead and it's criminal intent.'" That afternoon, Livers rushed out to Murdock together with his parents to grieve with the rest of his Stock family. "All I really know is it was gunshot," Livers explained. "I don't even know what caliber of weapon was used. . . . What was the motive behind this to get such good people?" The two investigators made up their minds that Livers was the premeditated killer, but they didn't want him to know that yet. So Lambert asked what type of person enters other people's house and takes their lives. "A sick person," Livers replied. "That is what I think, but I don't know. We are like you. We want to know the who, what, when, why, and how." In fact, Livers explained his sole purpose for agreeing to the formal police interview was to "get my name out of this. I was nowhere around that place that night that this happened," he professed.[1]

Unknown to Livers, these investigators had already devised a plan to make him confess to the killings, thanks to the help of Nebraska State Patrol Investigator Charlie O'Callaghan. O'Callaghan waited on standby in another room, ready to administer a lie-detector test Livers was sure to fail. When offered the chance to submit to a lie-detector test, Livers naively answered, "Fine with me." "I will go get him set up," Schenck said, as he left the interview room. O'Callaghan was a no-nonsense Irish investigator in his forties, and he was hardly an unbiased, neutral party. In fact, O'Callaghan had drawn up the search warrants to seize the cellular phone records of the prime suspect and other associates of Livers.

O'Callaghan already knew the Sampson brothers were under suspicion as possible accomplices, so he asked if Livers could think of anybody who might be of interest. Livers identified his cousin Nick Sampson. "I mean, he is a Sampson," Livers explained. "Just when he was growing up, he was not the brightest kid. He dropped out of high school. He reverted to drugs, and he did drugs, and, you know, he did stupid things with friends, just whipping donuts and tearing up fields."

Eventually O'Callaghan got down to business. He simply told Livers to answer "yes" or "no" to all his questions. Livers kept his feet still. He closed his eyes and faced forward. O'Callaghan attached two plastic tubes to Livers's fingers, which monitor the electrical impulses from the brain to the muscles. A blood pressure cuff was wrapped tightly around his arm. O'Callaghan ordered Livers not to burp, cough, or sniffle during the test. Livers closed his eyes and relaxed.

Q: "Reference to the death of Wayne Stock, do you intend to answer each question truthfully about that?"
A: "Yes."
Q: "While employed, did you take anything more than $50 from any employer?"
A: "No."
Q: "Were you involved in causing the death of Wayne Stock?"
A: "No."
Q: "Between the ages of eighteen and twenty-seven, do you remember doing anything that would disappoint your grandmother if she found out?"

A: "No."

Q: "Were you involved in the death of Wayne Stock?"

A: "No."

Q: "Are you hoping the polygraph will make a mistake today?"

A: "No."

Q: "Are you afraid I will ask you a question that I have not gone over word for word?

A: "No."

After the test, Livers opened his eyes and exhaled. "This is kind of tough," Livers exclaimed.

Earlier, he said he had never taken a polygraph before.

"I just want to get my name cleared," Livers declared.

O'Callaghan grabbed the polygraph charts spitting out of his machine. He told Livers he needed to review the charts without the suspect being present. This gave O'Callaghan a golden excuse to huddle with Schenck and Lambert to plot their strategy. The trio decided it was time to turn up the pressure cooker.

.　.　.

Schenck and Lambert stormed back into the interview room, scowling. "Guys, I had nothing to fucking do with this," Livers insisted.

"Let's just get this out in the open," Schenck barked. "We are seeing a different side of you."

"Let me speak, okay?" Lambert declared. "We have been watching you, okay? You are involved in this up to your ears, and if you think this will go away, this is a high-profile case. This will not go away."

"I didn't have anything to do with this," Livers insisted.

Lambert accused Livers of killing his uncle and aunt.

Today was Livers's one and only chance to save himself from a death sentence, Lambert advised.

"Your ass is on the line!" Schenck roared.

"You are on the line," Lambert vowed. "You are in the frying pan right now."

Livers was told he failed the polygraph exam miserably.

"You are off the charts!" Schenck screamed. "There is no messing around with that. You cannot fool it."

"The old Hell's Angels," Lambert lamented. "Three can keep a secret where two are dead. That is true. If you did it by yourself, then stand up and say so."

"I didn't do it by myself," Livers answered.

"Then who did it with you, Matt?" Lambert asked. "It almost came out of your mouth."

"Come on," Schenck ordered.

Livers slumped in his chair and wouldn't answer. The investigators sensed that he felt weak, helpless, and trapped.

"Matt, you know you want to say it," Lambert commanded. "Nobody deserves to die that way, Matt. We don't shoot dogs that way."

Livers looked at the floor. He avoided eye contact with the two visibly agitated interrogators. "We've had so many people sitting in that chair that think they are smarter than us, and they are not," Lambert bragged.

"No, I'm dumb as a brick," Livers replied.

Lambert disagreed.

"No, you are not dumb as a brick. Okay, you made a mistake."

"You fucked up," Schenck told him.

"You fucked up and now you have to pay for it," Lambert added.

"No more blubbering," Schenck demanded. "Just talk to me."

Livers sat speechless.

"I'm just blown away here," Livers responded. "I don't . . ."

"Come on, Matt, these things don't lie," Lambert interrupted. "The investigator who was sitting in here before, O'Callaghan, was trying to ease you into this. We don't work that way. We know the facts of the case now. We know who killed these people. We just want to know why.

"What button did he push on you at Easter time? What did he say to you or what did he deny you that would bring you back to their house in the wee hours of the morning and shoot them in their home?"

Schenck accused Livers of feeding the two investigators a "line of shit since the first day we started talking to you."

"It is time to let it go!" Schenck shouted. "We've let you go on about all the times you got laid off from jobs when you actually got shit-canned because you screwed up."

"Yeah," Livers answered.

Schenck asked Livers if he was a man.

Livers nodded in agreement.

"Then stand up," Lambert commanded.

Livers complied. He literally got out of his chair, and stood on his feet. "No," Lambert interjected. "Stand up and be a man."

"Own up," Schenck added.

"I am trying to," Livers sulked, sitting back down.

Schenck told Livers to stop shrugging his shoulders and looking around the room for answers.

"Because I will look at you and go piss on you!" Schenck roared.

"Electric chair, gas chamber, lethal injection," Lambert rattled off. "That's what kind of case this is. Those were farm folk that got shot like dogs."

"That everybody liked," Schenck added.

"That everybody liked," Lambert repeated.

"I know," Livers agreed.

Lambert stressed that Livers could not turn back the clock on what happened.

"I think there are some days that you lay in bed and you wish you were born in a different family," Lambert declared. "Am I wrong?"

"You're right," Livers agreed.

Lambert pointed out that none of Livers's relatives trusted him.

"In fact, I don't think half of them even like you," Lambert noted.

"They don't," Livers agreed.

Schenck pointed out how the Stocks had a lot of money and land, but they never gave their nephew any of their wealth.

"I've got nothing," Livers shrugged.

And Aunt Sharmon considered Livers the scum of the earth, Schenck told him. "Yeah, a pile of shit, I guess. I don't know," Livers agreed.

"If somebody fucked with me as much as they fucked with your mind, I'd be burning up inside," Schenck reasoned.

"I am," Livers admitted. "I was. I mean, it hurts. It hurts."

Now that the two detectives had broken down Livers mentally, Schenck capitalized on the moment, trying to draw out a confession—based on Schenck's theory for how the murders surely transpired.

Schenck said, "The truth is you got a gun. Right or wrong?"

Livers paused for a few seconds. Then he responded, "Right."

"And you took that gun back to your Uncle Wayne and Aunt Sharmon's house, right? Right or wrong?" barked Schenck.

"Right."

"And you walked upstairs in their house after hours. Right or wrong?"

"Right."

"And when you got to the top of the stairs, you walked back toward the bathroom, right?"

"Right."

"Okay. And you come around the bathroom and you know that house. You've been there many times, right?

"Right."

"And you know they are going to be asleep because it is really late, really early in the morning actually. And you walk up with that shotgun and you saw them laying in bed. Right or wrong?"

"Right, I guess."

"And you got up as close as you could without making too much noise, right?"

"Right."

"And you fired a shot at your Uncle Wayne."

"Right."

Livers agreed his aunt was screaming, but he didn't remember if she was clutching a telephone when she died.

"You don't remember?" Schenck shouted. "But you got pretty close to Aunt Sharmon, didn't you? Close enough to see her face pretty well."

"Yeah."

"And you were mad."

"Yeah."

"All that rage running through you."

"Right."

"And you fired a shot to shut her up. Isn't that right? I need you to say it out loud, buddy."

"Yes, sir."

Schenck asked the suspect to reveal where he shot Wayne.

"Yeah, I think I got him in the head."

Next, Schenck asked if Livers shot his uncle where it was hard to walk.

"The knee," Livers responded. "So he is trying to crawl to the office and then Sharmon was woke up screaming of course, I believe."

Livers paused before regaining his composure.

He added, "Then I pulled that trigger and shot her and then she screamed more and then I just . . ."

"You just what, buddy?" Schenck prodded.

"Put the gun to her face and blew her away," Livers confessed. "And then, as I headed out, I just stuck it to him and blew him away."

Livers claimed he left through the front door and retreated to the cemetery down the road.

"The car was waiting for you?" asked Schenck.

"Yeah, I think it was in the ditch, closer to the road."

"Where did that car come from?"

"I think it was my cousin Will's."

It was the perfect answer.

After Livers denied Will had any involvement in the murders, Schenck questioned if someone else had access to Will's car and keys.

"His brother Nick," Livers replied.

"His brother, Nick. Okay. Brother Nick know where he might be able to get a shotgun?"

"I think he has one."

"So Nick got you set up with keys, put a shotgun in the trunk for you, right or wrong?"

"Right."

Livers admitted he had washed his own clothes after the killings.

"Okay, how come you had to wash them? It's okay. You can tell me."

"Because I shit my pants."

"Okay, besides that unfortunate thing, was there other mess on you?"

"Blood."

.   .   .

Finally, Schenck asked the obvious and most important question. "Who was responsible for the deaths of Wayne and Sharmon Stock?"

"I was," admitted Livers.

"Now, tell me how you are feeling."

"Like shit."

"Are you breathing a little easier than you were before? It ain't going to bring them back."

"No. I fucked up."

Schenck pressed for the motive.

"Like you said, just pissed off."

When the two investigators pressured Livers to identify an accomplice, he obliged.

"Who was with you that night?"

"Nick Sampson."

As the hours rolled by, Livers's incriminating confession was all captured on the video camera mounted on the wall of the sheriff's department.

Schenck took a moment to compliment Livers.

"I have the utmost respect for what you are doing right now. I'm not trying to bullshit you. This is not an easy thing to do."

Since it was getting late in the evening, the two investigators took a break. They offered their confessor his choice of soda.

"Mountain Dew? I'll get that covered," offered Schenck.

Lambert said, "You did good today. I know you don't feel a lot better, but you're doing good."

Later on, other Cass County Sheriff's deputies fed the new prisoner his very first meal of the day, a bucket of delicious and mouthwatering chicken wings ordered from a local restaurant in Plattsmouth. As Livers devoured the wings and licked the bones dry, his two interrogators ducked out of the building. They had more work to do.

. . .

The sturdy brick building not far from the downtown Murdock post office was a popular hangout for area farmers and townsfolk. Above the entrance, two bulldog heads scowled down from a large wooden sign. The faded paint alerted thirsty patrons that the Bulldogs Bar & Grill offered ice-cold beer, fine food, and was open seven days a week. The fried chicken and fish fries were popular meals. The pork tenderloin, served with mashed potatoes, gravy, corn, and a dinner roll, was another down-home delight. The Bulldogs was known for its hospitality and well-attended karaoke and live music nights. The corner building on Nebraska Street had character and lots of country music blaring on the jukebox.

Well past dark, a black Chevy C-1500 truck bearing Nebraska license plates was parked in front of the tavern. Inside, the bar was noisy as usual. Draft beers flowed out of the tapped kegs. Food orders kept the kitchen busy. Locals enjoyed each other's company, just like any other night.

Chaos was about to unfold.

Around 9 P.M., the phone rang. One of the bartenders answered. The caller asked if Nick Sampson was in the kitchen. Yes he was, the barmaid politely answered. Suddenly, a half-dozen armed Cass County Sheriff's deputies and Nebraska State Patrol officers stormed into the bar. The commotion startled the patrons. Within a matter of seconds, Investigator Schenck spotted Nick in the back kitchen. The scruffy part-time cook was placed in handcuffs and marched past the stunned customers, who wondered what was going on. Police escorted Sampson through the front door and stuffed him into the backseat of a navy blue Nebraska State Patrol cruiser parked outside. Sampson, almost twenty-two, learned he was being arrested in connection with the first-degree double murders of local farmers Wayne and Sharmon Stock. This was a capital offense, which meant that Nebraska's death penalty could be invoked.

"What the fuck?" Nick blurted.[2]

Stunned, upset, and visibly depressed, Nick kept quiet during the forty-minute ride back to the Cass County Jail in Plattsmouth. He had no idea his cousin Matt Livers had just implicated him as an accomplice in the Stock murders. At the sheriff's facility, Nick traded his blue jeans and black T-shirt for an orange jail jumpsuit. But he disappointed the cops by refusing to be interviewed. He insisted he was innocent. He demanded an attorney. Nonetheless, Nick Sampson was thrown in a cell at the Cass County Jail, charged with two counts of first-degree murder. Late into the night, investigators from Cass County and the NSP executed search warrants at the residences of Nick Sampson and Matt Livers. In the town of Palmyra, authorities retrieved a .12-gauge Winchester model pump shotgun from underneath Nick's bed. The weapon was thought to be the obvious murder weapon. Police also recovered numerous spent shotgun shells and clothes inside Nick's rental house. Several miles away, Douglas County CSI Chief Dave Kofoed and his team of diligent CSIs cleaned out Livers's bedroom closet, over in Lincoln. The CSIs hauled away several black trash bags filled with the defendant's clothes, including six pairs of shoes. No weapons were recovered from Livers's residence. That night, police also impounded Nick Sampson's black truck and Matt Livers's red Pontiac Sunbird convertible for additional forensics testing. Around 2:30 A.M. investigators rustled Will Sampson and his fiancée out of bed, armed with a court-issued search warrant. Police tried to find weapons, blood, hair, soil, or other trace evidence to link Will to the murders. Investigators found none of that. They left Will's apartment without securing his arrest.[3]

·   ·   ·

Sometime during the night, Cass County Sheriff's investigators shared their good news with the victims' family. "Police said he [Matt Livers] made a confession," Kirk Drake remembered. "That's when it kind of hit home. It was like, 'Wow' he admitted to doing it.'"[4] The next morning, the Cass County Sheriff's Office staged a press conference to announce the arrests of Matt Livers and Nick Sampson. Approximately twenty print, television, and radio journalists

Cass County Sheriff Bill Brueggemann spoke at a press conference in April 2006 in downtown Plattsmouth, Nebraska, to announce the arrests of Matt Livers and Nick Sampson, who was Will Sampson's younger brother. *(Lincoln Journal Star Photo)*

from Omaha, Lincoln, and Plattsmouth gathered on the front lawn of the historic Cass County Courthouse to cover the milestone moment for police officials overseeing the Stock investigation.

"I would like to thank everyone who assisted with this investigation," long-time Cass County Sheriff Bill Brueggemann announced. "It is through good team work and effort we are able to ease the fears of the Stock family and residents of Cass County with the arrest of these two suspects." The sheriff cautioned the reporters that his investigators were still trying to determine the motive.[5]

.   .   .

That afternoon, Livers ate turkey and dressing for lunch after spending his first full night at the Cass County Jail. Despite being incarcerated, he willingly agreed to yet another interview with his interrogators. This time, Schenck and Lambert wanted him to put Nick Sampson directly inside Wayne and Sharmon's farmhouse at the time of the murders. After all, the massive blood spatter confirmed the presence of a second person lurking around the upstairs hallway.

"Matt, don't hide from me on this. Just talk to me, man. Did he go into that house, Matthew?" asked Schenck.

"Yes. He was in the house."

Livers confessed his cousin Nick fired the second shot into Wayne Stock's skull.

He added, "If I recall, the second shot took place in the hallway."

"Okay. I can agree with that," said Schenck.

Lambert asked, "One hundred percent sure he is the last person to fire that gun, and it's only the one shotgun between the two of you?"

"Yes, sir. Like you said, his head went everywhere."

The investigators needed to clear up the matter of the red marijuana pipe recovered in the driveway. Livers claimed the pipe belonged to Nick. Livers admitted, "He smoked a bowl, yes. I had my cigarettes." He claimed the pipe fell from Nick's pants as the two cousins ran from the farmhouse. He added, "I think he tripped and fell, kind of did a roll."

Still, Lambert and Schenck weren't quite sure what to make of that partially open window and the detached window screen with a tiny puncture hole found near the wooden patio. Livers flatly denied he or Nick tampered with any windows on the house. He and Nick came and left through the doors, Livers professed. His response seemed satisfactory, so the two investigators did not probe further.

7

BLOOD

Matt Livers's new reality settled in and smacked him like a brick in the face.

No more home-cooked dinners at his parents' house in Lincoln. No more lounging on his sofa to cheer for Tony Stewart or Dale Earnhardt Jr. during NASCAR season. Dreams of marrying his longtime sweetheart, Sarah Schneider, in the summer were shattered. Plans to attend commercial truck-driving school in Green Bay, Wisconsin, were deflated. Matt's life was in the hands of the Nebraska criminal justice system and the employees who controlled the Cass County Jail, where he was now a prisoner. Pictures of his face were plastered across several Nebraska newspapers, news Web sites, and television screens. At the jail, Matt traded his civilian clothes for standard orange jail garments. He slept on an uncomfortable bed behind steel bars. Jailers monitored his movements and kept a close eye on him. Despite all he had endured during the past twenty-four hours, Livers remained cooperative and compliant toward his police captors.

At one point, jailers escorted the new high-profile prisoner back into one of the Cass County Law Enforcement Center's windowless interrogation rooms. This time Livers drew a detailed diagram showing the interior layout of Wayne Stock's farmhouse. As part of the diagram, Livers labeled areas in the hallway where he and codefendant Nick Sampson allegedly stood. Livers knew the layout well since he had been inside several times over the years for family gatherings and holidays. That afternoon, NSP Investigator Charlie O'Callaghan also planned to administer another polygraph test. He aimed to gauge the veracity of Livers's statements about Nick Sampson's apparent involvement as the other gunman. At this stage, Livers's help was paramount because Nick was refusing to cooperate with police. But before the lie-detector test got underway, something unusual happened.

While the police video camera continued to record the exchange, Livers started rubbing his eyes. He paused for several seconds. The room grew uncomfortably silent. Something was clearly on Livers's mind. O'Callaghan surmised that Livers was about to unload another incriminating bombshell, perhaps ready to implicate others. He made an astonishing revelation all right, but it was not what O'Callaghan had in mind. Livers said, "Well, the absolute truth is, uh, I was never on the scene. I don't know if Nick is the actual person involved in this. I've just been making things up to satisfy you guys, and answering questions just from, you know, basically fitting in answers to what you guys have been asking."[1]

O'Callaghan's Irish blood began to boil. He grew testy. He raised his voice. He accused Livers of jerking him around.

"No, sir," denied Livers.

"No, you are. I'm telling you. You are!"

"No, sir."

Naturally, O'Callaghan was accustomed to criminals recanting their involvement after a sobering night of personal reflection inside the unfriendly confines of a jail cell. Livers's attempt to retract his confession was hardly a rare phenomenon. O'Callaghan reminded Livers that he had also tried to deny involvement in the murders at the start of his interview with Lambert and Schenck, only to confess after flunking the polygraph test. "You took a polygraph yesterday, and I gave it to you, and you were 100 percent involved with this," O'Callaghan grumbled, "and I have no doubt about it."

"Right," Livers agreed. "But the truth is I was never on the scene on this. I don't know if Nick is involved in this because we never, I mean, you can check my phone records. We never talked on Thursday or Friday about this. I mean this has been eating at me."

Livers explained he picked his cousin Nick only because he heard through the grapevine that Nick's brother's car was used in the slayings.

"What are you telling me this now for? What do you think it is going to accomplish?" demanded O'Callaghan.

"I'm just trying to come clean."

"You were there. . . . You've told us things that, unless you were there, you'd have no idea about."

According to Livers, his father learned details of the crime from one of Sharmon Stock's brothers, who had spoken with the investigators.

"And he told me about it," said Livers. "I mean the only reason that I know about the drug paraphernalia, I heard from Andy, Wayne's son, saying that when he pulled in and he nearly ran it over with his truck."

O'Callaghan demanded to know when Livers ever spoke with Andy Stock since it was Andy who discovered the bodies.

"I heard it from my mother on Monday, the day this happened, that even the [Cass County Sheriff's] investigator pulled in and nearly ran it over."

O'Callaghan was caught in a mudslide. He didn't want to make things worse for the ongoing investigation efforts, so he cut off the interview. He decided not to give Livers a polygraph test that day. Jailers escorted the prisoner back to his jail cell. None of the key investigators attempted to do any follow-up on the Livers recantation interview. No one sought to verify whether he was being truthful when he suggested being privy to certain intimate details about the crime scene. After all, Lambert, Schenck, and O'Callaghan had his incriminating confession, and that's all that really mattered now that Livers and Nick Sampson were headed to court.

.   .   .

The Cass County Courthouse, built around 1890, was an imposing maroon-brick structure atop a small hill at the far eastern edge of Plattsmouth's Main Street, only a block from the Burlington Northern Santa Fe Railroad tracks. Plattsmouth overlooks the scenic Missouri River in southeastern Nebraska and the Loess Hills region of southwestern Iowa in the distance. A refurbished toll bridge, built of steel in the late 1920s, moved motorists and heavy truck traffic between Iowa and Nebraska. The city of seven thousand, incorporated in 1855, was home to one of the oldest standing business districts in Nebraska. The courthouse, listed on the National Register of Historic Places, occupied half a block. The government building's distinguished architectural characteristics included a soaring clock tower. Corner towers had steeply pitched hipped roofs and gables. Original features of the building's interior remain unchanged, including thirteen-foot-high ceilings, tile flooring, and oak woodwork along the walls.[2] The small-town courthouse was a hub of weekday activity, but sensational murder cases that drew television news trucks from Omaha and Lincoln were a rare exception. The television news crews that camped along historic Main Street made many of the local folks heading into the courthouse for routine business somewhat uncomfortable. On April 27, 2006, Livers and Sampson had their initial hearings in a pint-sized county courtroom. In the gallery, brothers Andy and Steve Stock glared at Matt Livers with deep anger as armed sheriff's deputies escorted the young man in the orange Cass County Jail jumpsuit marked XL to a wooden table in front of the judge's raised bench. Livers sported a bleach-blond streak of hair that looked totally out of place against his natural-colored dark-brown goatee. He also wore clinking leg shackles and metal handcuffs. After taking his seat, Livers glanced over his shoulder to pan the small crowd of spectators. He looked nervous and scared. Family members wondered what possessed Wayne Stock's nephew to callously murder his uncle and aunt as they slept.

During the brief hearing, Cass County Attorney Nathan Cox, the soft-spoken, rusty-haired prosecutor, advised everyone that each of the two first-degree murder counts carried a sentence of life in prison without parole or capital punishment, if convicted. Livers sat expressionless and teary-eyed. He admitted to the judge that he was unemployed and had been without a job for nearly two months. He did not own any property of value either. As anticipated, Judge John Steinheider denied the defendant bail, given the seriousness of the crimes. The prosecutor put up no objections when the judge appointed Julie Bear, Cass County public defender, to represent Livers. Bear was a hard-working, smart, and conscientious lawyer. She was a true public servant. Most of her court appointments involved indigent clients who were involved with drugs, thefts, burglaries, domestic violence, and drunk-driving offenses. Although Bear had limited experience representing murder defendants, Livers and his family had no alternative. The Livers family could not afford private defense counsel. Those so-called hired guns easily commanded $25,000 or more to represent someone accused of murder.

After the routine court hearing finished, Cass County Sheriff's deputies held Livers by his arms and whisked him past several excited journalists holding cameras camped out in the hallway. News media eagerly captured video footage and still images of the shackled and glum-faced nephew accused of murdering his kind, well-liked relatives in their sleep. Several minutes later, the process was repeated. Sheriff's deputies hustled codefendant Nick Sampson into the same small courtroom. Sampson hadn't slept in a few days and appeared disheveled. His brown hair was ruffled. He hadn't shaved. As he sat alone at the defense table, Sampson repeatedly shook his head in disbelief. Court testimony revealed that Nick was fired from his full-time job as a welder after the notoriety of his high-profile arrest on double-murder charges. The judge denied bail, but agreed Sampson also qualified for a public defender. The court appointed Jerry Soucie, who worked for the Nebraska Public Advocacy Commission. Soucie's state-funded nonprofit organization primarily represented indigent clients facing potential death-penalty cases in largely rural counties of Nebraska. Later that day, journalists rushed out of the Cass County Courthouse to file their daily news accounts. The front-page headline for the *Omaha World-Herald* read, "Heinous crimes bring bail denial." Photos of Livers and Sampson in jail garb appeared on the front page of Nebraska's largest newspaper.

One of Livers's cousins, middle-aged farmer Jim Stock, told the newspaper, "It's hard to believe and hard to understand what the motive was. At the funeral, Matt and I shook hands, and he was shedding tears and grieving like the rest of us."[3]

· · ·

Unbeknownst to journalists and Nebraskans, Cass County law enforcement officials were growing very impatient and frustrated.

None of the physical evidence lined up as the cops had anticipated. Although Livers confessed his clothes were drenched with blood, all of his clothes seized from his bedroom closet in Lincoln lacked any blood. Additionally, none of the clothes removed from Nick Sampson's residence contained blood either. Making matters worse for police, the roommates for both murder defendants furnished them with plausible alibis. In separate police interviews, Susan Gill and Sarah Schneider insisted Matt Livers could not possibly have sneaked out of their rental house in Lincoln during the night of the killings. Sarah told the State Patrol that she and Livers both retired to bed around 11 P.M. on Easter night. They slept together in the same bed, as always. She found Livers asleep, clad in the same pajamas, when she awoke around seven that Monday morning.[4] Sampson's two female roommates furnished similar alibis. Lori Muskat insisted that Nick remained in bed with her the entire night of Easter. When she got up for work around 6:30 that Monday, her longtime boyfriend was still in their bed. She also pointed out to police that their two large dogs slept at the foot of their bed. The dogs growled and barked whenever someone left or entered their house. Lori never recalled hearing the dogs bark during the night in question. Their other roommate, Ashley Hageman, also corroborated Lori's account. Ashley never heard the dogs barking either, and she never heard their noisy and creaky front door open or shut during the entire night.[5]

Without any hard evidence tying Livers and Sampson to the Murdock farmhouse, the lead investigators became increasingly desperate. They hounded and badgered Kofoed and his crackerjack CSIs at the Douglas County Sheriff's

Office. The lead investigators began second-guessing the workmanship of the hotshot CSI team from Omaha. The investigators just couldn't believe that Kofoed and his team of highly skilled CSIs spent roughly eight hours tearing apart Will Sampson's car yet failed to find a single trace of blood. After all, Livers confessed he and Nick both used the car during the commission of the premeditated and bloody shotgun slayings. Furthermore, Livers confessed his own clothes were covered with blood after the close-range shotgun shootings. The CSIs from Douglas County were under relentless pressure to come up with some magical piece of evidence to corroborate the nephew's confession.

·　·　·

On April 27, NSP Investigator Bill Lambert asked Kofoed, the crime lab manager, to recheck the backseat of Will Sampson's car for signs of gunshot residue. Will's car remained at the Douglas County Sheriff's Office impound lot, not far from Kofoed's crime lab. Kofoed went back and rechecked the car a second time. He had a proven reputation for finding crucial evidence that others managed to miss or overlook. That afternoon, Kofoed signed his

An extensive exam of Will Sampson's car under Kofoed's careful watch and direct supervision found no blood, DNA, or trace evidence to tie the car to the farmhouse murders. Days later, Kofoed alerted lead investigators that he found Wayne Stock's blood underneath the dashboard, the only area Kofoed reprocessed that day. *(Author's collection)*

initials on a log sheet at the Sheriff's Office impound lot to check out the keys for Will's car. Instead of focusing on the backseat, Kofoed crawled underneath the driver's side dashboard near the steering column. The CSI director emerged with an oval-shaped piece of crime lab filter paper that turned pink. The filter paper signified a positive preliminary reaction for blood.[6] Back at his CSI administrative office, Kofoed called Lambert back around 4:30 P.M. Kofoed shared the exciting development. Lambert was thrilled and agreed to rush out to the county crime lab once he finished up his investigative report that evening. He arrived at the Sheriff's Office around 8 P.M. Kofoed escorted him to the impound lot and showed him the Ford Contour car, which was parked behind a barbed-wire fence and locked gate. Kofoed pointed to the spot under the dashboard where he found the blood. The bloodstain gave investigators the smoking gun needed to corroborate Livers's confession. "I mean it was like finding a needle in a haystack," Lambert later testified. "It was encouraging news."[7]

Kofoed saved the blood sample. Scientists at the University of Nebraska Medical Center's Human DNA lab later determined the filter paper specimen contained a full DNA profile matching murder victim Wayne Stock. Nebraska law enforcement officials let out a sigh of great relief. The recovery of Wayne Stock's blood directly tied Livers to the getaway car.

Unfortunately for Lambert, Schenck, Weyers, O'Callaghan, and Kofoed, the Stocks' killers hadn't been caught yet.

In fact, those late-night assassins were long gone from Nebraska.

8

ODD FIND

On the third day of the double murder investigation, the Douglas County crime lab packed up its crime-fighting tools. Kofoed and his fellow CSIs returned to Omaha after having spent three long, exhausting days and nights of processing the Stocks' bloody farmhouse. Unbeknownst to anybody in Nebraska law enforcement, a bizarre clue had been left behind at the two-story farmhouse along 286th Street.

On the fourth day of the case, detectives at the Cass County Sheriff's Office huddled. They reviewed hundreds of crime-scene photographs taken throughout the Stocks' home. These photos gave the detectives a snapshot into the minds of the assassins. The same perpetrators had maneuvered through the victims' home in complete and total darkness before taking the Stocks by complete surprise. Crime scene photos showed no evidence of robbery. The house had not been ransacked. All of the rooms were remarkably undisturbed. As the detectives reviewed some of the more mundane crime photos, one eagle-eyed Cass County Sheriff's detective spotted a shiny obscure object resting on the kitchen floor. Other investigators concurred with Sheriff Lt. Larry "Ike" Burke's sharp-eyed observation. Sure enough, a foreign object might have been overlooked at the farmhouse double murders. That afternoon, investigators rushed back to the remote country farmhouse. Burke was proven right. Inside the kitchen of the murder house, Sgt. Sandy Weyers bent down to the floor.

And there it was! A yellow-gold ring tucked underneath the kick plate near Sharmon Stock's kitchen sink. The odd discovery featured a unique engraving. Black lettering read, "Love Always, Cori and Ryan." The cautious investigators were baffled. They didn't know who their new clue belonged to. The ring was put into a secured paper bag. Bill Kaufhold of the Douglas County crime lab

In the bottom right-hand corner of this crime scene photograph, taken inside murder victim Sharmon Stock's kitchen, was an engraved ring of unknown origin. (*Author's collection*)

was assigned to take possession of the strange, shiny object. Afterward, the Douglas County CSI lab took several photos of the gold ring and placed the item into its evidence storage unit.[1]

The murder victims' family all shared the same reaction. They had never seen the ring before. The ring definitely did not belong to Wayne or Sharmon, their grown children told authorities. Even the names on the ring—Cori and Ryan—didn't register with the family. At first, Cass County Sheriff's investigators assumed the ring belonged to Ryan Paulding, murder suspect Matt Livers's best friend. Livers had happened to stay at Ryan Paulding's residence in Texas during those three weeks leading up to the killings. Nebraska authorities probed deeper into Paulding's background and his relationship with their confessed killer. Police obtained a search warrant to retrieve Paulding's phone records. However, none of the investigative efforts to tie Paulding to the engraved gold ring panned out. No evidence suggested that Paulding traveled from Texas to Nebraska to participate in the murders of the Stocks.[2] The lack of immediate answers left the cops scratching their heads. They even grew skeptical about the ring's potential relevance to the homicides. Given that the

At the time of his arrest, Nick Sampson's .12-gauge shotgun was seized by police from underneath his bed. Investigators presumed the shotgun was used kill the Stocks. *(Author's collection)*

investigators were already stretched thin in the early days of the case, their attention turned to other more obvious clues.

For approximately two weeks, the ring stayed in a sealed evidence bag as local cops unsuccessfully built their case against Livers and Nick Sampson. Aside from the bloodstain Kofoed found inside Will Sampson's car, nothing else surfaced to tie the cousins to the scene of the crime. Other aspects of Livers's confession began to unravel. One of the more troubling signs came when NSP ballistics expert Mark Bohaty concluded that the .12-gauge Winchester shotgun seized from Nick Sampson's bedroom was definitely not the murder weapon.[3]

As the evidence trail became ice cold, NSP Investigator Bill Lambert remembered how the ring on the Stocks' kitchen floor was out of place. Lambert sensed the ring hadn't been researched fully. He knew from his numerous interviews with relatives that Sharmon Stock always kept her entire house, especially her kitchen, immaculate and neat. The crime scene photos confirmed this fact. Room after room appeared as neat as a pin after the murders. The ring was ultimately submitted for DNA testing at the University of Nebraska Medical Center. The lab tests results threw Lambert and Schenck another curveball. The independent lab analysis found a mixed DNA sample showing two unknown contributors. The DNA residue left on the ring did not match the DNA characteristics of either Matt Livers or Nick Sampson, the two men already in jail for the murders.

This was just the latest kick in the gut for the lead investigators. The shiny red-colored marijuana pipe recovered from the Stocks' gravel driveway also excluded the DNA characteristics of Livers and Nick Sampson. If the DNA residue deposited on both the dope pipe and engraved ring excluded the pair of cousins already charged with two counts of first-degree murder, then who did the DNA belong to? Who were Cori and Ryan?

9

RING OF TRUTH

Dave Kofoed assigned Christine Gabig to track the engraved ring's origin. Gabig, a trace evidence expert, seemed right for the task. She was like a dog on a bone, Kofoed remembered. She scoured jewelry books and magazines to understand the significance of the serial imprint on the ring bearing the letters and numerals AAJ10K. She discovered that the last three symbols stood for 10 karat gold. Gabig also gleaned that the letters "AAJ" revealed the jewelry manufacturer's trademark. Two North American companies had used those letters; one had been out of business and without an address since 1994. If the ring belonged to that company, the mystery behind the ring would surely hit a brick wall and end there. Fortunately, Gabig discovered a working phone number for the other company, A & A Jewelers Inc., which was located in Buffalo, New York.[1]

Gabig's cold call caught one of the female employees in the shipping department by complete surprise. That woman wasn't quite sure what to do. The employee notified her manager that someone from a Nebraska police department was on the line. Operations manager Mary Martino dropped her heavy workload to take the unexpected call.

. . .

Gabig's call in May 2006 could not have come at a worse time. Martino was preoccupied with closing her company's offices in Buffalo. She was one of three employees left to liquidate the A & A Jewelers operation. About two hundred employees had just been let go. The company in New York was in the midst of bankruptcy and in the process of disconnecting its telephone in a matter of days. During the call, Martino confirmed that Gabig was, at the

This engraved ring with the unique inscription "Love Always, Cori & Ryan," ultimately cracked the Stock murder case. DNA left on the ring would prove deeply damaging to one theory of the crime and pivotal to another, after an extensive "needle in a haystack" search traced it back to a particular owner. *(Author's collection)*

very least, on the right track. The AAJ imprint definitely matched the A & A jewelry company manufacturer's serial number. Additionally, Walmart was one of A & A's biggest retail customers, Martino advised. Gabig conceded she didn't have any additional useful information to pass along except for the ring's unique inscription, "Love Always, Cori & Ryan."

"That's like looking for a needle in a haystack," Martino replied.[2]

But Gabig persisted. She pleaded for Martino's help. This ring was mysteriously found at a gruesome double homicide in rural Nebraska. Everyone else appeared unwilling to assist her, Gabig admitted. Martino didn't shrug off the call. Rather, she promised to see if she could be of any help, realizing the case involved double murder.

Unfortunately, Martino didn't have much to go on. All she knew was that her company manufactured the ring and created the unique engraving. She had no idea which of the literally thousands of Walmarts scattered across the country may have sold that ring and whether the purchase order still existed. In any case, Martino promised to get back in touch with CSI Gabig if she found anything noteworthy.

After the call, Martino headed straight to A & A's warehouse, which stored copies of tens of thousands of back records for jewelry purchases from all over. She started with Box 1, which inventoried the sales receipts for Walmart stores 1 through 25. She inspected every single sales record in the box but came up empty. Next, Martino moved on to Box 2. It contained sales receipts from stores 26 through 30. Again, no luck. Martino inspected Box 3, Box 4, Box 5, and so on. She spent several hours manually inspecting dozens of boxes, trying to find the elusive sales receipt for the "Love Always, Cori & Ryan" engraved ring.

Martino went through sales receipts for approximately one hundred Walmart stores. She found nothing. She was exhausted. She felt hopeless and emotionally drained. "I thought this is going to be impossible doing this," Martino said.

.   .   .

Back in Nebraska, CSI Gabig contacted the Walmart stores around Omaha and Lincoln, hoping the ring was purchased there, but her enthusiasm was dashed when local Walmart officials denied the ring came from one of the eastern Nebraska stores. Gabig's efforts reached an impasse. It was all up to the Buffalo jeweler who had never even been to Nebraska before. By now, Martino could have called off the records search, realizing it was becoming too labor intensive. After all, A & A shipped its jewelry to more than three thousand retail stores across the country.

But Martino didn't quit. "I heard homicide. I heard it was important," Martino recalled.

Martino enlisted help from the A & A corporate headquarters in Toronto. They devised a computer grid listing the Walmart stores across North America that did business with A & A Jewelers. The computer grid also included possible dates the ring was sold, along with the special inscription.

Martino's amazing persistence eventually paid off.

"After three days of searching," Martino remembered, "I got up from my chair, and I said, 'I found it! I found it!'"

At long last, she did.

The A & A purchase order showed that a female customer bought the ring in December 2004 at Walmart store no. 1012. Martino faxed the sales receipt to the authorities in the heartland.

This time, Nebraska investigators were in for another shocker.

This ring came from the Walmart store in Beaver Dam, Wisconsin. The southcentral Wisconsin city had a growing population of sixteen thousand. Beaver Dam was about forty miles northeast of Madison and about seventy miles northwest of Milwaukee. According to the sales receipt, someone named Cori Zastrow spent about $130 to buy the ring for her boyfriend. NSP Investigator Bill Lambert had never heard Zastrow's name mentioned at any point during the Stock murder case, but he checked her out. Back in Nebraska, investigators now surmised that Zastrow and her boyfriend Ryan might be associates of Livers and Nick Sampson. The murder case in Murdock, Nebraska, had now widened into Wisconsin.

In mid-May, Lambert notified the Dodge County Sheriff's Department in Juneau, Wisconsin, that he already had two local men in custody in connection with a brutal double murder in rural Nebraska. Then Lambert explained the odd piece of jewelry left at the Nebraska crime scene. He explained how the ring was purchased in Beaver Dam by a young lady named Cori Zastrow.[3] Dodge County Detective Mark Murphy agreed to help investigate the matter. Lambert sent Murphy a list of questions to ask her. Naturally, Cori Zastrow and her mother Louise were quite surprised when a Dodge County patrol car rolled into their driveway on the evening of May 17, 2006. The mother and daughter politely greeted the local detective and let Murphy inside.

Cori was a nineteen-year-old commuter student at the Madison Area Technical College. A responsible young lady who had no prior criminal history, she also kept busy by working as a part-time secretary for her mother's fraud investigations firm. Cori drove a 2002 silver Grand Am bearing Wisconsin plates. Neither schooling nor her part-time job required her to travel outside Wisconsin. Cori and her mother insisted they had never been to Nebraska. Cori denied knowing anybody who lived there. She and her mother remembered staying home for Easter weekend. All of their travels were local and routine, the detective learned. The mother and daughter were stunned to learn the ring Cori bought for her former boyfriend approximately eighteen months earlier managed to surface at a horrific and bloody double murder some five hundred miles away in rural Nebraska.

·   ·   ·

Back in 2004, Cori Zastrow fell in love with a young farmer named Ryan Krenz. Ryan, who worked on his parents' dairy farm on the outskirts of Beaver Dam, came from a typical Wisconsin farm family. Deer hunting was a big family ritual. Like thousands of Wisconsinites, the Krenzes donned their neon-orange hunting jackets every November. Ryan embraced the farm life. He also owned a bright-red 2002 full-size Dodge Ram 2500-model pickup, complete with an extended cab.

With the romance blossoming, Cori went ahead and placed an order for a specially engraved gold ring at her local Walmart. She then gave the ring to Ryan as a special gift. However, a few weeks later, their romance fizzled and the couple broke up. Although the two young adults remained close friends, Cori let Ryan keep the ring, she told the detective.[4]

After leaving the Zastrows, Detective Murphy decided to interview Ryan Krenz about the circumstances of this engraved ring. The following evening, Ryan and his parents sat down for a formal police interview at the kitchen table with the curious Wisconsin detective now helping Nebraska authorities piece together a multi-state double murder mystery. Now age twenty-one, Ryan confirmed his former girlfriend's account. He and Cori had dated. She gave him the ring. Their relationship soon soured. After the breakup, Ryan remembered stashing the ring inside the glove compartment of his Dodge Ram truck.

He hadn't seen the ring for several months, he estimated. As for Ryan's truck, the Wisconsin police already knew the full set of facts regarding that story.

.   .   .

Back on Saturday, April 15, 2006, Ryan parked his big red truck in his family's gravel driveway as usual. Then suddenly, a family crisis ensued. Ryan's older brother suffered serious injuries in an auto accident, and was airlifted to a trauma center about eighty miles away near Appleton. One of Ryan's close friends rushed over to the Krenz farmhouse to drive Ryan to the hospital. That evening, Ryan was relieved to learn his brother's injuries were not life-threatening. Sometime after 10:30 P.M., Ryan got a ride back to his farmhouse. He went straight to bed, thankful his brother's injuries had not been fatal. The next morning was Easter. When Ryan went outside around 7:30, his truck was gone.

At first, he figured one of his friends stopped by and borrowed it when he was at the hospital in the Fox Valley on Saturday night. Ryan called all his friends. One by one, they denied borrowing his truck. Ryan realized that someone had stolen his truck after he got a ride to the hospital.

Ryan called 911. A Dodge County Sheriff's cruiser came to the Krenz farm to take the stolen vehicle report that Easter Sunday. Ryan told the deputy that he left his truck unlocked and the keys were inside the ignition. The Sheriff's deputy estimated the truck was taken sometime after 7:30 the previous night. The truck had logged about 31,000 miles and was worth about $18,000. Information about the missing truck was entered into an active national police database for stolen vehicles.[5]

Back in Wisconsin, April 16 and April 17 passed without any news regarding the stolen truck's whereabouts. When the truck was finally located, it was almost twelve hundred miles away.

.   .   .

On the evening of April 18, a passing motorist alerted law enforcement to a dirty abandoned truck stranded near Opelousas, Louisiana. St. Landry Parish Sheriff's Deputy Josh Godchaux approached the empty Dodge Ram truck parked along the shoulder of state Highway 10 and Interstate 49. The Louisiana deputy found the doors were locked and the truck had minor front-end damage. The occupants were long gone. The truck bore Wisconsin license plates and was registered to Ryan Krenz of Beaver Dam, Wisconsin. Godchaux quickly realized the truck was reported stolen. He had the truck towed to an impound lot in Louisiana for safekeeping. A radio dispatcher in Louisiana alerted the Dodge County Sheriff's Office in Juneau, Wisconsin, about the truck's recovery.[6]

Experienced Dodge County Detective Jim Rohr was assigned to follow up on the stolen truck report. Rohr had more than twenty years on the force and was one of his agency's smartest detectives. The silver-haired investigator let the evidence tell the story rather than let his own guesswork guide his criminal investigations. Rohr initially figured Ryan Krenz's truck was just another routine auto theft. When the Wisconsin detective discovered the truck was driven all the way to Louisiana, Rohr suspected one of the thieves surely had ties to the Deep South. But that was not the case at all. Rohr discovered that a Beaver Dam resident, Betty Kehl, had contacted police in reference to the stolen red truck. Kehl told police that she spotted two teenagers around 7:30 P.M. on Saturday, April 15, walking toward the Krenz farm along Canary Road. The creepy-looking boy and girl looked about sixteen and eighteen. Both wore black Goth attire and looked totally out of character for the neighborhood.[7] Detective Rohr's intuition told him this was a good tip to follow up.

10

LEOPOLD AND LOEB

Greg Fester had led a train wreck of a life growing up between the communities of Beaver Dam and Horicon in southcentral Wisconsin. His criminal history could be traced back to age ten. At twelve, Fester confronted two students at his middle school with a twelve-inch butcher knife. By the time he was fourteen, he wound up on a law enforcement sex offender registry and ended up at an alternative school. Fester set small arson fires and committed random acts of vandalism. He shot out car windows with pellet guns for kicks. "This was a kid who grew up with law enforcement in the back of his pocket," remarked Horicon Police Chief Doug Glamann. "Every police officer on our department knew who he was, where he lived, and every one of them would do a second look-over every time we saw him out in public."[1]

As Fester got older, he grew more violent and impulsive. His life was clouded by heavy drug use. At seventeen, he fathered a child, but Fester had no role in raising the infant. In December 2004, Fester approached the teenage mother outside the Beaver Dam High School. He warned her to stay away from his current girlfriend. Fester grabbed the ex-girlfriend with one arm and pulled out a knife, holding it near her waist. He shoved her backwards and threatened to kill her. The knife incident on Beaver Dam school property resulted in Fester's expulsion. The police arrested him for use of a dangerous weapon, a serious misdemeanor. Under a summer 2005 plea bargain, Fester was convicted of disorderly conduct and put on probation for one year.

By April 2006, Fester, age nineteen, had racked up at least twenty separate arrests or juvenile citations. Illegal drugs consumed his life. He constantly smoked marijuana. He owned dozens of bongs and pipes to feed his high. Fester also dabbled in heroin and cocaine, but he didn't use those drugs as frequently. He also experimented with Dextromethorphan. Dex is the ingredient in over-the-counter cough suppressants. When taken in excessive dosages, it can spark hallucinations. Around town, Fester recklessly rode around on a noisy dirt bike. As a result, police officers made frequent house calls to discuss the matter with his parents. Fester was also prescribed Ritalin and Mirtzapine to treat hyperactivity and depression. His parents allowed their unruly and out-of-control teenager to move into one of their rental apartments, an upstairs loft in downtown Horicon. Fester looked like a weirdo in this mostly conservative community with a population of about four thousand. Besides having a cross-dressing fetish, the teenage punk with long straight black hair wore spiked dog collars around his neck and painted his fingernails black. He slapped thick white makeup on his face and pretended to take on the persona of his idol, rocker Marilyn Manson. When Fester walked past unsuspecting local residents along the downtown city sidewalks, he deliberately widened his eyeballs and was delighted when he freaked people out, especially the elderly. Fester hated school. He despised police officers. He didn't work. He had no respect for others. He had no career ambitions or long-term goals. And yet he was genuinely adored and idolized by his new younger girlfriend.

Unlike Fester, Jessica Reid came from a broken home. Her father was not part of her life. Growing up in the Milwaukee suburb of West Bend, Reid made the junior high honor roll and her school's dance team. At age thirteen, Reid saw her world change when her mother and stepfather split up. Over the next couple of years, Jessica's mother, Rhonda Davis, constantly picked up and moved from town to town. Jessica was enrolled in five different schools over that period. She had no stability in her home life.[2] "Jessica was always sweet-natured, kind-hearted," said her grandmother Marge Mortensen. "When her parents divorced, I think her whole world fell apart."[3]

Eventually, Reid landed in the same town as Greg Fester and the two crossed paths. She found school boring and the classroom unchallenging, so she quit attending.

When she was sixteen, she was arrested for disorderly conduct, possession of drug paraphernalia, and truancy. In 2006, the skinny girl with long sandy-blond hair turned her back on her education. She moved in with a group of guys from Horicon. Consequently, the Horicon Police Department also kept a close eye on that place, which had a reputation as a party house. Shortly after her seventeenth birthday, Reid fell madly in love with one of the social outcasts at the party house, Greg Fester. Reid became enthralled by the Gothic lifestyle and yearned for more. She and Fester didn't go on traditional movie date nights like other normal teenagers in their Wisconsin town. Instead, they sneaked into creepy cemeteries under pitch-black skies to have sex. They found it fascinating to have sexual intercourse surrounded by hundreds of solemn granite headstones and corpses buried underground. During that time frame, Fester and Reid also became more daring. They began breaking into rural abandoned and vacant properties for adrenaline rushes. And they managed not to get caught.

By late March 2006, Fester and Reid stole a van and drove it into a remote field toward the Appleton area. With no one around, Fester poured a can of gasoline on the van. He used his lighter to set it ablaze. The teenage hoodlums watched orange flames consume the van. They fled before anyone called police. In the coming days, Fester and Reid decided to go for broke and make a fresh start along one of North America's oceans. They wanted to rid their pathetic lives of Wisconsin once and for all. Even though Reid and Fester didn't own a vehicle, they did have a plan.[4]

Over the noon hour on April 11, Jessica Reid watched from a distance as local resident Ned Thompson went inside one of the stores in downtown Horicon to run a brief errand. Reid raced toward Thompson's white Mercury Mountaineer and jumped inside. She then backed into another parked vehicle, causing a huge scene. After regaining control, Reid peeled around the corner. She parked in front of Fester's apartment on East Lake Street. "Let's go!" she screamed. "We're getting out of here!"

"What do you mean?" Fester reacted.

"We're leaving. We have a vehicle," she bragged.[5]

Fester fetched his acoustic guitar and a small wooden box that held most of his favorite bongs to smoke dope. Reid grabbed a keepsake portrait of her mother and her baby sister for the long journey ahead. Fester and Reid also possessed a couple of stolen credit cards and an ATM card to buy food and gasoline. Then, out of nowhere, a group of eyewitnesses to Reid's crash spotted them piling their belongings into the stolen SUV. Reid and Fester panicked. They retreated back inside Fester's downtown apartment building. The teenagers ran through a maze of hallways and adjacent buildings to avoid the pursuing police officers. Although Reid and Fester managed to avoid capture, her purse and his black leather wallet turned up inside the stolen auto. The Horicon Police now knew the identities of their suspects, if only they could find them.

. . .

That afternoon, Fester and Reid wandered several miles outside of town. They stuck mainly to deserted landscape to elude any cops still on the lookout. After safely passing through the small town of Hubbard, population sixteen hundred, the pair of Goths came upon a rural residence along Raasch's Hill Road. There, Fester and Reid noticed an orange Chevrolet truck parked in the driveway. No one was home at Craig Schattschneider's place. Better yet, the truck was unlocked with the keys still dangling from the ignition. That afternoon, Reid inhaled one last drag from her cigarette, which bore traces of her pink lipstick. She flicked the butt into the stranger's driveway. The coast was clear. Reid positioned herself behind the wheel. Fester climbed into the passenger's seat. When Reid shifted into reverse, she backed over a tiny tree in the yard, but otherwise made a successful getaway. Over the next several hours, Wisconsin's twenty-first-century version of Leopold and Loeb breezed through several small towns, including Mayville, Theresa, and Campbellsport. Much to their relief, no flashing blue-and-red lights and sirens gave chase as the pair rolled past endless stretches of unplanted farms and cow pastures in the stolen truck. Since Fester and Reid were in the mood for pure fun, they veered off the main roads and went mudding. They careened over hills and large dips, leaving the truck muddy and filthy. Soon their adrenaline rush wore off and turned into boredom. They left the truck stranded about thirty miles from Horicon. Needing help, Reid used her phone to call her ex-boyfriend, John Plzak. He came by, picked them up, and let them hide out back at his apartment in West Bend. The next day, a Sheriff's deputy from Washington County stumbled across the abandoned orange truck on the outskirts of West Bend. The truck's rightful owner led police to a discarded cigarette butt in his driveway that bore Jessica Reid's pink lipstick.

Authorities in Wisconsin had linked Reid and Fester to a pair of daytime truck thefts in a relatively short period of time, but the auto thieves were nowhere in sight. Over the next few days, Fester and Reid smoked dope and partied with others at Plzak's apartment. Actually, Plzak had been a nice and steady guy for Reid before she broke things off. He was three years older, but treated her kindly and with respect. He genuinely cared for her and did his best to treat her right. On one of those mornings when they were hiding from police, Reid got out of bed and admitted to Fester that she had had sex with Plzak the previous night. Fester grew furious, but Reid promised to make everything right with him and find them a new place to stay. Fester became impatient. He called his dad to come get them. Greg Fester Sr. made the hour-long drive to West Bend to retrieve his son and Jessica Reid and bring them back home to Horicon. Before leaving West Bend, Fester grabbed Plzak's shiny silver-and-red marijuana pipe and slipped it into his own jacket pocket. During the ride home, Fester's father relayed how police in Horicon were looking for them. Naturally, Fester and Reid didn't want to go to jail for stealing a pair of vehicles. They asked to be dropped off at the Kwik Stop on Beaver Dam's north side. Greg Fester assured his father that he would contact the police. Of course, he never did. Before it grew dark, the pair of teenage misfits walked past several cow pastures and farms on the outer edge of Beaver Dam. Around dusk, they came upon a white wood-framed multistory farmhouse with a red barn. A shiny red truck parked in the gravel driveway drew Fester's attention. He motioned for Reid to follow as he approached the vehicle. The teenagers found the doors unlocked and the keys in the ignition. This red truck was their ticket out of Wisconsin. They had their chance to reach the sandy beaches of the ocean after all.

Around 7:30 P.M., Fester and his wild, crazy girlfriend climbed into the red Dodge Ram truck bearing Wisconsin license plates A55056 and drove off into the night. That stolen truck belonged to Ryan Krenz, the same young man who had just left the farm to visit his seriously injured brother at one of the area trauma centers.

. . .

Three nights later, Fester and Reid ran out of gas along the interstate in Louisiana. They had no money left when they set out on foot, trying to avoid police capture. During their adventure, the Wisconsin teens trudged through miles of dense forest and wilderness, sporting only their backpacks and a few possessions, including their precious remaining tablets of Dex. After wandering for hours, they came upon a furniture store on the outskirts of Washington, Louisiana. Fester walked into the store and displayed a red plastic gas can as part of his con. The kind-hearted store owners, Mary and Francis Vidrine, took pity on the teenage couple and had no idea they were fugitives, thinking they were just down on their luck. The Vidrines drove Fester and Reid to nearby Opelousas to hop on a Greyhound bus. The store owners even put $300 on their business charge card to buy Fester and Reid a one-way fare to Michigan. Michigan? Fester knew he had a cousin who lived near Benton Harbor.

Fester used the cross-country bus ride to Michigan to rest and snooze. Reid popped some tablets of Dex into her mouth. As she enjoyed the drug-induced high, Reid began jotting down her thoughts into her notebook. But the bus trip was a colossal misadventure. Upon reaching Michigan, Fester discovered his cousin had moved far away. Reality sunk in. The wild teens had no money, no vehicle. They found themselves stranded again in another unfamiliar state. Reid became fed up and homesick. She called her mother. Her mother drove all the way from Wisconsin to retrieve her rebellious daughter and the Marilyn Manson–wannabe boyfriend.

. . .

Unbeknownst to Reid and Fester, authorities in Wisconsin were still in hot pursuit of those responsible for the rash of vehicle thefts. The following night, Reid was arrested back at her mother's house in Horicon. The next day, Reid lied to Dodge County Detective Jim Rohr when he asked if she stole Ryan Krenz's red truck. "I know it sounds like I'm lying," she told Rohr. "You really need to talk to Greg about this truck." When the silver-haired detective asked if her fingerprints would surface on the truck, Reid gave an odd response. "I won't be mad at you if you charge me with this because I know it's not your fault," she said.[6]

Later that afternoon, Horicon Police Officer Jason Roy pulled into the driveway of Anthony "A. J." Wilson's hangout. Roy knew Fester was a frequent visitor. Wilson was on court probation at the time, and he knew the local cops on a first- and last-name basis.[7]

"Yeah, Roy, he's inside my residence right now. Come on in and get him," Wilson politely responded. Once Roy entered, the officer and Fester made eye contact. Fester darted from the living room and raced toward the kitchen. A door slammed. Fester ran downstairs to hide in Wilson's basement. Wilson urged Fester to surrender. "Come on out, Fester, he knows you're here," Wilson hollered. A few minutes later, Fester came out of the basement. He put his hands in the air. A pat-down search revealed no weapons or illegal contraband, but it yielded a drug pipe and one spent .410-gauge shotgun shell tucked inside a pocket in Fester's leather jacket. Back at the Horicon Police Department, Fester's leather jacket and contents were placed into evidence storage for safekeeping. He was arrested on suspicion of violating probation. Additional charges were pending in connection with the series of recent auto thefts.

When asked why he had been arrested, Fester replied, "I was stupid and made some stupid mistakes." Unlike his girlfriend, Fester confessed to all three auto thefts in the Horicon and Beaver Dam areas, including the theft of Ryan Krenz's truck along Canary Road. As a direct result of Fester's incriminating admissions, a police car was dispatched to detain Jessica Reid.

This time, Jessica was thrown into jail. She now faced an additional count of auto theft, plus an obstructing an officer count. She was very mad at Fester, she told Detective Rohr. "If he would have just shut his mouth, none of this would have happened," she complained.

Now Reid was curious about what else Fester may have revealed to police. "What did Greg say?" she asked, fidgeting. "I really want to know what he said." Reid claimed she didn't recall how they ended up in Louisiana, about sixty miles from Baton Rouge. She admitted they both smoked marijuana during their cross-country joyride. They committed at least one gas drive-off, but she couldn't remember which state that was in. Detective Rohr asked if she broke into any homes during their spree. "Greg did that," she declared. "That one's all on him."[8]

She claimed to serve as Fester's lookout as he broke into one house that they trashed somewhere in Iowa or Oklahoma, she guessed. Reid was booked into the Dodge County Detention Center. Later that evening, a female inmate decided to notify the jailers about a chilling conversation she had had with Reid.

. . .

The inmate alerted jailers that Jessica Reid reportedly witnessed her boyfriend kill someone in another state. "What do you think they could get me for?" Reid reportedly asked her new cell mate. Rather than question Reid, Detective Rohr confronted Fester back at the jail. Fester confirmed he had burglarized a vacant house and left it trashed, perhaps in Iowa or Minnesota, but that was all he was ready to admit. "I did not shoot a single person," Fester whimpered. Detective Rohr wasn't going to take Fester at his word, so he issued a bulletin to other law enforcement agencies in a multistate region. Dodge County, Wisconsin, had two teenagers in custody who admitted to trashing a house in rural Iowa or Minnesota, and their fingerprint cards were available upon request. The boyfriend and girlfriend generally traveled along rural, remote areas to avoid law enforcement, Rohr noted. "The female suspect confided with another inmate that her boyfriend shot a male subject and that the female subject tried to clean up some of the blood, but was worried that she left her fingerprints at the scene," the bulletin read. Anyone with an unsolved shooting or homicide in a rural setting was told to contact Det. James G. Rohr of the Dodge County Sheriff's Department. The bulletin was transmitted in late April 2006 to authorities in North Dakota, Minnesota, Iowa, Illinois, Wisconsin, and Michigan.[9] Unfortunately,

Nebraska wasn't on anybody's radar in Wisconsin until the middle of May, when the ring found in the Stocks' kitchen was traced back to the Walmart store in Beaver Dam. By then, Matt Livers and Nick Sampson had already spent a few weeks in jail facing double murder charges.

By late May, police in Wisconsin determined that Ryan Krenz, Cori Zastrow, and her mother Louise Zastrow had absolutely no involvement with the rural Nebraska homicides. Their DNA samples did not match the DNA residue found on either the marijuana pipe or the engraved gold ring. On the other hand, Wisconsin authorities strongly suspected Fester and Reid may have been present at the Nebraska slayings. Their fingerprint files, along with some of their personal artifacts, were sent to the Nebraska State Patrol for further lab analysis. All the while, Reid and Fester apparently remained unaware that authorities in Wisconsin were investigating them in connection with a rural Nebraska double murder.

. . .

A shrewd detective, Dodge County's Rohr came up with the perfect plan to keep it that way. On May 30, Fester agreed to let Rohr reinterview him at the jail. Rohr tricked Fester into thinking that some police agency in Iowa had contacted Rohr in reference to a crime involving a vandalized house. "This information was false and was used as a ruse to obtain a buccal swab from Gregory Fester for his DNA," Rohr stated.[10] Fester volunteered to comply and let the detective put a wooden stick into his mouth to obtain his DNA sample. Rohr then used the same ploy with Jessica Reid. Their DNA samples arrived at the Nebraska State Patrol on June 2, 2006, and were sent to the University of Nebraska Medical Center for rush-delivery scientific analysis. The results were clear: the mixed sample of DNA residue contained on both the marijuana pipe and the gold ring matched the DNA characteristics for both Fester and Reid. Conclusive and irrefutable scientific DNA evidence from Wayne and Sharmon Stock's farmhouse pointed to two culprits, neither of whom was Matt Livers or Nick Sampson.[11]

Now authorities in Nebraska had a real problem on their hands.

11

WISCONSIN

It took homicide investigators Bill Lambert and Earl Schenck about eight hours to drive from Omaha to Juneau, Wisconsin, to confront the unfamiliar teenagers whose own DNA put them at the scene of the Stock murders. Lambert and Schenck convinced themselves the creepy teenagers had to be acquaintances of Matt Livers and Nick Sampson. At the Dodge County Detention Center, Fester openly wondered why the pair of Nebraska cops traveled to Wisconsin to interview him. He confessed that he and Jessica Reid had stolen the red truck belonging to Ryan Krenz on the Easter weekend. Fester recalled they drove through Illinois, Iowa, Oklahoma, and maybe Texas and Louisiana. Along the way, they broke into houses and cars to scrounge money for gas and food. But Fester insisted he did not remember passing through Nebraska. Lambert and Schenck inquired if Fester had any family or friends in Nebraska. Fester paused for a brief moment. Then he suddenly claimed he once met a guy named Thomas about a year ago at a local house party in Wisconsin hosted by Fester's friend, Jonathan Wendel. Fester claimed this Thomas character was also a fellow pot smoker, so they chatted a lot at the party and exchanged phone numbers. The two Nebraska investigators were intrigued. Schenck remembered that one of Nick Sampson's best friends in Murdock was named Tom Todd. Schenck let Fester go on and talk freely about this Thomas character, presuming he must be talking about Tom Todd, but Fester was of no help. He was unable to provide the police with any more details regarding this supposed mystery friend from Nebraska. Fester admitted he did not even know this Thomas's address or last name. "Thomas was not the pot smoker I thought he would be," Fester shrugged. He claimed his

Trac phone contained his contact information for Thomas. However, during the interview being recorded that phone was out of minutes and remained inside Jessica Reid's bedroom at A. J. Wilson's apartment, Fester recalled.[1]

.   .   .

As far as their escapades with the stolen Krenz truck, Fester admitted he and Reid had burglarized a house somewhere in Iowa. Fester also confessed to breaking into another house during their trip, but he did not know where that was. Investigator Lambert sensed the other house was the Stock farmhouse. Fester described how one house was older while the other house appeared newer. The older house Fester and Reid vandalized was on a dirt road, but the newer house had brown siding and was along a gravel road, Fester pointed out. The tan house was smaller, Fester clarified. "Like one floor," Fester remembered, "but you could go upstairs."

Lambert presented Fester with five photos of the Stocks' farmhouse. "Yes, that's one of the houses we broke into," Fester declared. "I remember that siding." Fester figured the intrusion occurred around midnight. He remembered the sky being pitch-black. After they found all the doors locked, Jessica pried off a window screen in the backyard to gain entry, Fester confessed. At that point in the interview, Lambert displayed a photo of the window screen resting against the farmhouse. "That's the one," Fester confirmed. Inside the house, Fester recalled he heard snoring from upstairs as he lurked around the first level in total darkness. The investigators questioned if Fester remembered the location of the staircase. "Yeah, you go through a pantry-like room into the kitchen and then through the kitchen and turn right and go upstairs." However, Fester maintained he stayed in the kitchen and living room the entire time, and never once ventured upstairs. He denied stealing anything from the home, but couldn't speak for Jessica. "I didn't see her the entire time we were in the house," Fester mumbled. He shrugged and said that he didn't know how long he and Reid stayed in the farmhouse. He said he remembered they left through a back door.

In a firm and commanding tone, Investigator Schenck spoke up.

Fester had just admitted to burglarizing a house in Cass County, Nebraska, he advised. Fester reacted with total surprise. He had no idea he and Jessica had ever passed through Nebraska, he replied. Schenck demanded that Fester reveal who else joined them at the farmhouse, but Fester denied anyone else was there. "No, just me and Jessica," Fester answered. Schenck grew upset.

He didn't believe Fester's account. He knew full well that Livers confessed he and Nick Sampson were the two gunmen. But Fester remained adamant that no else was there except for himself and his girlfriend. When asked if he lost any personal artifacts near the house, Fester answered no. He also denied knowing the homeowners. "No, I don't know them at all," Fester responded. He squirmed in his chair after Lambert revealed the farm couple were found slain the very next morning after Fester and Reid burglarized the place. As the questions heated up, Fester demanded a lawyer. The investigators obliged and halted the taped interview. Fester was returned to his jail cell.

.   .   .

Later that afternoon, Schenck and Lambert brought in Jessica Reid for a separate interview. Like Fester, she, too, wondered why two Nebraska cops drove five hundred miles to interview her. Like Fester, she also faced a trio of auto theft charges from Wisconsin, but by now, she was free after posting a modest bail. Lambert and Schenck showed her a photo of Ryan Krenz's mud-caked truck recovered in Louisiana. "Holy crap!" she responded. "It's

Greg Fester and Jessica Reid stole this Dodge Ram truck on Easter weekend, April 2006, at a rural farmhouse outside Beaver Dam, Wisconsin. The pair took turns driving the truck through Iowa, Nebraska, and across the southwestern United States over the course of several days. They abandoned the truck in Louisiana after running out of gas. *(Author's collection)*

very important that you be totally honest with us," Lambert warned. "And don't try and bullshit us." Reid confirmed she and Fester stole the red truck outside Beaver Dam, Wisconsin. From there, they drove into Illinois and later crossed a bridge over the Mississippi River into Iowa. Eventually, they drove south, mostly traveling along back roads to avoid police. She and Fester also used various illegal drugs during their cross-country journey. The Gulf of Mexico was their destination, she said. "He wanted to go to the ocean," Reid said of Fester. "But we didn't make it there. We ran out of gas."[2]

Along the way, the teenage transients broke into abandoned houses at random to pay for their travels. "At one house we found some money, but it wasn't much. Like $200," Reid confessed. Lambert presented Reid with a photo of the gold ring with engraved black lettering that read, "Love Always, Cori & Ryan." Reid looked at the photo and tried denying she ever saw the ring before. Lambert knew he had caught the seventeen-year-old girl in a web of lies. Lambert raised his voice. He declared that the engraved ring had come from inside the red truck she and Fester stole. He explained how laboratory tests confirmed the ring contained her DNA along with Fester's DNA. "I'm serious," Reid said, fidgeting. "There were no rings in that truck." Lambert explained the scenario for which the ring was found. The criminal investigation had already determined that Krenz last saw the engraved ring inside his truck. The ring showed up on the kitchen floor of a house in Nebraska and was now in the possession of law enforcement. Lambert turned up the heat. He produced a photo of the red-and-silver marijuana pipe. "Does that look familiar?" Lambert asked. "That's a pot pipe that was found in the driveway outside that house. And it's been sent to a laboratory."

Suddenly, Reid grew defensive. Then she blurted, "Did I rob a house? 'Cuz, if they want their stuff back and all that other stuff, if I robbed a house, I'm sorry." Reid tried to claim she stole $200 from the house. Then the amount stolen in her story grew to $500. "And I do remember losing this pipe," she admitted. Reid also confessed she had in fact possessed the engraved gold ring. "How did the ring get into the house?" Lambert inquired. "I lost it," she erupted in laughter. "I just lost it somehow. I just remember looking down, and it was gone." When she first broke into the farmhouse, she remembered she had placed the oversized man's ring onto her thumb. "And it was too big for my thumb," she admitted. Reid admitted she must have lost the ring on the kitchen floor. "What is this about?" she asked in a dead-serious tone. Wisconsin Detective Jim Rohr interceded during the interview. Rohr advised that the Nebraska investigators still had plenty of questions to ask. Reid maintained that she drove the stolen red truck into the gravel driveway of the unlit farm-house and parked behind the house. She and Fester made sure there were no barking dogs present before setting foot on the farm. Lambert broke the news that the farmhouse was in Murdock, Nebraska.

"Murdock, Nebraska?" she inquired. "Murdock," Lambert repeated. "Does that even ring a bell?" Reid reacted with total surprise. She didn't appear to be lying. "I've never heard of that town in my life," she laughed. "I had no idea we were in Nebraska. I thought we were still in Iowa."

Like Fester, Jessica Reid gave the very same answer to the Nebraska inves-tigators when they demanded to know who else met up with them inside the Nebraska farmhouse. "And there was no else with you?" Lambert growled. "You didn't meet some people?" Reid just shook her head. After Lambert revealed that the homeowners were found shot to death in their bedroom, Reid denied killing anybody. "Oh God, I've never killed anybody, okay? I really didn't. This is so seriously. . . ." "Yes, this is serious," Lambert agreed. "That's why we are here." Reid whimpered, insisting she only stole money from the residence. Then she began to sob. Tears rolled down her cheeks. "I don't want to go to jail for murder because I didn't do it," she cried. "If Greg killed anybody, I don't know. If he did, I'm sorry." Again, the investigators expected her to cough up names of other accomplices, including Livers and the Sampson brothers. "Was anybody else around?" Schenck asked. "It was just us," Reid professed. "I swear to God."

Schenck noted how the blood of the murder victims was found on the gold ring. "And what our crime lab analysis is telling us is that whoever had this ring on had it on at the time the shots were fired," Schenck explained. Finally, Detective Rohr spoke up. He reminded Reid she had confessed to another female inmate back in April that she may have left her fingerprints at a crime scene as she tried to clean up some blood. "And you were wondering what you could be charged with," Rohr explained. "I have a statement from that inmate." "From what inmate?" Reid asked. "I never talked to these inmates that I was with in jail."

Lambert and Schenck weren't there to play any more games. They bore down and told her to identify who killed the homeowners. Reid shrugged. She took a long breath. "I don't know. I don't know. I don't know. I don't know what happened," she insisted hysterically. Lambert ordered her to identify the other assailants who were with her and Fester. "No one was there," she answered. Lambert and Schenck grew visibly agitated. They even tried to scare her into confessing the names of other accomplices, bragging that Nebraska, unlike Wisconsin, had a death penalty. "If I would have killed anybody, I would tell you," she claimed. "But I didn't kill anybody."

Lambert admitted he did not believe Reid killed anybody either. "I think you have information," Lambert told her. "I was with Greg," she cried. "I didn't even know I was in Nebraska." Schenck assumed that Fester and Reid had surely met up with the codefendants at the Bulldogs Bar & Grill, where Nick Sampson worked as a cook. So he asked if Reid remembered visiting a "Podunk little town" with a tavern, a reference to Murdock, the farm community of less than three hundred, just a couple of miles from the Stock farm.

But Reid again frustrated the two Nebraska cops. She and Fester never passed through any such downtown. Next, Schenck showed her a photo of the brown Ford Contour owned by Nick Sampson's brother, Will. He hoped that photo would jog her memory. "Where is this car from, Nebraska?" Reid inquired. That car was seized by Nebraska police, Schenck exclaimed. "Because it has blood from the scene in the car," he bragged. "The same as the blood on the ring that you dropped on the floor of the kitchen." "I've never seen this car in my life," she professed. Lambert displayed a mug shot of a scruffy, brown-haired young man, Nick Sampson. "I have no idea who that is," Reid responded. "I'm not even kidding you. I've never seen that guy in my life."

Schenck displayed a photo of Nick Sampson's brother, Will, but Reid denied meeting up with him either. Furthermore, she didn't recognize the photo of the Bulldogs Bar & Grill. She had never set foot inside that building before. Schenck displayed a photo of confessed killer Matt Livers. "I could make fun of this picture," Reid laughed. "He looks really fat, but no, I've never seen him either. I have never seen any of these people that you are showing me right now. I have no idea who they are."

Lambert became infuriated. He looked her squarely in the eye and hollered for her to come clean and reveal what brought her and Fester to Nebraska. "I thought we were in Iowa," she insisted. "I really seriously thought to God we were in Iowa. I did not know we were in Nebraska."

"You are in a lot of trouble!" Lambert shouted. "You are at a crime scene. Two people are dead."

"Oh man, this is too crazy," she responded.

"Yeah, it's crazy!" Schenck yelled. "It's a double homicide, and it carries the death penalty in Nebraska with the electric chair."

The investigators urged Reid to cooperate and identify the people in the mug shots, otherwise her life as a seventeen-year-old was over. They sternly warned her of what would happen to the rest of her life. Reid realized she was in a bleak situation, so Reid grabbed the photos off the interview table to study them. Lambert assured her not to be afraid of the faces in those mug shots. "We can take care of these people," Lambert advised. "You need to take care of yourself or you will have no life. If you don't get the death penalty by some remote chance, then you will rot on death row in some maximum-security prison in Nebraska until you pass away." Lambert's message sank in loud and clear. She listened intently as the NSP investigator shifted the conversation back to the country farmhouse along the bumpy gravel road. "I don't think you stumble across this house in no-man's land," Lambert observed, "far off the beaten path. I don't believe that for a minute."

Reid gazed at the mug shot of Nick Sampson. Now she decided to confess that this individual and some other person who was with him joined her and Fester at the farmhouse slayings. "It was just bang, bang, bang, bang, bang," Reid exclaimed. "And I was like, 'Oh my God!' And I freaked out and me and Greg left." As Reid's nerves frayed, the investigators gave her a cigarette break to relieve some stress.

"You know what?" Schenck told her. "I don't think you shot him. I really don't."

"Neither did I," Lambert volunteered. "Never did."

The investigators pressed her again to identify other accomplices. Schenck showed her another photo of Matt Livers. "I do not recognize this guy," Reid answered. Instead, she gravitated to a police photo of Nick Sampson's brother, Will. With that, she begged for mercy.

For sure, Reid was an accessory to a serious crime. "You let it go for months until now!" Schenck barked. "You think we weren't going to find out? Look what brought us here to you. The ring—the ring that was on your hand! That has a serial number on it that was tracked to New York, which was tracked to Walmart here. That was tracked to a girl who bought it for her boyfriend, who said his vehicle was stolen—which you stole. That's how. You ever hear that your sins will find you out? Well, it is true."

Reid finally admitted she did go upstairs. She maintained she saw one of the victims get shot. Her damning admission matched up perfectly for investigators. They, of course, already knew about the silhouette of one of the assailants on the upstairs wall. "We knew that," Schenck confirmed. "Just keep going. You're doing good."

Reid remembered how the male victim's brains were sprayed across the hallway. She freaked out, she said, and darted downstairs when some of the blood sprayed on her clothes. She ran out the back door as fast as she could to get back in their stolen truck. "That's what I have stuck in my head for the rest of my life!" she screamed. "Some guy's brains being splattered all over the floor." During her mad dash for the door, the ring flew off her thumb, she admitted. "I was running out of the house pretty fast," she recalled. Lambert dug into his investigative folder and pulled out a morbid photo of Wayne Stock's bloody corpse in the second-floor hallway. "Does that look familiar?" Lambert asked. Reid shrieked. She looked away. "I don't want to see that. I want to get home," she begged. But Reid was not going home, Lambert assured her. "How many times have you seen a guy's head split like a melon in three pieces in different directions?" Lambert asked her.

Schenck made one more valiant attempt to get Reid to identify Matt Livers as her coconspirator. He told her to reexamine the mug shot of Livers. "I would recognize him because he's got a weird head," she quipped. "I don't recognize him." Schenck turned his attention back to the photo of Nick Sampson. "So you said this guy was scary?" Schenck asked. "Yeah," Reid nodded. "He just gave off this vibe like he was an evil person. I didn't know if he wanted to kill them or not. I just knew he wanted to take their money." With that, Lambert opened a bottle of water and took a drink. "You know what this comes down to, though," Lambert surmised. "You didn't steal the vehicle, this wouldn't have happened. You would not have ended up in Nebraska."

As Reid looked through the small stack of mug shots, Lambert still couldn't fathom why she did not remember any of their names. "You didn't know these guys from Adam?" Lambert groused. "You didn't know them at all? Hey Rob, hey Bob, Bill?" Reid shrugged and sat silent. "You walk into a bar," Lambert advised. "You meet two total strangers. They look at you and go, 'You can break into a house?'"

"Well, we had no money, no food. All we had was a truck," Reid replied with a smirk.

During an interview break, Reid anxiously asked Detective Rohr how she was doing. "You are doing the right thing," Rohr answered. "You know this really sucks," she complained. "It's on my record now." She begged Rohr to get her placed on work release. "There won't be getting out of jail on this one," Rohr promised.

. . .

Later in the day, Rohr filed an additional felony charge of bail jumping against Reid. When she moved back into A. J. Wilson's house following her release from custody in late April, Jessica had failed to notify the court about her change of address. The additional felony let police put Reid back in jail as they sorted out her role in the Nebraska murders. The very next day, Rohr filed an affidavit with a local Wisconsin judge seeking to execute a search warrant at Wilson's house in Horicon where Reid had stayed.

The search of Wilson's house became the key turning point in the case.

12

DIARY

A half-dozen Wisconsin police officers swarmed A. J. Wilson's house in Horicon on the afternoon of June 6, 2006, seeking access to a black cellular phone in Jessica Reid's bedroom and other potential clues. As the officers milled through the house, A. J. led them to a package hidden in a dining room china hutch. Behind a portrait of A. J. Wilson's father, Dodge County Det. Michael Reissmann found a small Camel-brand cigarette box with the words, "To Greg," scribbled in black marker. Inside, the box contained a folded two-page letter addressed to Greg Fester.

An excerpt read: "And this bullet well it's the only thing left. And I loved it, but that's something we will talk about one day. But its here also bcuz that was something I did for you, me and for you to love me as much as I love you. Love always, Jessica, XOXO."[1]

The empty box of Camel smokes also contained a red .12-gauge spent shotgun shell casing—identical to the kind recovered from the Stocks' farmhouse.

Astonishingly, the shotgun slug and Jessica's weird love letter for Fester were not even the biggest evidence finds that afternoon.

In Reid's bedroom, Wisconsin police came across a diary, but this was no ordinary teenage girl's journal.

On page 13, Reid wrote: "I killed a man. He was older. I loved it. I wish I could do it all the time. If Greg doesn't watch it, I am going to just leave one day and go do it myself. He's not communicating with me very well for some reason anymore. I know who I am kind of now. I just have to get there first. I miss the south. It's cold up here."[2]

· · ·

Inside this Camel-brand cigarette box, police in southcentral Wisconsin made a chilling discovery. A shotgun shell was hidden inside the box, a souvenir from the Stock slayings, plus a folded letter, in which Jessica Reid wrote that she saved the shotgun shell as a token of her love for Gregory Fester. *(Author's collection)*

That evening back at the Dodge County jail, Fester took full responsibility for firing the final shot into the back of the farmer's head. He blamed Reid for shooting the lady. But Lambert and Schenck were not satisfied. They assured him that other people in Nebraska were already in custody, so it was in his best interest to cooperate to gain leniency at sentencing. Just as they had done with Reid the previous day, Lambert and Schenck pushed Fester to implicate others in Nebraska. They provided him with a total of four police mug shots to study, including a photo of Nick Sampson's buddy, Tom Todd. Fester agreed to identify a pair of purported accomplices, just as the Nebraska investigators wanted him to do. But he thoroughly confused the cops by rejecting the mug shots of Matt Livers and Nick Sampson. Instead, Fester gravitated to the photos of Will Sampson and Tom Todd. Of course, Fester couldn't identify the names of any of the people in the mug shots because he really had no clue who they were. Trying his best to fool and please the gullible Nebraska investigators, Fester meekly referred to the photo of Will Sampson as the "brown-bearded guy." He wanted to go along with the investigators' newly adopted conspiracy theory.

Fester's second police interview in as many days deviated greatly from his first. The previous day, he had steadfastly maintained that only he and Jessica were present at the tan farmhouse. In the second interview, Fester claimed he remembered the downtown business district of Murdock buzzing with lots of lights and energy. Hot cars. Sexy blondes. Blaring bass from car stereos. Black gangster dudes. Fester's story about seeing black gangsters wandering around downtown Murdock on Easter Sunday should have raised a red flag that his story was preposterous. Murdock was about as all-white as any small town in Nebraska. Furthermore, Cass County authorities would have known from previous interviews with locals that downtown Murdock was practically a ghost town on Easter Sunday night. The Bulldogs Bar & Grill closed by 9 P.M. because business was slow in the little town of 270. Instead, Fester tried telling Lambert and Schenck that he and Reid drove into Murdock to score dope from this mythical person named Thomas. Soon a big guy with a thick beard approached their stolen truck and exclaimed, "Let's go off somebody!" Fester said he and Reid agreed to give Thomas and the big bearded guy a lift to some nearby farmhouse. The bearded guy supposedly brought a long-barreled shotgun for the ride. "I was hoping nobody was home, but it turned out extremely horrible," Fester said.[3]

According to Fester, the four intruders converged at the top of the staircase. "And the big guy just went right in there and started shooting. . . . Big guy handed me the gun and was like, 'Shoot him or I'll kill you.' I stepped up and aimlessly pointed it and looked away and shot." Lambert interjected. "A guy who has a gun that is a threat to you gives you his gun that is loaded and says, 'Shoot him or I'll kill you!'" Lambert grumbled. "How is he going to kill you?" "These people brought me to this house, and he is fucking killing people," Fester professed. "This is fucking insane. This is not fucking right at all. I mean, this is sick. This is fucking disgusting shit."

After the killings, Fester claimed he drove the two males back to the nearby town and dropped them off near the bar. "Big guy told me, 'Don't say anything or I'll fucking kill you. I'll hunt your family down.' Thomas is like 'Peace' whatever, fuck you, kind of. Both walk off."

Lambert wondered if people were still present at the Bulldogs Bar. "Not many, though," Fester answered.

After hearing Fester's outrageous story, the cops confronted him about the mementos seized from Reid's bedroom. "She showed you one of those spent shells and said, 'See what I'm saving for you?'" Lambert quizzed.

"No," Fester stammered. "Honestly, I didn't know about that. I'm not going to lie."

Schenck and Lambert decided to remain in Wisconsin for a third day.

. . .

On June 7, Jessica Reid calmly sat down for her second interview with Schenck and Lambert. She was totally unaware of the evidence trove taken from her bedroom the previous day. Before the interview started, Rohr, the local detective, served as the moderator. He briefed Reid that the two Nebraska investigators had already spoken with Fester again. "Well, how did it go with Greg?" she inquired.

"A lot has happened in the last twenty-four hours," Rohr advised. "All I can tell you is, girl, you got to be honest. And you got to say what happened here." On cue, Lambert and Schenck entered the interrogation room together. The looks on their faces reflected their unhappiness with Reid. They told her how they had gone through her bedroom at A. J.'s house after obtaining a search warrant from a local judge.

The Wisconsin police found lots of interesting stuff, Lambert noted.

"Like what?" she wondered. "Like shoes, clothes with stains on them . . . like letters that you wrote!" Schenck roared. "You got some explaining to do. I'm willing to tell you right now, I am at the end of my rope over this whole thing with you and young Gregory."

Reid realized the Nebraska cops had uncovered her darkest secrets.

"Greg blew a guy's head off," Reid finally confessed. "And he shot a hole through the lady's face."

"Really?" Schenck fired back. "And you didn't have nothing to do with that?"

Schenck pulled out Reid's notebook. He read from the entry dated April 22, 2006, which was five days after the Stock murders: "I killed someone. He was older. I loved it. I wish I could do it all the time. If Greg doesn't watch it, I'm going to just leave one day and I'll go do it myself."

"You are in a lot of trouble, young lady!" Lambert screamed.

"I didn't kill this guy, though," Reid insisted, fidgeting. "I didn't have a gun. How am I supposed to kill somebody without a gun? I watched Greg do it."

"Quiet!" Schenck interrupted.

The two Nebraska cops were just getting warmed up. Next, Schenck alerted her to the secret love letter tucked inside the Camel cigarette box at A. J.'s residence. "And this letter was really interesting because it was concealed under some stuff, and then I found the little surprise that you left for Greg. . . . You brought some stuff from the crime scene home with you. That was really nice of you," Schenck said sarcastically.

"That was it?" Reid pleaded. "That was all? You guys, I am not kidding. I did not kill anybody."

"You know what?" Schenck barked. "You're seventeen years old and you've just thrown the rest of your life away, Jess."

Schenck reread from her diary: "I killed someone. I loved it. He was older and I wish I could do it all the time."

Tears ran down Reid's face.

"Yeah, you better be crying," Lambert declared.

"That was not me," Reid sobbed.

"Oh really?" Schenck commented. "This is your handwriting on all the letters. I got news for you. You're not going to get 'Candy' tattooed across your lower back when you get out of jail because you ain't getting out of jail."

"I didn't kill anybody," she moaned. "I'm not kidding you guys, okay? I need a gun to kill somebody. I didn't have a gun."

"There were guns there," Schenck advised. Schenck told her that the murder victims owned several firearms in their home.

"Where did you get the gun?" Lambert demanded.

Reid replied that the shotgun used as the murder weapon was already in the stolen truck. "What about the bar?" Lambert inquired, referring to the Bulldogs Bar & Grill in downtown Murdock. This was the local dive Reid identified in one of the police photographs the previous day as the meeting place for hatching the murder plot. "That was all a lie," she insisted. "All of it was a lie. I am not kidding."

Rather forcefully, Reid went back to her initial interview statement. She and Fester were the only ones involved in the homicides, she proclaimed.

"You are so full of crap," said Lambert.

Schenck added, "And we're done, and so am I." He leapt from his chair and darted for the door.

"That's what happened, though," insisted Reid.

Lambert replied, "We'll see you in Nebraska."

"Are you kidding me?"

"No, we are not kidding you," answered Lambert.

"I just told you what happened, though. I really don't know who those people are that you showed me. That guy and that guy and those four guys—I have no idea who they are."

Before he left the room, Lambert revealed that people in Nebraska had already confessed to their involvement in the homicides as well.

"Oh my God! Just put me in my cell, and I'll just sit there for the rest of my life. Because this is—wow!"

Lambert and Schenck ordered her to sit back down in her chair.

Reid asked, "Well, what did they confess to?"

Lambert dodged her question, but he assured her that she and Fester did not just stumble across the farmhouse.

"But that's what happened," she insisted.

After the two Nebraska investigators walked out of the interview, the mild-mannered Wisconsin detective spoke up in their defense.

Rohr assured Reid the slayings were not just random.

"You go right into that house. You go right upstairs. You go right to a bedroom where they're sleeping."

"I was following Greg, though."

"How would he know where to go? Someone was there that knew where these people were. It's very clear, Jess. There's no getting around that. I don't know why you want to cover for someone else out of this."

Rohr asked why Fester exited the truck brandishing a loaded shotgun.

"Protection," she answered.

"Ah, protection when you're going into somebody else's house? Excuse me?"

"It's a farmhouse."

"I don't care," replied Rohr.

"We thought of that one, too. You know, we didn't know that these things were going to happen. If I had known, I would have stayed home with my mom."

"And then you write these letters like this," the detective pointed out.

"It's pretty crazy. But this wasn't me. It was not me. I am a good person. I'm not a bad person like this . . . I'm not a murderer. I didn't do this," she insisted.

"You were right there with him, Jess. You are feet away from some guy who gets his head blown off."

"Yeah, that's pretty crazy," Jessica admitted.

"You go into that house with Greg with the gun. You say you were just there to rob."

"That's what I was there for," she agreed.

"You never got $500, did you?"

"No."

"That was a lie too because you wouldn't run out of money by the time you got to Louisiana if you had $500."

Reid said the murder weapon was gone and smashed into pieces. After the slayings, she and Fester drove all night before they stopped again. She remembered they pulled off a road where Fester got out and smashed the shotgun and left the pieces in a roadside ditch.

. . .

Rohr continued to discredit Reid's statement that the shotgun came from Wisconsin. Ryan Krenz, the truck owner, never reported any weapons stolen, Rohr noted.

As Reid grew more trusting of Rohr, she asked him to shut the interview door for a moment. She wanted to talk freely out of earshot of the two Nebraska cops, who might be in the hallway.

"I didn't blow this lady's head off," she began.

"Who did?"

"Greg."

Furthermore, Reid had no idea about any people in Nebraska in jail for the slayings. She blamed the Nebraska investigators for refusing to let her tell the truth.

"You know who was in this house?" asked Jessica.

"Who?"

"Me and Greg. Me and Greg."

Suddenly, Schenck barged back into the room. He had overheard her conversation.

Schenck had devoted countless hours to investigating the Stock murders. He had elicited a confession from Matt Livers. He had arrested Nick Sampson at the Bulldogs Bar based on Matt's incriminating statements. And now this bold unfamiliar Wisconsin teenage girl was making statements on videotape casting his arrests into grave doubt. Schenck was aware that these interview tapes would be turned over to the criminal defense lawyers for Sampson and Livers at some point.

"You realize that what we are talking about here right now is being recorded," Schenck barked. "And while you were in here talking to Detective Rohr, it was being recorded?"

Schenck had been solving crimes longer than Jessica was out of diapers, he assured her. "I've been working crimes like this and others for a long time. And the evidence doesn't lie," he bragged.

Reid said, "I want to tell you guys the whole story, but you guys are ignoring me. Greg was lying to you guys yesterday, too. I know he was. Because of one question: 'Was there anybody with you?' No. No. No. I want somebody to believe me. I really do. I want you guys to believe me. . . . The real story is actually harder to tell because the only person who was killing was Greg."

"Yeah, and you're lying," scoffed Schenck.

He asked why she wrote those letters about killing the older man.

Reid stuttered.

"Why? Answer that question! Why would you write those letters?"

"Because I feel like I killed those people too. I didn't turn Greg in."

Jessica smiled. She admitted she got an adrenaline rush from participating in the murders.

"And enjoyed it?" probed Schenck.

"Watching it? Yes."

Lambert told her to explain why somebody already in jail had confessed to the homicides.

"I have no idea."

"It's because they were there, Jess."

"Oh man! This is so unbelievable you don't even know what's going on in my head right now."

To prove she was telling the whole truth, Reid served up a previously unknown clue.

Two different shotguns—not just one—were used in the Nebraska slayings.

One came from an abandoned house that she and Fester burglarized along the way. The second came from the same house in Wisconsin where she and Fester stole the red truck.

"Well, where in the house did you steal it?" inquired Lambert.

"The gun cabinet."

"The gun cabinet?" he repeated.

"Yeah."

As she described the details of the metal gun cabinet inside the Krenz farmhouse, her mind drifted back to the night of the killings.

"We went into this house. Greg crawled into the window and let me in through that door. . . . So we went upstairs and heard the guy snoring so we got even more excited and went up there. I went into the bathroom and

Greg went in the room and he turned the light on for some dumb reason and I turned around and I was like 'What are you doing? Are you dumb?' And then he went back into the room and the lady, I guess, was waking up. She was rolling over to get out of bed because the light was on and Greg turned around and he shot the guy in the leg and then those were the two that were wrestling. And then I had a gun too. I didn't shoot the guy, but I remember shooting. . . . It freaked me out. . . . And this wasn't a small gun. It didn't have as much of a kick as the gun that Greg's did or whatever and then I shot or whatever and then I don't know where the bullet went. But all of a sudden I heard . . . Greg standing next to the guy, and he shot him in the head and his head blew off. And then I couldn't hear anything, but he ran into the room and he shot the lady . . . And then he got up and he was like 'Oh my God!' and he ran down the stairs, and I just ran after him because I didn't know why he was running down the stairs. And my jacket was sitting on the kitchen floor . . . and I saw I lost my ring, so I grabbed my jacket and just was running through the house. We broke both the guns up and we stuck them in a ditch. I know the whole story. That's why I know the house. That's how I know this. . . . Because I know there was nobody else there. It was just me and Greg."

At the end of her interview, Lambert promised Reid that she and Fester would definitely face murder charges back in Cass County, Nebraska.

.   .   .

After three long days and nights in Wisconsin, investigators Schenck and Lambert drove back to Nebraska. The pair of teenagers would remain in Wisconsin, pending extradition. A flatbed semitrailer transported Ryan Krenz's red truck from Louisiana to the Douglas County Sheriff's Office crime lab in Omaha for additional forensic tests. Not surprisingly, the cab of the truck contained some bloody clothes, towels, and other personal belongings left behind by Fester and Reid. By early summer, a total of four people faced two counts of first-degree murder in the Stock deaths. Two were cousins from Nebraska. Two were a pair of Gothic teenagers from central Wisconsin.

.   .   .

Then, all of a sudden, it appeared that even more arrests were imminent.

13

CONSPIRACY

Back in Plattsmouth, Nebraska, the Cass County Courthouse sent a belated press release on late Friday afternoon, June, 9, 2006.

"On June 8, 2006, the Cass County Attorney's Office charged both Jessica M. Reid and Gregory D. Fester II with two counts of first-degree murder and two counts of use of a firearm to commit a felony in connection with the deaths of Wayne and Sharmon Stock. Arrest warrants have been issued for both Reid and Fester. Both individuals are in custody in the State of Wisconsin on the Cass County warrants. Cass County will immediately begin the extradition process."[1]

This was stunning and unexpected news for the victims' families and everyone following the case, including the public defenders for Livers and Nick Sampson. "Murdock Slaying Case Leads to Wisconsin," read the front-page headline of the June 10, 2006, *Omaha World-Herald*. The arrest affidavits involving Fester and Reid were filed under seal with the court by the Cass County Attorney's Office, which blocked the public and press from gaining access to information about the surprising turn of events, at least for the time being.

. . .

Meanwhile, competitive Nebraska reporters and I, who were all chasing the story, contacted court officials in Dodge County, Wisconsin, who graciously provided several pages of fresh court documents that outlined a significant part of Investigator Schenck's criminal complaints against the two newcomers, Fester and Reid. Interestingly, the court documents filed in Wisconsin totally ignored Jessica Reid's persistent statements that only she and Fester

After this stolen, red-painted truck from Beaver Dam, Wisconsin, was positively linked to the April 17, 2006, Nebraska farmhouse slayings as the real getaway vehicle, the Cass County Sheriff's Office in Plattsmouth, Nebraska, came up with an entirely new theory to explain the murders. Investigators then set out to prove that victims Wayne and Sharmon Stock were slain as part of an elaborate multiple-state conspiracy involving two teenagers from Wisconsin and various young adults residing in Nebraska and Texas. *(Author's collection)*

were involved. Instead, the records presented the story indicating that Reid and Fester met up with two men in front of the Bulldogs Bar in downtown Murdock on Easter night and later joined them at the farmhouse. The court records made it clear that Reid identified Nebraska defendant Nick Sampson as one of the killers. The court records did not identify the other supposed accomplice.[2] Additionally, the court documents lodged against Fester also bolstered the newly adopted theory of a multistate sophisticated murder conspiracy. In fact, the notion that Fester and Reid acted alone was the last thing anybody at the Cass County Sheriff's Office was even considering. Instead, Cass County embarked on proving a new theory that Nick Sampson's close friend Tom Todd was also one of the Stocks' killers. According to an affidavit for a search warrant filed on June 8, 2006, in Cass County Court, Cass County Sheriff's Investigator Matthew Watson alleged that Tom Todd gave Fester and Reid directions to the Bulldogs Bar in Murdock and then joined them in the commission of the murders. According to that search warrant, Cass County Sheriff's officials now contended that Fester and Reid drove Tom Todd and Will Sampson from the Bulldogs Bar to the remote farmhouse. Watson submitted court briefs alleging that Todd, Will Sampson, Reid, and Fester forced entry into the Stock home.[3] After hearing two gunshots, "Fester advised that he saw William Sampson pull the gun away and then Thomas Todd fired a round from the gun he had. Fester described this gun as a smaller shotgun that loaded at the breach. Fester advised that once Thomas fired, the male victim stopped moving," Cass County Sheriff's Investigator Matthew Watson stated in the warrant.

Only a matter of hours after the press release announced the arrests of the two Wisconsin teenagers, Cass County Sheriff's deputies moved in and raided Tom Todd's house on Kansas Street in his normally peaceful hometown of Murdock. The search warrant sought "blood, clothing, hair, dirt or other trace evidence identified with the victims Wayne and Sharmon Stock, plus weapons and ammunition." Todd, age twenty-one, shared a single-story brick house with a friend, Fred Wilson, also age twenty-one. Todd graduated from Elmwood-Murdock High School, and most of his family had roots in rural western Cass County. Todd bypassed college to take a job building grain bins. He typically worked from five to seven weekdays. His criminal history was minor. A high school fight landed him probation for a third-degree misdemeanor assault conviction. In his free time, Todd played guitar and rode a four-wheeler. He regularly socialized with a half-dozen local friends from Murdock, including Nick Sampson, whom friends affectionately called "Doodle." Occasionally, Todd frequented the Bulldogs Bar & Grill, where Nick worked. In the midst of the police raid at Todd's house, authorities brought Todd back to the Cass County Sheriff's office for intense questioning. There, Todd surrendered DNA samples, fingerprints, and palm prints, but he forcefully denied any involvement in the deaths of Wayne and Sharmon Stock. Todd told Lambert and Cass County Sgt. Sandy Weyers that he called in sick for work on April 17—the morning Andy Stock found his parents' slain bodies—but that hardly meant that he was the killer. Todd did not know the Stocks personally or hold any animosity toward them.[4] He had no motive to kill them, he repeated. Todd said he first learned of their deaths from a coworker. He had not spoken with either Nick or Will Sampson about the slayings before or after the Easter weekend. Todd asserted he had never visited the Stocks' farmhouse in his life. In fact, he didn't even know the couple's exact address. He knew of the couple but did not know them personally. Likewise, Todd had not spoken with Matt Livers in probably at least four or five years. Todd shrugged when asked to remember his pattern of activities on Easter. He knew he returned home in the evening and went to bed at the usual time. He urged investigators to interview his roommate to verify his alibi statement that he was home the entire night of the Stock slayings. Todd also insisted he had never visited Wisconsin in his life. He denied knowing Jessica Reid, Greg Fester, or Fester's close associate, Jonathan Wendel. Todd said he had no interest in weapons and didn't own any shotguns. Although Todd's roommate owned a .30–30 caliber rifle, Todd denied ever firing the weapon.

Finally, Todd agreed to take a lie-detector test to clear his name. Sure enough, Nebraska State Patrol Investigator Charlie O'Callaghan was already on standby, ready to administer Todd's polygraph test. O'Callaghan was the same investigator who had determined that Livers failed his polygraph exam, setting off the chain of events that led to the arrests of Livers and Nick Sampson.

O'Callaghan drew up the following relevant test questions for Todd:

Q: "Whether or not you were at the Stock home on the night of their deaths, do you intend to answer truthfully each question about that?"
A: "Yes."
Q: "Were you at the Stock home on the night of their death?"
A: "No."
Q: "On the night of the Stocks' death, were you at their home?"
A: "No."

O'Callaghan concluded Todd flunked the polygraph. "It is the opinion of this examiner that Thomas Todd is being deceptive when he denies being at Wayne and Sharmon Stock's home on the night of their deaths," O'Callaghan stated.

Todd fumed. He insisted he had absolutely nothing to do with the killings. "No way, 100 percent sure, no way, I don't care about the test!" Todd yelled. At 3:07 A.M., the weary suspect stormed out of the interrogation room at the Cass County Sheriff's headquarters. Todd demanded an attorney. He refused to answer any more questions from Weyers, Lambert, and O'Callaghan. Disappointed, Nebraska law enforcement officials had no hard evidence to arrest Todd and link him to the Stock murders, so a Cass County cruiser drove him back to his residence in Murdock in the middle of the night.

During the raid on Todd's residence, Cass County sheriff's deputies seized his telephone bill, a blue glass bong, and a bowl to smoke marijuana. Authorities confiscated Todd's roommate's gun-cleaning kit along with a pair of flashlights. A brown coat with unknown stains thought to be blood was also taken. Tennis shoes and work boots were also snatched. The police raid failed to produce any shotguns the investigators so desperately hoped to find. Still, the persistent investigators from Cass County weren't quite ready to back off Todd as a viable suspect as part of their evolving conspiracy plot. The following week, Todd's roommate Fred Wilson agreed to be interviewed and also take a lie-detector test. In this instance, NSP Investigator O'Callaghan concluded that he found no deception in Wilson's statement insisting that Todd was in their home the entire night of Easter. Frustrated Nebraska law enforcement officials had to back off Todd, once and for all.[5]

There was simply no shred of evidence pointing to Tom Todd as a suspect in the deaths of Wayne and Sharmon Stock. Nothing.

.   .   .

In Wisconsin, Dodge County Sheriff's Detective Rohr tried to verify Jessica Reid's interview statements. Rohr contacted Ryan Krenz, the farmer whose red truck was stolen and driven to Louisiana. Krenz agreed to account for all the firearms in his family's gun collection. The family had one gun cabinet and two safes that stored an assortment of various firearms for fall hunting season. Rohr's tenacity paid off again. A .12-gauge Remington 870 owned by Ryan's father was missing from a gun cabinet. (Ryan had not checked for any missing weapons after he discovered his truck was stolen on Easter Sunday because he had no reason to suspect any weapons were taken.) In addition to the stolen Remington, Krenz discovered several older .12-gauge ammunition rounds were missing from the storage drawer. Rohr realized he was onto something.

He rushed out to the farm. He obtained consent to retrieve a few dozen individual .12-gauge shotgun rounds, plus several rounds of .410-gauge ammunition to compare with the ammunition used to kill the Murdock, Nebraska, farm couple.[6] Next, Detective Rohr sought to verify Fester's statement about getting directions to Murdock, Nebraska, from some drug associate named Thomas, who supposedly joined Fester and Reid at the farm to orchestrate the killings. On June 10, Fester's friend of three years, Jonathan Wendel, told Rohr during an interview that he was absolutely certain that Fester had no friends in Nebraska. Fester definitely did not have any friends named Tom, Tommy, or Thomas either, Wendel assured the Wisconsin detective. Wendel denied knowing anyone in Nebraska, and also denied having any acquaintances with those names living outside Wisconsin, Rohr determined. Next, Rohr lined up an interview with Reid's former housemate, A. J. Wilson, plus three other close associates of Fester. In separate interviews, all of them agreed that

Fester never talked about having a friend in Nebraska named Tom or having any contacts at all in Nebraska. Authorities also obtained the records from Fester's cellular phone seized from Jessica Reid's bedroom. The phone did not include any contacts named Thomas. Moreover, an exhaustive forensics search of Fester's cell phone revealed no incoming or outgoing calls made to any Nebraska area code by Fester or Reid. Rohr's extensive investigation determined that Fester's claim of having a friend named Thomas in Nebraska was totally false. Prior to Jessica Reid's extradition to Nebraska, she agreed to a series of one-on-one interviews with Detective Rohr.

With the Nebraska cops long gone, Reid felt at ease to speak more freely. Now she openly admitted that she shot the male victim, Wayne Stock, during the farmhouse burglary. Reid again insisted that no one else other than herself and Fester was involved in the Nebraska homicides. Jessica confirmed she had entered the upstairs bedroom when Fester shot the screaming woman holding the telephone. In fact, some of Jessica's clothes still had splotches of the male victim's blood, she admitted. Rohr later retrieved Fester and Reid's clothes and shoes from their jail lockers. Then he mailed the garments to Nebraska authorities for follow-up DNA testing.

Nobody was more relieved about the break in the case out of Wisconsin than the two public defenders for Livers and Nick Sampson. But the arrests of the two out-of-state teenagers soon turned into a major letdown when it became patently clear that Cass County authorities had no intention of releasing Livers and Nick Sampson. Both men remained lodged in the Cass County jail, each without bail. Nick Sampson's feisty attorney Jerry Soucie issued a press statement on June 19, reiterating his belief in Sampson's innocence. Soucie asserted that the court affidavits submitted by the Nebraska investigators—mainly those alleging that his client met up with the Wisconsin teenagers outside the Bulldogs Bar—were simply untrue. "In response to the claims that have appeared in the press relating to these Wisconsin documents, Mr. Sampson does not recognize the names of these two individuals," Soucie stated. "He does not recognize their photographs, and he certainly has no knowledge of meeting or speaking with them on April 15, April 16, or April 17, 2006, or at any other time."[7]

. . .

Soucie revealed the major allegations against Nick Sampson had been negated by information Soucie uncovered on his own and had since shared with Cass County Prosecutor Nathan Cox. Moreover, the forensic science evidence used to bring murder charges against the Wisconsin teens was "diametrically contrary" to the evidence used for arresting Nick Sampson. Soucie urged people to call him or the prosecutor if they saw or had contact with any persons matching the description of Jessica Reid or Greg Fester or the shiny red Dodge Ram truck they stole in Wisconsin and used to commit the murders. He also asked anyone to come forward if he or she had seen a tan car parked at the rural cemetery less than a mile from the Stocks' farm near Bluff Road and 286th Street on April 16–17. Unbeknownst to Soucie, NSP Investigator Lambert was quietly piecing together more information about Fester and Reid's role in a rural Iowa vandalism incident that happened several hours before their arrival in Murdock.

. . .

The weathered farmhouse sat along a hilly dirt road in northcentral Iowa, about thirty miles from Des Moines. On April 16, the property endured one of the worst acts of vandalism Guthrie County Sheriff Roger Baird had ever encountered. Unfortunately, law enforcement in rural Iowa had no leads or suspects for more than two months. Then, on June 21, Lambert called. He notified the small-town Iowa sheriff that two teenagers from Wisconsin were in custody for a double murder in rural Nebraska, and both had confessed to trashing an older vacant farmhouse along a dirt road somewhere in Iowa. Lambert also relayed that the teens admitted to stealing a .410-gauge shotgun and a bucket of coins for gas and food during their travels. Luckily for the Iowa farmer, Gary Hines, he was not home when Fester and Reid pulled into his gravel driveway along 250th Street that Easter Sunday afternoon. Hines had left around 8 A.M. to attend a family gathering in Boone, about an hour's drive northeast. After a long day, Hines grew tired. He stayed overnight at his girlfriend's place in Burton, Iowa. He returned around 8:30 A.M. on Monday, April 17, only to find his place looked like a tornado had blitzed through. Meanwhile, authorities about 140 miles west of Guthrie County, Iowa, had another crime unfolding—the discovery of the Stocks' bodies in their Nebraska farmhouse. In Hines's case, he found his windows and mirrors smashed. Thousands of shards of glass littered his carpet. Vandals cracked and destroyed his stove, microwave, and porcelain toilet. Flour and sugar bowls were dumped. Picture frames, television sets, hanging lights, and glass cabinets were all shattered. Even the refrigerator had not been overlooked. About $50 of meat had thawed and spoiled because the vandals intentionally flung open the freezer and fridge. Curiously, the thieves bypassed Hines's large stash of hard liquor, which included vintage Tequila. Instead they stole a twelve-pack of Coca-Cola Classic. Sheriff Baird and his deputies documented the destruction, which was extremely unusual and senseless for rural Guthrie County. They found no fingerprints in the house, despite the extensive damage. On June 22, Lambert made the two-hour drive to tour the Iowa farm, which had been in the Hines family for more than a century. Outbuildings and the garden looked fine, but the farmhouse appeared dated.[8] Gary Hines said how he was grateful the thieves did not to break into a new metal outbuilding that stored dozens of expensive personal possessions. Hines showed the inquisitive Nebraska investigator a small garden hand shovel used by the criminals to pry open his back door to get into his house. Hines pointed out how the vandals stole a box of his red Winchester .410 Super X no. 7 ½ shotgun shells that was kept inside a kitchen cabinet. Lambert collected some of the shells to compare with the ammunition shells used to murder the Stocks. During the walk-through interview, Hines showed Lambert the empty corner in his upstairs bedroom where he last saw his .410-gauge Monitor antique shotgun. Hines used the old shotgun sparingly, mainly to shoot varmints and rodents inside the barns or around the garden. The 1920s shotgun was a family relic and had been passed down through the generations, Hines said proudly. The missing .410-gauge shotgun was a breach-load, single shot. It had a blue barrel and chrome receiver with a dark walnut stock. The stock had a black plastic butt plate, and underneath it bore the family's name or initials G. H. or G Hines. Later Hines directed the Nebraska investigator into the empty upstairs bedroom of his late parents. Hines explained that his father, Robert, died about ten years ago and his mother, Phyllis, died about four years ago. From this room, he told Lambert, the thieves stole a small green tin can containing about $150 worth of quarters from the dresser top. Lambert, though, had a strong suspicion that Fester and Reid had stolen other keepsakes from Hines's late parents' bedroom. On April 19, Louisiana authorities inventoried the stolen truck belonging to Ryan Krenz only to recover an out-of-place gold wristwatch and a Navy Seabees belt buckle. When Lambert showed Gary Hines a couple of these photos, the Iowa farmer immediately recognized the gold wristwatch as a Bulova brand. "It looks like something my father would have worn," Hines added. Gary Hines's deceased father was a World War Two veteran, who had proudly served in the U.S. Navy Seabees. Gary Hines urged Lambert to contact his brother Leland Hines, who lived in Louisiana. Later that same night, Leland Hines relayed over the phone to Lambert how both he and his father had served in the Navy Seabees. Leland's wife bought them matching belt buckles about twenty years ago. Leland's father always affectionately wore the special belt buckle. The Seabee emblem was silver on the face with a blue background. Leland Hines e-mailed two photographs to Lambert at the Nebraska State Patrol offices in Omaha. Without question, Leland Hines's Seabee belt buckle was identical to the one recovered from the stolen truck abandoned by Fester and Reid in Louisiana. Lambert's hard work had paid off. Irrefutable physical evidence linked the Wisconsin teenagers to another random farmhouse burglary during their crime spree, this one in rural Iowa, preceding the farmhouse slayings in Murdock, Nebraska. Astonishingly, Nebraska investigators still refused to concede that Fester and Reid had acted alone. Livers and Nick Sampson still faced a possible sentence of life in prison or the death penalty once their cases went to trial. That July, Weyers and O'Callaghan hopped on a plane bound for Texas.

They set out to prove that Livers and Nick Sampson deliberately recruited the Wisconsin teenagers to drive five hundred miles to kill the Stocks inside their quiet farmhouse.

14

RANSOM THEORY

In the 1990s, Patrick "Ryan" Paulding and Matt Livers became best friends in their high school's special education program back in Abilene, Texas. Paulding and Livers both had IQs of about 70, making them borderline for a diagnosis of mild mental retardation. Ryan's father considered his own son's mental capacity comparable to that of a ten-year-old. Paulding had a connective tissue disorder that affected his cognitive motor skills. At age thirty-one, he staged Hot Wheels matchbox fantasy races on his apartment floor for pleasure. In the days leading up to the Stock murders, Paulding hosted Matt Livers at his bachelor pad near Dallas. Although Paulding immediately became a person of interest, Nebraska authorities were forced to back off when DNA and fingerprints excluded Paulding from the trail of evidence left at the farmhouse killings. By mid-summer, Nebraska cops refocused their suspicions on Paulding.[1]

. . .

On July 6, Paulding volunteered to meet with Cass County Sgt. Sandy Weyers and NSP Investigator Charlie O'Callaghan in the Mansfield Police Department, a Dallas–Fort Worth suburb of fifty thousand. Both Nebraska investigators remained convinced that Paulding's best friend had masterminded the vicious killings of the Stocks even though virtually all the physical evidence now pointed directly at the two transients from Wisconsin who happened to be on a cross-country crime spree. After brief formalized introductions, Paulding told the Nebraska investigators that he still believed in Livers's innocence.[2]

"Why are you convinced Matt's innocent?" asked Weyers.

"He'll stick his neck out for anybody. He's the greatest guy. He'd give you the shirt off his back."

"So you know he's admitted to killing his aunt and uncle?" Weyers pressed.

Paulding responded that the deputies were nagging Livers. "He had enough."

Weyers assured Paulding that innocent people don't take a polygraph and never return home.

She added, "I don't want an innocent person in jail either, but I believe you know more about Matt's life than what you're telling me. Did it ever occur to you that Matt might have something to do with this?"

"Never," he declared.

"Why are you so convinced? You say you're like brothers. The guy's been fired from his job for his temper, did you know that?"

Paulding shrugged. He slumped in the hard leather police chair. He denied his best friend ever mistreated him or Matt's fiancée, Sarah Schneider. There had never been any fights, confrontations, or violent tendencies.

That afternoon, Paulding agreed to take a lie-detector test administered by Mansfield Police Det. Ralph Standefer, who devised the following relevant questions:

Q: "Before Easter of this year, did you ever lie to stay out of trouble?"
A: "No."
Q: "Did anyone tell you what was going to happen to the Stocks prior to their death?"
A: "No."
Q: "Did you participate in any plan to cause the death of the Stocks?"
A: "No."

After the test, Standefer left the room for about ten minutes to huddle with Weyers and O'Callaghan. When he returned, Standefer pulled his chair directly in front of Paulding, then gave him a stern lecture. Paulding had flunked the test.

Specifically, Paulding showed deception related to the question of whether he knew of a preconceived plan to murder the Stocks.

"Guess what? You failed that question," Standefer told him.

Paulding appeared dumbfounded.

Standefer rationalized that he understood Paulding cared about his friend Matt. "I don't think Matt's a bad person either because otherwise you would not be friends with him," Standefer said. "But you know what? Our friends do things we don't necessarily approve of. Matt made a mistake."

The Texas polygraph examiner tried to convince Paulding that Livers took responsibility for the killings only after he failed a polygraph test. "Matt came in and didn't tell them the exact truth at first," Standefer explained. "Don't make the mistake of being the only liar in this investigation. Even Matt's not that dumb. . . . Matt is the person who murdered Wayne and Sharmon Stock. That is what the investigation has revealed. That hurts you because you're friends with Matt."

"He never told me anything about his intentions," Paulding insisted.

Standefer pounced on the word "intentions." He asked Paulding what word Livers used to indicate he intended to kill his uncle and aunt. "It could be 'kill,' 'murder,' 'make them disappear' . . ."

"Kidnap," responded Paulding.

Standefer demanded to know what Livers intended to do after kidnapping Wayne and Sharmon. "He's here for three damn weeks, man! He had a plan."

"I guess Matt told me he was going to kidnap them. Get Wayne's money and somehow Nick [Sampson] was involved."

Later on, Texas Ranger Brad Harmon entered the tiny windowless interrogation room. Harmon pressed Paulding for more details about the two Wisconsin teenagers. "There's a lot of people involved," Harmon warned.

But Paulding insisted he had never met anyone from Wisconsin. And Livers never told him about enlisting others from Wisconsin, Paulding added. He began crying when Harmon reminded him that Livers was in a jail cell awaiting trial on double murder charges because he confessed. With tears flowing, Paulding recalled how his best friend continued to proclaim innocence, even in jailhouse letters he sent to Paulding. Livers even mentioned joining a Bible study group at the Cass County jail, Paulding relayed. Paulding's father was a Baptist minister. "In thirteen years, he hasn't been interested in the church," Paulding said, weeping. "He hasn't been interested in God. I guarantee this changes our friendship big time. I don't trust him. I may tell little white lies, but to fucking lie that you killed someone. He fucking lied to me and that really hurts. . . . I guess he kept a lot of things from me."

"What did he tell you his plan was?" asked Harmon.

"He was going to kidnap them, I guess, take his money."

Paulding claimed that Livers grew agitated after hearing his uncle Wayne Stock purportedly did not approve of Livers's plans to attend truck-driving school.

. . .

The next day, July 7, investigators tried a different tactic. They simply asked Paulding to circle "truth" or "lie" next to several written questions. Those questions were then used as the basis for a second polygraph test conducted by Standefer. These were the following relevant questions:

- Matt Livers discussed a plan to kidnap the Stocks with me?
- The plan included taking money from the Stocks and afterwards killing them?
- Matt Livers approximately an hour after the murders of the Stocks contacted me and told me he did it, meaning he, Matt Livers, killed the Stocks?
- I was not in Nebraska when the Stocks were killed?
- I have not withheld any knowledge about anyone from Wisconsin being involved in the Stocks murder?
- I have not withheld from the investigators any further details regarding the Stocks death?

For all six written and oral questions, Paulding answered "true."

After Paulding finished the lie-detector test, Standefer left for several minutes. Then he returned shortly.

"Well, you missed the boat yesterday, and you missed the boat today, too," announced Standefer.

This time, the Texas lawman voiced displeasure. "I will tell you specifically what it's about. It's about the Wisconsin thing. . . . This was your last opportunity to be a truth teller or a liar. Guess what? The truth teller's gone. That only leaves one. I did everything I could for you. You failed it, and I'm going to let them know."

After Standefer left, Paulding sat alone for more than ten minutes before an angry Sergeant Weyers entered and started shouting.

"The polygraph shows you know these people! What's in this for you? What are you getting that you are willing to keep your mouth shut?"

"I do not know anybody from Wisconsin."

"But you do!"

Paulding whimpered that he didn't know anybody from Wisconsin. Secondly, Livers never spoke about any acquaintances in Wisconsin. Livers never said his cousins, Will and Nick Sampson, knew others in Wisconsin either.

"You want us to believe you over some polygraph test? And that is never going to happen. . . . The polygraph shows you know these people," Weyers insisted.

Later she displayed the grisly crime scene photos.

"You know damn good and well what the plan was for these people. You cannot tell me that somebody who can do that to someone in their family, even a stranger, is not a horrible, sick individual."

She displayed a photo of Wayne Stock facedown in a pool of blood.

"Look at him! Blew his head right off. He didn't just shoot them. He massacred them! It's sick!" she exclaimed.

Another photo showed Sharmon Stock's disfigured face.

"Look at her!" Weyers continued. "Here's her head. Blew her frigging jaw right off her head. It's sick, and all you want to tell me is you can't recall. . . . That is Uncle Wayne and Aunt Sharmon, never, ever to play with their grandkids again. Never, ever to go to the functions of their kids. Their kids have no parents. Their grandkids have no grandparents. Their life is over. Now tell me what the plan was and don't give me any B.S."

After studying the photos, Paulding indicated that Livers spoke of a plan to shoot them.

"Did he ask you to help him?" asked Weyers.

"No. I'm 100 percent positive."

"Did he ask his cousin Nick to help him?" she inquired.

"I believe so. I guess Nick was so aggravated with Wayne. That's what I assume."

"How were they going to do this?"

"I want to say Wayne's shotgun, and Nick had one too."

"They were going to use Wayne's shotgun?"

"Yes," replied Paulding.

"Did Matt tell you anything about these Wisconsin people?"

"No."

"Nothing?"

"Nothing," Paulding answered.

Weyers displayed a photo of Greg Fester, the Wisconsin teen.

"I have no idea," he said.

"Ever see him before?"

"Not that I know of."

Weyers displayed a photo of Jessica Reid, Fester's girlfriend.

Paulding also denied ever having seen her before.

Weyers reached an impasse. After two long probing days in Texas, she had had enough.

"Your whole future is at stake, and you got your good buddy Matt Livers to thank for that," Weyers declared.

Paulding trembled.

She continued, "Everything you've told us today, I've had to spoon-feed to you. . . . That is not going look good when we talk to the prosecutor."

Paulding may very well face conspiracy to commit first-degree murder charges in connection with the Stocks' deaths and be brought back to Nebraska, she warned. "If jail doesn't scare you, or prison doesn't scare you, you better dig real deep because withholding information like you're doing is a conspiracy of first-degree double murder," Weyers barked. "I'm just telling you what the scales are. If you think we're your enemies now, wait until this all pops up."

O'Callaghan delighted in the chance to scare the daylights out of Paulding. "We're crawling up your ass with a microscope," O'Callaghan vowed. "This is not going away for you. We will know more about you than you will ever want us to. We're getting close to finding something you don't want us to find out about. . . ." But things in Texas did not go as well as planned for the Nebraska investigators.

Weyers and O'Callaghan had to let Paulding go home. They had insufficient probable cause to make an arrest.

.   .   .

For the past several months, Matt Livers had spent his days and nights in a lonely Cass County jail cell, unable to marry his sweetheart. He had a dismal future with two first-degree murder charges hanging over his head. Each carried life in prison without parole or the death penalty. And somehow Livers persevered despite being a public pariah in a high-profile double murder case. He adjusted to the isolation and loss of freedom. In the jail, he obeyed the rules. He was polite to his captors. He spent a lot of his time writing letters to his fiancée, Sarah Schneider. His letters were printed in capital letters because he never learned to write cursive in school: "WHY WOULD I SAY I DID SOMETHING WHEN I NEVER HAD ANYTHING TO DO WITH IT? WHAT IN THE WORLD IS WRONG WITH ME? AM I RETARDED OR WHAT? IM JUST NOT SURE I HAVE BEEN TRYING TO ANSWER THIS QUESTION NOW FOR A LONG TIME."[3]

When he learned through the newspaper about the Wisconsin break in the case, there was a sliver of optimism. Then it quickly dissipated when he realized the Cass County prosecutor was not going to dismiss the charges against him. Resigned to his new way of life, Livers spent his time in quiet self-reflection. He tried not to dwell on his disastrous plight. After all, his case was still months away from a jury trial in early 2007.

A small transistor radio, his newfound Christian faith, and visits from his mom, dad, and fianceé were his source of strength. Livers attended Sunday afternoon worship services in the Cass County jail gymnasium. He signed up for a jail ministries Bible study program. He started reading Bible passages. He wrote more letters to his fiancée: "JUST GOT BACK FROM CHURCH I THINK THE WORD THAT THEY PREACHED ABOUT TODAY WAS MENT [sic] FOR ME TO HEAR TODAY. THE WORD WAS WE ALL SIN IN ONE WAY OR ANOTHER BUT NEVER GIVE UP I WILL GUIDE YOU THROUGH IT. AMEN TO THAT. I NEEDED TO HEAR THIS I ALSO ASKED FATHER + SON TO SAVE ME SO TODAY 7-30-06 IVE BEEN SAVED BY OUR AWESOME FATHER + SON OF ALL MIGHTY!!! AND I FEEL GREAT!!!"

Livers mentioned how he prayed for their relationship three times every day. He thanked Sarah for her constant words of encouragement: "AS YOU SAID OUR LORD AND SAVIOUR FATHER AND SON OF ALL MIGHTY IS ON OUR SIDE. THEY WILL END THIS MESS WHEN THEY FEEL THE TIME IS RIGHT IN THEIR EYES. THEY KNOW THE TRUTH AND KNOW I WAS NEVER A PART OF IT. FATHER AND SON OF ALL MIGHTY WOKE ME UP A FEW NIGHTS AGO AND SAID IF THIS GOES ALL THE WAY TO TRIAL IT WILL BE OK. . . . I JUST KNOW WITH THEM ON OUR SIDE EVERY THING WILL WORK OUT FOR THE BEST. IVE [sic] MADE IT THIS LONG SO IF U HAVE TO WAIT A WHILE LONGER. I CAN AND WILL DO IT. . . ."

After Labor Day, the leaves of southeastern Nebraska turned maroon and burnt orange. Temperatures in the seventies made life more bearable. Another season of Nebraska Cornhuskers football was underway. And twenty-five miles south of the Cass County jail, thousands flocked to historic Nebraska City to visit the AppleJack festival, the state's most time-honored community festival. Livers desperately longed for the chance to recline on his sofa and snuggle up with his fiancée in Lincoln. The month of October marked his sixth full month in the county jail. He wrote Sarah: "I JUST HOPE AND PRAY THIS NIGHTMARE ENDS REAL SOON, AS I SAY IN EVERY LETTER ARE [sic] AWESOME FATHER + SON OF ALMIGHTY WILL END THIS WHEN THE TIME IS RIGHT IN THEIR EYES. AGAIN I HOPE THIS HAPPENS REAL SOON. . . . P.S PLEASE SEND ME SOME MORE JR and STEWART PICS AND A COPY OF THE UPDATED POINTS PLEASE. THANK YOU."

Livers hoped the photographs of two NASCAR stars would brighten his otherwise miserable and humiliating situation living among robbers, child molesters, burglars, drug addicts, and assorted habitual criminals in the Cass County jail.

. . .

Jerry Soucie was the fiery, red-faced and white-haired public defender for Nick Sampson. He learned in May that DNA evidence excluded his client's DNA. In fact, not a single piece of physical evidence linked Nick Sampson directly to the slayings, except for the trace of blood found under the dashboard of Nick's brother's car. But if Nick Sampson had no involvement in the killings, why did his first cousin finger him as an accomplice? Soucie didn't have a strong and compelling argument until the shocking arrests in Wisconsin of Greg Fester and Jessica Reid. That July, Soucie filed a motion seeking his client's release on a $50,000 personal recognizance bond, pending trial. It was a somewhat outrageous request because first-degree murder defendants were rarely ever released from jail in Nebraska before trial. On July 9, a team of Cass County Sheriff's deputies marched Nick Sampson into the courtroom of Judge Randall Rehmeier. Nick wore the traditional orange jail jumpsuit, leg shackles, and steel handcuffs. Several friends and family members packed together on the wooden pews to show moral support. Cass County Prosecutor Nathan Cox argued against Sampson's release from custody, citing two key pieces of evidence. The first was the confession implicating Livers and Nick Sampson as the killers. The second was the blood of Wayne Stock discovered inside the car of Nick's brother, Will.

But Cox was not finished. He revealed in open court for the first time that three individuals tied Nick Sampson to the murders: Livers, Jessica Reid, and now Ryan Paulding. Cox told the judge that Paulding recently admitted to law enforcement that Livers and Nick Sampson had planned to kill the Stocks for months. Cox indicated in court that a conspiracy probe remained very active and more arrests might be forthcoming. Not surprisingly, Judge Rehmeier concluded that Cox met his burden of proof to justify Sampson's continued detention. Nick's case was slated for a jury trial in December, and his frustration reaching a breaking point.

He angrily blamed his cousin Matt Livers for his terrible plight. His girlfriend, Lori Muskat, tried to play peacemaker. She had warned Nick that he must leave Matt Livers alone once both of them were freed. But Matt Livers would never be freed, Nick told her during one of their many jailhouse visits being monitored by law enforcement. Lori insisted that Nick's own public defender believed in Livers's innocence. Finally, Nick speculated his cousin did not commit the killings, but perhaps was present when the murders occurred. Lori vehemently disagreed. That was not what "the chick," a reference to Jessica Reid, had told her own mother, Lori replied. Nick Sampson shook his head. The entire case was screwed up, he lamented. Eventually, conversation shifted to wedding bells. They had been together for three-and-a-half years. She wanted to get married, she hinted. Nick told her to slow down. First, he needed to get his life back in order after his release. Above all, he needed a new job. On the other hand, if a jury found him guilty, Nick would spend the rest of his life in prison or on death row.

15

TIPSTER

The Cass County cops continued to fail in their efforts to link the Nebraska cousins to the new defendants from Wisconsin. Absolutely nothing added up after months of feeble attempts. The summer's blockbuster arrests of Fester and Reid sparked frank discussion in Nebraska's small-town coffee shops, taverns, and barbershops about whether their trusted Sheriff's investigators botched the original case by arresting the wrong people. And yet Cass County investigators remained bound and determined to prove everyone wrong.

In many respects, the theory put forth of an elaborate and well-intentioned murder conspiracy was like a bowl of Saltine crackers. Each cracker represented a different suspect or figure. Cass County investigators assumed the cracker representing Ryan Paulding, Matt's best friend from Texas, would reveal the connection between Matt and Nick and the Wisconsin teens, but that never happened. In fact, that cracker crumbled when Paulding recanted his entire statement about a kidnap plan soon after the Nebraska authorities left Texas. He claimed he had been coerced by the police into making a false statement. At the very least, Cass County investigators realized Paulding's credibility as a prosecution witness was so shaky and unreliable that nothing he said on the record to police could be trusted and taken seriously at the upcoming trials for Matt Livers or Nick Sampson. The second cracker, representing Murdock resident Tom Todd, proved totally worthless, so it, too, crumbled. No physical evidence was found in Todd's residence in Murdock during the police raid. That unknown stain found on Todd's clothing did not turn out to be human blood after all. An exhaustive review of cell phone logs conclusively proved that Tom Todd had no connection with the two Wisconsin transients, Fester and Reid. In fact, a court affidavit filed by the

Cass County Sheriff's Office claiming that Fester saw Todd and Will Samp-son shoot and kill the Stocks in the upstairs bedroom was totally inaccurate and 100 percent wrong. Bogus court documents identifying Nick Sampson's brother Will as one of the killers was like another broken cracker. Cass County investigators failed to establish any direct tie to connect Will to the crimes. And Jessica Reid did not do the Nebraska cops any favors. She insisted she and Fester acted alone and never set foot inside the Bulldogs Bar & Grill. But then, just before Cass County's entire conspiracy theory was reduced to a bowl of crumbs, along came a strange and baffling tip from Kirby Drake, one of the influential siblings of murder victim Sharmon Stock.

. . .

On April 17, Drake helped persuade the hometown Sheriff's investigators to focus entirely on Matt Livers, the victims' estranged nephew. Now, three weeks after the Nebraska news media plastered the new jailhouse mug shots of Wisconsin teenagers Fester and Reid everywhere, Drake was moved to contact Sergeant Weyers. According to Drake, once he saw Fester's mug shot in the newspaper, he "knew" he had seen Fester at least once before in Murdock's Bulldogs Bar & Grill.[1] Drake told police he prided himself in re-membering people's names and faces. He also remembered he had frequented the Bulldogs Bar only three times in the past year, including New Year's Eve with the Stocks. Besides New Year's Eve, Drake recalled visiting the bar for his birthday on January 10, 2006, and to pick up a large dinner takeout or-der on Easter Sunday—only hours before his sister and brother-in-law were slain. Drake recalled he ordered four pot-roast dinners and one shrimp and popcorn chicken dinner on Easter. Looking back, Drake believed he spotted a red pickup with Wisconsin plates parked outside the Bulldogs Bar on Easter. That particular afternoon, Drake ordered two draft beers as he waited for his food order from the kitchen. Suddenly, a new face inside the bar gave Drake an "uneasy feeling." A young man with dark hair halfway down his back walked past him and headed toward the kitchen and restrooms, Drake told police. Drake claimed he asked one of the patrons about the new stranger in town and one of them immediately answered, "Gregory Fester II from Wisconsin . . . a friend of Nick Sampson's."

Drake mentioned that the young man lurking around the bar had no facial hair, grungy-looking sagging jeans with a chain-type wallet dangling from his pants pocket, and a black T-shirt. Drake also remembered the Bulldogs had only two cooks at the time and one was Nick Sampson. After his food was ready, Drake paid his bill and left. As he went outside, Drake also claimed he saw a large dog in the back of a red truck bearing Wisconsin license plates and he laughed. He said he wondered why anybody from Wisconsin would drive to Nebraska with a dog in the back of their pickup. Drake described the dog as a larger lab mix, light brown with a spot about eight inches in diameter on its right side. Coincidentally, Nick Sampson also had two large dogs that matched the same general description.

Naturally, Cass County investigators were excited. Drake's tip gave them an opportunity to shore up their miserably failing multistate conspiracy probe. They made it easy for Drake by furnishing him with a photo lineup consisting of six different long-haired dudes. One of the mug shots included the very same photo of Fester that had been splashed across the Nebraska news media during the previous month. Drake circled that particular mug shot. Then he eagerly agreed to take a polygraph. The examiner was none other than NSP Investigator Charlie O'Callaghan.

Not surprisingly, O'Callaghan found Drake's story credible. After all, Drake could be an extremely helpful star witness for the prosecution at the upcoming murder trials for Matt Livers and Nick Sampson. "It is the opinion of this examiner that Kirby Drake is being truthful when he identifies Gregory Fester as being the same individual he recognized in the Murdock, NE., Bulldog[s] Bar prior to the deaths of Wayne and Sharmon Stock," O'Callaghan stated.[2]

In the end, Drake would not serve as a star witness for the prosecution. His interview statement was unsubstantiated, which was another big letdown for local law enforcement. To their credit, Sgt. Sandy Weyers and Sheriff's Investigator Matt Watson made every attempt to verify Drake's comments. About a dozen witnesses recalled Drake was in the Bulldogs Bar, but none of his other statements were corroborated or deemed factual. "All parties denied ever having seen or met Greg Fester," Weyers stated.[3]

Additionally, none of the customers at the Bulldogs recalled seeing any red truck parked out front bearing Wisconsin plates on Easter Sunday. No one saw a large brown dog similar to one of Nick Sampson's dogs in any of the trucks parked near the Bulldogs on Easter Sunday. Bar owner Trudy Berkey and two employees emphatically denied that Reid and Fester ever set foot in the bar on Easter or any other prior occasion. Berkey assured the Cass County deputies that no stranger had frequented the Bulldogs on Easter Sunday. She confirmed that Nick Sampson dropped in around three for a ham steak, mashed potatoes, and gravy. He was in town to cut his mother's lawn. After staying about ninety minutes, Nick drove back to his house in Palmyra,

Nebraska. As Nick sat in jail awaiting trial, the Cass County Attorney's Office had a big problem on its hands.

.   .   .

On the first Friday in October, Cass County Attorney Nathan Cox calmly walked into the district courtroom across the hallway to dismiss both counts of first-degree murder against Nick Sampson. Before taking questions from pesky and inquisitive news reporters, Cox read from a prepared statement. He began by complimenting the Cass County Sheriff's Office and Nebraska State Patrol for working tirelessly and doing a tremendous job in the investigation. "Recently, Judge Rehmeier ruled that law enforcement had properly arrested Nick Sampson," Cox said. "However, the standard that the prosecution must meet at trial is proof beyond a reasonable doubt. After considering the evidence discovered to date in the Stock murder cases, I have come to the conclusion that the Nicholas Sampson case, at this point, does not meet that standard. This decision was not made lightly. Significant evidence used

Cass County Attorney Nathan Cox, with Chief Deputy Attorney Colin Palm behind him, announces that double murder charges against Nick Sampson are being dropped. In December 2006, Cox dropped his prosecution against Livers upon realizing that Livers had given a false confession. *(Lincoln Journal Star Photo)*

to establish probable cause is not available currently for trial as the rules of evidence and the Constitutional rights of the accused do not allow us to present certain evidence against Nick Sampson at trial."[4]

Of course, Cox was referring to Matt Livers's incriminating confession implicating Nick as his lone accomplice. By law, prosecutors could not force Livers to testify against his codefendant, since Livers had not gone to trial himself. "I have decided that the only prudent choice at this time is to dismiss the charges against Nicholas Sampson without prejudice," Cox continued.

Cox reassured the victims' family that his office and law enforcement would continue to exert every effort to hold the perpetrators of the senseless murders responsible. "In conclusion, the cases against the three other defendants currently in custody for these homicides are proceeding to trial. I am confident in the state's cases and their successful prosecution."

Livers's jury trial remained on schedule for January 2007. Later that morning, Nick Sampson emerged as a free man for the first time in six months. He walked out of the adjoining Cass County Law Enforcement Center in blue jeans and a gray hooded sweatshirt. The carefree Murdock native jumped into the arms of his crying fiancée, Lori Muskat. Others present for the emotional reunion included his mother Debra, his sister Crystal, his brother Will, and about a dozen friends who had faithfully stood in his corner from the beginning. On the lawn of the historic Cass County Courthouse, Nick's outspoken public defender Jerry Soucie addressed the news media for what seemed like a historic occasion in its own right. "On April 26, 2006, state and local law enforcement officials stood outside the Cass County Courthouse and announced that the murders of Wayne and Sharmon Stock had been solved with the arrest of Nick Sampson and Matt Livers," Soucie barked in his familiar forceful tone.[5]

"Five months and ten days later the charges against Nick Sampson have now been dismissed. The truth is law enforcement was wrong. The real investigation had only begun. I know I speak for Nick, his family, friends, and supporters in expressing our gratitude that the county attorney has done the right thing."

Soucie emphasized his client was totally innocent of murdering the Stocks. Nick was arrested before investigators performed any forensics testing on Nick's shotgun, clothes, the engraved ring, bloody flashlight, marijuana pipe, shoe prints, and tire impressions found at the farmhouse. All of the subsequent forensic testing excluded Nick, included someone else, or could not identify anyone, Soucie explained. Nick also had an alibi and those two witnesses were interviewed by law enforcement. "I want to emphasize that these charges

Nick Sampson speaks with reporters moments after charges were dropped against him prior to his upcoming double murder trial. His public defender, Jerry Soucie, holds a photo of the engraved ring found at the farmhouse crime scene in Murdock, Nebraska. The ring helped free his client and proved that the two Wisconsin teenagers were the real killers. *(Lincoln Journal Star Photo)*

were not dismissed based on some legal technicality or evidentiary ruling by the court that made further prosecution impossible," Soucie clarified. "No evidence in this case has been suppressed. The charges have been dismissed because there is simply no evidence upon which this case could be tried. Nick Sampson did not commit this crime. He did not aid or assist anyone else to commit this crime, and he has absolutely no direct or indirect knowledge regarding who killed Wayne and Sharmon Stock or why."

Soucie credited the recovery of the engraved gold ring on Sharmon Stock's kitchen floor with cracking the case. "Nick's nightmare began on April 25 when local law enforcement officers made the decision to arrest him without any evidence except for the statement of Matt Livers," Soucie declared. "This arrest was made without any attempt to first verify any of the things said by Mr. Livers. This represented a bad case of tunnel vision and the investigators failed the basic requirements of Homicide Investigation 101."

Soucie unleashed more vitriol toward the Nebraska State Patrol and Cass

County. "It was obvious from the beginning that Nick Sampson had absolutely no motive or reason to harm Wayne or Sharmon Stock," Soucie said.

In fact, only one interaction surfaced during the murder investigation, an incident from 2004 when Nick and Matt borrowed the four-wheelers out of Wayne Stock's machine shed on a winter day and rode through the barren hay fields. Wayne Stock got mad and yelled at Matt for borrowing the ATVs without his permission. Nick, on the other hand, was only a shirttail cousin of the Stocks. "That such an incident could form the basis for Nick holding a grudge for years and then serving as the motion for committing these two murders as revenge is simply absurd," Soucie contended.

In fact, the police theory that Matt and Nick plotted the murders during a phone call prior to Easter should have been easily debunked by law enforcement. Phone records revealed the two cousins had not even spoken to one another on the phone during the previous four months prior to the murders, Soucie noted. During the double murder investigation, police obtained phone records for more than fifty separate numbers from more than two dozen users and subscribers in Nebraska, Wisconsin, and Texas. E-mail wasn't practical since Nick and his roommates didn't have computers at their house in Palmyra, and neither did the Wisconsin teens. "The time line and phone records do not show any connection between Nick Sampson or Matt Livers for that matter and anyone from Wisconsin including Jessica Reid, Gregory Fester or anyone remotely connected to either Reid or Fester," Soucie boasted.

He excoriated the Nebraska police for leaving his client to languish in a jail cell for four full months even after the real killers from Wisconsin were identified and had confessed. "The developments in Wisconsin during the first week of June with the arrests of Reid and Fester should have made it painfully clear that what Matt Livers said was not credible and demonstrably false," Soucie determined. "This will become even more apparent as the prosecutions of Reid and Fester continue and hearings are held in Livers's case."

After Soucie finished bashing the local cops, he switched gears and singled out one Wisconsin detective for special praise. After all, it was the Wisconsin police who doggedly determined the murder weapons brought to the Murdock farmhouse had come from two other prior burglaries, the first in Wisconsin, then a second in Iowa. This fact obliterated the Nebraska investigators' theory that Matt, Nick, or someone within their tight circle of friends had furnished the weapons as part of a well-planned conspiracy. "I want to especially thank Det. Jim Rohr of the Dodge County Wisconsin Sheriff's Office for his work following through in investigating the involvement of Reid and Fester after the local investigators left Wisconsin," Soucie said. "I am not at all sure that the Cass County and State Patrol investigators would have discovered important evidence exculpating Nick Sampson without Detective Rohr's persistence and patience."

So, on a beautiful Friday afternoon with blue skies and puffy white clouds lazily drifting across the southeastern Nebraska skyline, Nick Sampson realized his nightmare had ended. No more orange jail jumpsuits. No more perp walks through the Cass County Courthouse in front of television camera crews and newsprint photographers. No more law enforcement–monitored phone calls and visitations at the humbling jail facility. No more lonely days and depressing nights in an isolation cell. "I had nothing to do with this crime. No involvement in this case whatsoever. I was in my home in Palmyra the entire night," Nick Sampson eagerly told Nebraska reporters, marking his first public comments since his April arrest. "Jail will break you in a heartbeat. On my second day in there, I was bawling like a three-year-old. Isolation—it takes getting used to."[6]

After he faced murder charges, Nick's fiancée Lori moved into Nick's mother's house in Murdock. With Nick in jail, she could no longer afford to pay the rent. "We were a two-income family, now it's bad," Nick commented as he sipped a can of Pepsi. "Luckily, I have one job left—at the Bulldogs."

His friends from the Bulldogs smiled and cheered. They planned to host a welcome-home party at the small-town bar to cheer up his spirits. When reporters asked Nick to comment about the Cass County Sheriff's Office, Sampson rolled his eyes.

"I don't think they know how to investigate a murder," he snapped.

16

FREEDOM

Even though Nick Sampson was released from jail, law enforcement in Cass County still hoped to send Matt Livers to Nebraska's death row or prison for the rest of his life despite a plethora of compelling evidence lined up against the two Wisconsin teenagers.

Luckily, Livers's public defender Julie Bear believed completely in his innocence. Bear knew something wasn't right with her client's supposed confession, especially after Fester and Reid surfaced. She knew Matt's confession got most of the crime scene facts totally wrong.

For instance, Matt claimed to be present during the Stock murders; neither Fester nor Reid identified Livers as being present.

Livers claimed that he and Nick Sampson each shot the Stocks; both Reid and Fester admitted they were the ones who fired the fatal shots.

Livers did not identify Reid or Fester as being present during the murders or being involved in any way. DNA evidence left at the crime scene proved Fester and Reid were present at the time of the murders.

Livers claimed that Nick Sampson dropped a marijuana pipe in the driveway after the shootings. DNA testing conclusively established the drug pipe contained a mixed sample from Reid and Fester, not the DNA of Nick Sampson or Matt Livers.

Livers claimed that a single shotgun was used to kill the Stocks. Spent shell casings at the crime scene showed two weapons were used.

Livers claimed that Nick provided the .12-gauge shotgun. Ballistics tests eliminated Nick's shotgun as the one involved. Evidence established the pair of shotguns used to kill the Stocks were stolen and brought to Nebraska by Fester and Reid.

Livers claimed that Nick disposed of the murder weapon. Fester and Reid admitted they threw the murder weapons into a ditch somewhere between Murdock, Nebraska, and Washington, Louisiana.

Livers claimed that he shot Sharmon Stock after shooting Wayne Stock in the leg. Livers claimed that Sharmon continued screaming and was then shot in the head. The crime scene and autopsy contradicted this scenario.

Livers claimed that he and Nick plotted to kill the Stocks during a cell phone call the Thursday or Friday before Easter. Law enforcement obtained the cell phone records for both Livers and his girlfriend and should have known that no such call ever took place. In fact, there were no phone calls between Livers and Nick Sampson during any of the months prior to the killings.

To determine Livers's full psychological profile prior to his double murder trial set for early 2007, the Cass County court granted permission for Dr. Scott Bresler of Ohio to evaluate the double murder defendant. Bresler, a former University of Nebraska forensic psychologist, was now at the University of Cincinnati in the Department of Psychiatry and Behavioral Neuroscience. As part of his rigorous evaluation, he reviewed the investigative police reports and studied the videotapes of Livers's eleven-hour interrogation and confession. Bresler traveled to Nebraska to interview Matt's parents and Matt's fiancée. He devised a number of psychologist tests, including the Weschler Abbreviated Scale of Intelligence, the Personality Assessment Interview, the Paulhus Deception Scales, the Validity Indicator Profile, the Gudjonsson Suggestibility Scales, the Gudjonsson Compliance Scale, and the Repeatable Battery for the Assessment of Neuropsychological Status (commonly known as list-learning and story memory). By the time Bresler finished his work, the distinguished Ohio psychiatrist understood why a terribly flawed and horribly incompetent police interrogation wrecked Matt's self-confidence and left him stumbling and stammering as two angry investigators spoonfed him a confession that had more holes in it than a piece of Swiss cheese.

. . .

On November 30, 1977, Matthew David Livers was born at a small-community hospital in Syracuse, Nebraska, a town of one thousand with a strong German heritage and a short drive from Lincoln. Matt's early years brought many challenges, including delayed motor and speech skills. "Matt will amount to a zero nothing," a school psychologist informed his mother.[1] Matt attended normal kindergarten in the Elmwood-Murdock school system. He also went for additional therapy at an Educational Service Unit program called Project

Me, about twenty miles away in Springfield, Nebraska. The program aimed to mainstream Matt and other children with academic difficulties into a regular first grade classroom. In grade and middle school, Matt had a short attention span. Back then, people didn't understand his learning disabilities. Kids teased and bullied him. Some took his lunch money. On multiple occasions, Matt returned home from school in tears. He had very few school friends. School officials, for their part, felt Matt exhibited really bizarre behavior growing up in Murdock. By 1992, Matt's family relocated to Abilene, Texas, thanks to a job opportunity for his father. Moving to Texas offered Matt a fresh start, too. The special education program at Matt's new high school included many other students like him, including Ryan Paulding, who ultimately became his best friend. But Matt did not altogether escape teasing and bullying in Abilene. On occasion, he sneaked out of school before the bell rang to avoid other teenagers eager to pick on him. All of Matt's classes were concentrated in the special education program. Consequently, his few friends at Wylie High School were also slow and learning disabled. Yet other aspects of his teenage years were normal. Matt obtained his driver's license. He held a part-time job at a local Taco Bell restaurant to pay for his car. In May 1996, Matt beamed as he wore his cap and gown and walked across the stage to receive his diploma, just like hundreds of classmates. Since college wasn't practical, Matt took a job at the local Abilene Airport with a private security company. He enjoyed security work. He thought of himself as being like a real police officer, minus the firearm. Soon Matt moved back to Nebraska with his parents and took a job at the large Kawasaki assembly plant in Lincoln. By 2000, Matt followed his parents back to Texas, this time relocating to Victoria, a city of sixty thousand, about thirty miles inland from the Gulf of Mexico. In Victoria, Matt worked a slew of jobs: laborer, security guard, and lot porter for a car dealership. In December 2001, he met Sarah Schneider. She was already pregnant and in the midst of a divorce, but she and Matt hit it off. By 2003, Matt and Sarah decided to move to Lincoln, Nebraska, after Matt's parents again pursued career opportunities in Nebraska. Not far from the University of Nebraska–Lincoln campus, Matt and his steady girlfriend rented a modestly priced, forest-green, two-story house in an urban neighborhood. The couple's relationship was strong and fulfilling. They never fought. Their only major argument occurred when Sarah confronted Matt about his penchant for making impulsive buys on the eBay Web site. But somehow life in Nebraska had its share of downs. Matt was fired from a couple of positions as a laborer. His job as a security guard at the Novartis plant abruptly ended prematurely after he kicked a hole in a wooden door during an outburst. Then a month later, Matt was still unemployed when his wealthy uncle and aunt were slain in their Murdock farmhouse only hours after Matt joined them for an Easter luncheon. Virtually everybody in the immediate family fingered Matt as the obvious killer. Then Matt's confession eight days later cemented their belief that he was cold, cruel, and bloodthirsty. Then the shocking summer arrests of Fester and Reid in Wisconsin left everyone confused, and the critical elements of the case against Matt and Nick Sampson were called into question. By late November, Dr. Bresler's ten-page report contained a number of disturbing observations to prove why Matt's confession was hooey.

.   .   .

On April 25, Lambert and Schenck took Matt from his home and traveled sixty miles to the Cass County Sheriff's Office for his interview. In essence, Matt was captive. He had no way of getting home on his own, even if he wanted to end the interrogation, Bresler noted. Also, Matt had only a can of Mountain Dew but no breakfast that morning. He did not receive any food until the end of the night, after a series of confrontational interrogations and a stressful polygraph test. Matt had offered to take the polygraph test to clear his name. He admitted to not sleeping well the previous night. He felt nervous and spoke of being intimidated by the long cables hooked up to the polygraph machine in the law enforcement interrogation room. He also complained about the hardness of his metal chair and having to undergo a grueling eleven-hour interrogation without the benefit of any food. In fact, Matt repeatedly asked for a blanket after the police set the thermostat low to make the room unbearably cold for their suspect.

He denied a total of eighty-nine times that he killed his relatives before finally breaking down and agreeing with the investigators' theory of how the murders transpired. In total, Matt made 139 separate denials during the entire interrogation, Bresler noted. During his first interview evaluation with Dr. Bresler, Matt appeared both nervous and anxious. He often smiled for no reason as he wore his standard jail garments. The forensic psychologist noted Matt's ideas made sense, and Matt spoke in a normal rate, volume, and tone. But his mood appeared depressed. He fully understood he was in jail because he told the police he murdered his aunt and his uncle. Matt actually believed he would get to leave the police station if he confessed to the double murder. "I wanted to go home," he told Dr. Bresler.[2] During his examination, Dr. Bresler administered a series of intelligence tests on the defendant. On the vocabulary test, Matt compared to a thirteen-year-old. On a similarities test, he compared to a ten-year-old. On block design and matrix reasoning, he compared to a seven-year-old. Matt demonstrated a much higher verbal IQ score than his performance IQ tests showed. Overall, he displayed a general intellect capacity that placed him in the borderline mildly mentally retarded range. His verbal skills were stronger than his nonverbal skills, leading people engaged in conversation with him to think Matt was more high-functioning than he really was. Dr. Bresler made his most striking assessments when applying the Gudjonsson Suggestibility Scales. Matt had a strong tendency to make up information to fill in his lack of knowledge or memory gaps. Dr. Bresler noted this particular trait was more prevalent in people of diminished mental capacity. He tested Matt on the Gudjonsson Compliance Scale, which is a twenty-question true-or-false test that gauges avoidance of conflict/confrontation and one's eagerness to please someone. An average score is 9. Anything above 16 is extremely rare and a sign of an unusual trait. Matt scored an 18. "These scores reflect that Mr. Livers has a very elevated degree of trait compliance," Dr. Bresler concluded. "Research supports that persons with elevated Gudjonsson Compliance Scale scores are more likely to give in to interrogation, generating a confession but later retracting it."

According to Dr. Bresler's final analysis, Matt Livers's confession was clearly false. The two screaming cops had coerced him into false admissions of guilt. Foremost, he had a very low intelligence and appeared learning disabled. Those factors alone made him vulnerable to being manipulated by others of stronger intellect. Also, Matt had worked in security guard jobs. He liked "police-type" work. He trusted police and believed in their good nature. Throughout his entire interrogation, Matt typically responded with "yes, sir," or "no, sir" answers. Furthermore, he had no prior criminal history. He had never been confronted in an environment where he was interrogated or mercilessly grilled by the cops. Moreover, Matt would not suspect that police may fabricate evidence to link him to a crime as a ploy to solicit his confession, Dr. Bresler noted. On at least eighty-eight different occasions, investigators Lambert and Schenck cut off Matt's pleas of innocence. They made disparaging comments about his life. "The police threatened that Mr. Livers would be killed for his role in this crime. At one point, a police investigator tells Mr. Livers that he will be 'hanged from the highest tree,'" Bresler highlighted. Consequently, Livers became more fearful, frustrated, and depressed. "These conditions certainly could have led him to produce a false confession with the purpose of terminating the unwanted police encounter,"

Bresler wrote.[3] Matt's behavior in his post-confession interview was telling. He cried as he recanted his day-old confession. He gave logical explanations for his knowledge of certain facts about the Stock murders. Police, however, halted that videotaped interview after assuring their defendant he had to be lying, Bresler observed. "However, it is possible that after rest, food and some calm reflection, Mr. Livers may have felt more comfortable to reveal that he made up the confession and that he was innocent. In other words, he returned to the pattern of denying involvement in the murders, a pattern in which he asserted his innocence over 100 times before he confessed to the crimes the previous day," Bresler wrote the court.

Dr. Bresler's final report floored Cass County Attorney Nathan Cox. Cox immediately sought out a second opinion. He turned to Dr. Mario Scalora, the nationally distinguished University of Nebraska forensic psychologist. Scalora had evaluated hundreds of inmates within the Nebraska Department of Corrections and often served as an expert witness for both prosecutors and defense attorneys. Scalora agreed to offer his own independent analysis about the legitimacy of Matt's confession.

.   .   .

December 5, 2006, the Cass County District courtroom was reserved for what was supposed to be the start of a three-day-long pretrial hearing to determine whether Matt's confession would be admissible at his upcoming January trial. At 9:45 A.M., the bailiff said, "All rise!" Cass County District Judge Randall L. Rehmeier walked into court and took his seat behind his raised bench. Nathan Cox and Chief Deputy Attorney Colin Palm appeared for the prosecution. Public defenders Julie Bear and Susan Bazis appeared on behalf of Matt, who was not present. The judge explained that the purpose of the morning's hearing was to take up a number of key pretrial motions, mostly filed by the public defenders. Then he made the startling announcement: "In the interim period of time, the State has filed this date a motion to dismiss."

Court: Is that correct, Mr. Cox?

Cox: That is correct, sir.

Court: Okay. And the State wishes the court to enter an order dismissing the case then?

Cox: That's correct, sir.

Court: And with regard to the matter, then, the court will at this time grant the motion to dismiss. And I'll enter the order accordingly that's been submitted. . . . That will complete the matter, and you are excused from the proceedings.[4]

Finally, after nearly eight months in jail, Matt Livers was free to go home, just like his cousin Nick Sampson. The Cass County Sheriff's Office was left wiping egg off its face for arresting the wrong two people. To his credit, Cox toughened up and politely addressed the Nebraska news media in the courthouse hallway. He told the press that two independent forensic psychologists concluded that Livers's initial confession was false. "My expert has come to the conclusion that based on the information that we currently know, the statements of Matthew Livers are unreliable to the point of not being useable at this time," Cox said. "This combined with a number of inconsistencies that I have not been able to reconcile, as they relate to Matthew Livers's statements, I have determined that the only option at this time is to dismiss the charges against Matthew Livers until such time as those inconsistencies are resolved, if they can be resolved."[5]

Once Cox finished, reporters swarmed Julie Bear, the Plattsmouth public defender lawyer, who quietly went about her business at her Main Street law office a few blocks from the courthouse. Bear just prevailed in the biggest case of her legal career. She graciously thanked Nathan Cox for dropping the double murder charges against her client. "This dismissal is the right thing to do legally, morally, and ethically," Bear told the news media. "Matt has always been respectful and trusting of law enforcement, and he trusted the investigators when he volunteered to meet with them in any way he could to solve a horrific crime. Unfortunately, the interrogation process utilized tactics that were coercive and techniques that did not serve the interest of justice."[6]

She praised Dr. Bresler, the forensic psychiatrist who helped her understand the phenomenon of false confessions. She thanked Steven Drizin, the Northwestern University legal scholar on false confessions, who headed the Center on Wrongful Convictions in Chicago. Drizin reached out to her after learning of the arrests of the Wisconsin teenagers back in June. He served as a legal consultant at no cost. Lastly, she praised Jerry Soucie, Nick Sampson's public defender. Soucie was a tremendous resource, she added. Bear assured everyone that mental health experts for the defense and prosecution came to the exact same conclusion—Matt's confession was demonstrably false and inconsistent with the crime-scene evidence. "Yet the investigators overlooked the inconsistencies in the confession and falsely accused an innocent man of a crime he did not commit," Bear stressed.

Sadly, the Murdock murders created a double tragedy for the Stocks. "This family has been victimized twice," Bear explained, "once in the loss of a parent, brother, aunt and uncle, and again with the needless arrest of an innocent man. This has forever fractured family relationships, cast doubt upon innocent people, and interrupted the grieving process for the family. This case came perilously close to being a tragedy on many levels, and there have been devastating consequences as a result of a poorly conducted interrogation."

By the lunch hour, Bear joined Matt's family in the lobby of the Cass County Sheriff's Office for an emotional and tearful reunion. Matt's parents Dave and Barbara Livers cried when their son emerged from the jail wearing blue jeans, a black sweatshirt, and a red Nebraska Cornhuskers baseball cap. He had a wide smile. This time, he could go home for good. Matt gave a giant bear hug to his fiancée, Sarah Schneider.

"It's over!" Livers shouted. "It's over now. I'm going home. Amen." More tears of joy flowed as Matt clutched his parents. Finally, he hugged Bear, the public defender who had achieved his freedom against unbelievable odds.[7]

Journalists chased after Matt and his family as they exited the Sheriff's building. Matt's fiancée, a registered nurse, told the author she never doubted Matt's innocence for a second. "He was home with me in bed the entire night that this happened," she reckoned. A television reporter asked Matt what it was like being in jail for so many months.

"Tough," he snapped.

Moments later, the Livers family sped away from the Cass County Law Enforcement Center. The nightmare of their last year was finally behind them, but the scars that damaged family relationships would never go away.

17

JUDGMENT

Officials in the Cass County Sheriff's Office were angry with Cass County Attorney Nathan Cox's decision to dismiss double murder charges against Matt Livers and set him free. But Cox, a noble and honest man, made the right call in the end, and that's what really mattered most. An innocent man would not stand trial for his life in Cass County.

Shortly thereafter, Wisconsin teenager Jessica Reid pleaded guilty to two counts of second-degree murder. Theoretically, Jessica could be released after serving as little as ten years' prison time or up to life in prison. Fester also pleaded guilty to two counts of second-degree murder, plus one count of using a weapon to commit a felony. The guilty pleas of the Wisconsin transients restored some credibility for the prosecutor's office. Then, as sentencing neared, one of God's soldiers on Earth came to Reid's defense. The Rev. Val J. Peter, executive director emeritus of Girls and Boys Town, notified Cass Count District Judge Randall Rehmeier that he had counseled and prayed with Jessica inside the Cass County jail since her transfer to Nebraska in July 2006. In his seventies, the feisty Father Peter had been the former longtime leader in Omaha of the original Father Flanagan's Boys' Home in Nebraska. Father Peter was one of Omaha's most colorful and controversial priests, and he had recently garnered front-page headlines in the *Omaha World-Herald* for counseling a troubled teenage girl from a small western Iowa town who had set her family's house on fire with a can of gasoline. That girl had tried to kill her sexually abusive stepfather, but instead the arson tragically killed two younger siblings. Now Father Peter was going to bat for Jessica Reid, another troubled teenage girl who also came from a dysfunctional home life. In his letter, Father Peter urged Judge Rehmeier to give Jessica a sentence of less than life. That way she could repay her debt to society and become a productive citizen someday. Reid came from a broken home. She had no religious or moral training. "And as Father Flanagan often said, 'Without any doubts, we can hardly blame a youth for that lack of training,'" Peter wrote. "Please take that into consideration."[1]

Reid's parents never taught her the rudiments of right or wrong. She did not know the Lord's Prayer. She grew up in a family absent of morals, rules, and without any religious foundation, Peter noted. "When she walked into that house with Gregory Fester, she had not the slightest premonition that he would senselessly, maliciously, wantonly kill 2 wonderful people so undeserving of this fate," the priest wrote. "She had no hatred in her heart. She was just unaware that anything made much difference."

At the close of his letter, Father Peter informed Judge Rehmeier, "You have my respect and esteem in this difficult task."

.   .   .

On March 19, 2007, approximately one hundred brokenhearted friends and family members of Wayne and Sharmon Stock piled into the third-floor Cass County District courtroom. Andy Stock was joined by his sister Tammy Vance and his brother Steven. In the days prior, Andy Stock gave the court a victim impact statement. He described how his life was consumed with fear, pain, and paranoia after discovering his father's shattered head and blood smeared across the upper walls and hallway. Trudging out to his parents' empty farmstead to manage the Stock Hay Co. was burdensome. "Every morning, the first thing I see is the bedroom window where the entire trauma took place that April night," Andy stated. "The lack of blinds on the upstairs windows reminds me that they had to be removed because of the blood splatter. The lack of movement on the farm reminds me that no one is there to greet me with a smile that morning. I am again put through the hell as the phone starts to ring for the day, and I have to explain time and time again why Wayne cannot be reached."[2]

Andy wasn't the only Cass County resident still reeling from the nightmare. The murders of Wayne and Sharmon also impacted the area's farm children.

Some kids grew scared and got butterflies in their stomachs when they saw an unfamiliar face approaching the front door of their parents' home. Kids checked the doors and windows of their homes to make sure they were locked. Some children struggled to sleep for days after the murders while others woke up in the middle of the night, panic-stricken.

. . .

Now age twenty, Fester no longer resembled the Marilyn Manson wannabe that he was before he murdered the Stocks. In jail, he chopped off his long black hair, which reached well below his shoulders. On the afternoon of his sentencing, Fester's bangs dangled toward his chin. His oval-shaped eyeglasses gave him a John Lennon look. Prosecutor Nathan Cox asked the judge to impose the maximum penalty—life imprisonment—for Fester. "This really is a train wreck of a life that we're looking at," Cox said bluntly.[3]

Prior to April 17, 2006, life in Murdock had a picturesque, Norman Rockwell–like setting, Cox recounted. Locals greeted strangers at the post office, gas stations, and other businesses with kindness. Rural residents left their doors unlocked at night because they had nothing to fear. But that all changed. The community was shattered because of Fester and Reid, the prosecutor noted. Residents of Cass County now locked their doors at night. Some families slept with shotguns next to their bedside for protection. The

Sheriff's deputies in Nebraska escort Gregory Fester from the Cass County Courthouse in Plattsmouth, Nebraska. In March 2007, Fester received two life prison sentences with no chance for parole after pleading guilty to murdering Wayne and Sharmon Stock during a cross-country crime spree with girlfriend Jessica Reid. *(Lincoln Journal Star Photo)*

Stocks' children and grandchildren were forever robbed of sharing holidays and other special memories together with Wayne and Sharmon. "The loss to Murdock has been incalculable," Cox stressed.

The judge asked Fester if he wanted to make any statement prior to sentencing. The courtroom grew silent. Fester reached into his pocket. He unfolded a crumpled piece of paper. Cass County Sheriff's Investigator Earl Schenck Jr. leaned against the wall in the courtroom, eager to hear what Fester had to say. Incredibly, Schenck still refused to believe that the two teenagers from Wisconsin were the only real perpetrators.

"I stand before you today a broken man," Fester began, trembling. "Not because this day will reveal my punishment and fate, but because for almost a year, my heart has known the horrible truth. That I am responsible for taking the two, two innocent people's lives. There is no price that I can pay that will ever make that right. . . . There is not a day that goes by that I don't feel pieces of my heart dropping into my soul. One set of very bad decisions can change one's life instantly."[4]

Fester's mother wept bitterly. His father remained composed, emotionless.

"I don't think I can cheapen the Stocks' beautiful lives with trivial explanations," Fester told the court. "Every day that I know they missed, every holiday, every smile, will haunt me for the rest of my natural life."

Fester wiped his eyes multiple times as he explained that "sorry" is not a strong enough word for how he felt. "Nothing will ever take away the pain that I am responsible for either. They say that time can heal all.

"I think that's false in this case. I know it's hard to see me as a young man with any kind of future after the pain that I've caused, and maybe I don't deserve one. But I wish I could take that, go back to before I came to Nebraska, but I can't. I can't change anything."

Fester's court-appointed public defender Alan Stoler asked the judge to impose a rather lenient sentence of forty-one to fifty-two years. Generally speaking, most prison sentences are halved under Nebraska's good-time credit laws. Fester accepted responsibility for the killings. His troubled youth, his past psychiatric problems and habitual drug use were mitigating factors, Stoler argued unconvincingly. Fester dropped his head and stared at the floor as the silver-haired judge in glasses gave Fester consecutive life sentences with no chance of parole for killing Sharmon Stock and Wayne Stock in cold blood.

Fester was marched out of the courtroom and back to his cell block.

Jessica Reid was up next.

Her public defender Thomas Olsen urged Judge Rehmeier not to restrict her to a life in prison. Olsen's voice boomed as he asked the court if it made any sense for a seventeen-year-old girl with a relatively minor criminal record to go on a cross-country crime spree. Did it make sense for Jessica to break into unfamiliar houses for an adrenaline rush? Did it make sense for Jessica to steal a stranger's truck and then flee Wisconsin, the only state she had ever lived in? Did it make sense for Jessica to burglarize a farmhouse in rural Nebraska? Did it make sense for her to fire a shotgun blast at the head of a middle-aged man she did not know?

"Absolutely not," Olsen reasoned.

Moreover, Jessica had never hunted. She had no prior experience handling guns, let alone high-powered shotguns, her lawyer informed the court. Olsen pleaded for leniency. Jessica admitted responsibility, and her actions helped exonerate the two innocent Nebraska cousins, Olsen pointed out. Like Fester, Jessica got her moment to address the court. The judge granted her permission to turn around and face the crowded gallery. The baby-faced teenage girl stared into dozens of sad faces. Her body shook. Her eyes welled.

Jessica Reid is escorted into the Cass County District Courtroom for her sentencing in March 2007. She and Fester thought they burglarized a farmhouse and orchestrated the murders while traveling through Iowa, not Nebraska. *(Lincoln Journal Star Photo)*

Her voice cracked. "Um," she said. "I just want to say, I'm deeply sorry for all the pain I've caused."

The courtroom grew eerily silent. Several more seconds passed. Finally, overcome by emotions, Reid just sat down. She never finished whatever else she planned to say. In all likelihood, Jessica probably wanted to say she deserved a life sentence. She had already said so during her interview with the probation officer as part of her presentence report. "If it was my family, I think I would deserve life," Jessica admitted. "I can't be selfish. That night we took everything they had. They can't even see their grandchildren, their children. I still have a life. I can eat and listen to music. Those are things that they will never be able to do again. People deserve a second chance, but if it were my family, I would say life with no parole. I think that's what I deserve."[5]

Prosecutor Cox agreed. He asked for a sentence of life without parole. The fair-minded Cox reminded the judge how several days after the barbarous act Reid began writing her haunting diary, which recounted the Stock murders. Cox opted to read some unimaginable excerpts from Reid's wicked diary: "I killed someone. He was older. I loved it. I wish I could do it all the time."

Courtroom spectators were aghast and outraged. Reid's diary sickened them. But there was more. Cox reminded the court that Reid saved one of the shotgun shell casings as a souvenir for her boyfriend, Fester. To his credit, Cox was a righteous and highly ethical prosecutor who had come full circle about the hard cold facts of the case. Cox assured everyone in the courtroom that an overwhelming trail of physical evidence, including crime scene DNA, showed Fester and Reid were the killers. Convincing facts proved that the two transient killers acted alone and drove a stolen Dodge Ram truck out of Beaver Dam, Wisconsin. These two had selected the Stocks' country farmhouse outside of Murdock for a completely random burglary, Cox explained. Cox never once uttered the names Matt Livers or Nick Sampson during either sentencing hearing.

Before pronouncing Reid's sentence, Judge Rehmeier read a lengthy police interview explaining Reid's version of the crime. For many in the courtroom, this was the first factual account they had heard regarding the execution-style crime. Amazingly, Fester and Reid never even stole a nickel from inside Wayne and Sharmon's farmhouse late that Easter Sunday night in 2006. Their coldhearted killings traumatized a tight-knit Nebraska community and reverberated across the entire state. "The offenses involved here were brutal, senseless crimes," Judge Rehmeier declared. "By all accounts, the victims were wonderful people, respected by members of their community and church and loved very much by their family. They experienced fear and horror, which is hard to imagine. They were brutally murdered in the sanctity of their own bedroom, their own home. . . . It's hard in this case to consider anything less than life sentences."

Reid looked stunned and distraught by the judge's verdict. Barely eighteen, she could expect to live out the rest of her life inside Nebraska's only secured women's prison, ninety miles west of Omaha, in York.

.   .   .

After adjournment, many of the victims' relatives gave emotional, teary-eyed hugs to one another before departing. Near the courthouse lawn, Andy Stock told news reporters he was pleased with the sentences. He declined to say whether the apologies offered in court by Fester and Reid made any impact on his family. Sharmon's family was relieved the double murder case had drawn to a close. The families expressed their sincere gratitude and appreciation to Prosecutor Nathan Cox.

.   .   .

And so one of Nebraska's most terrorizing small-town double murder cases in decades had, indeed, drawn to a close. Or did it? Remember, the blood of Wayne Stock was found under Will Sampson's dashboard during the first week of the case. How did it get there?

The truth surrounding this particular mystery had yet to unfold.

18

FINDER

Practically everyone in Nebraska who followed Dave Kofoed's career at the Douglas County Sheriff's crime lab was totally ignorant of Kofoed's shady past. His dark side precipitated his employment into CSI police work, which began around 1990.

. . .

David Wayne Kofoed came from a well-known Omaha family, the oldest of five highly competitive and very successful boys. His father was a high-ranking sergeant at the Omaha Police Department. One of Dave's younger brothers, Bart, was a prep basketball star who then went on to play for several years in the National Basketball Association, a key teammate of perennial NBA All-Stars Karl Malone and John Stockton of the Utah Jazz. Growing up in Omaha, Dave Kofoed was an outstanding athlete himself, in football and in wrestling, at the prestigious Creighton Prep High School. During college, he turned into a bodybuilding buff. Kofoed won the title of Mr. Nebraska and then, in 1979, the more coveted title of Mr. Midwest for his perfectly chiseled physique. He also followed his father's footsteps by enlisting in the United States Marine Corps. As a Marine, Kofoed flew A-4 Silverhawk fighter planes. He became a success.

He rose to the rank of 1st lieutenant and earned a rifle sharpshooter badge. By the summer of 1984, Kofoed's squadron was assigned to VMAT-102 in Fallon, Nevada, which is not far from Reno.[1] By his late twenties, Kofoed had a reputation for being a wild guy and a party animal in the Marines. On weekends, he and his fellow Marines piled into a van and frequented Reno's gambling casinos. Gambling was a new experience, and Kofoed became fond of the blackjack tables. He found the adrenaline rush of blackjack comparable to flying fighter jets. Unfortunately, Lady Luck was not Kofoed's friend. He quickly amassed losses—heavy losses. He borrowed cash from his fellow Marines to gamble some more.[2]

After a couple of months of military duty assigned to Fallon, Kofoed's squadron returned to its usual base in Yuma, Arizona. One day back at his familiar military barracks, Kofoed took advantage of an opportunity when nobody else was around. He opened an unlocked filing cabinet that contained the personal documents and credit card statements of his fellow Marine roommate, Jerry Osgood. Later that same evening, Osgood received a totally unexpected call down at base headquarters. A Western Union representative was on the phone. The representative needed to know to which of the two Western Union locations in Fallon, Nevada, Osgood wanted to have his $1,500 wire transfer sent. Osgood was floored. He stated he had never authorized Western Union to wire $1,500 cash to any of its locations near the Reno gambling casinos over in Nevada. But someone else had. Someone posing as Osgood had placed a phone call from inside Osgood's apartment, using Osgood's credit card number to facilitate the $1,500 wire transfer. Fortunately for Osgood, he stopped the money transfer before it went through. Western Union advised him it would investigate the matter on its end. After the disturbing phone call, he bumped into his squadron's executive officer. Greatly troubled, he explained what had just transpired. Later that evening, Osgood returned to his apartment at the base. He nonchalantly relayed the incident involving the fraudulent wire transfer to his roommate, who happened to be Dave Kofoed. Ultimately, Kofoed admitted to the shameful act of dishonesty. Indeed, he had tried to gain access to Osgood's credit card with the intentions of wiring himself enough cash to gamble at Reno's casinos. Kofoed tried to justify his actions. He explained that he had learned how to read cards from one of his uncles, who apparently was a professional gambler. Kofoed intended to use the $1,500 wire transfer to employ his uncle's card-reading technique and then repay Osgood with his winnings, plus interest, he told him. At the time of the credit-card incident, Kofoed admitted he was about $50,000 in debt to the gambling casinos. Osgood relayed Kofoed's admissions to his military superiors. The squadron's executive officer investigated the situation. Kofoed was given two options. He could abruptly resign his commission or face a nasty court martial. Kofoed chose to quietly resign from the Marine Corps. Officially, Kofoed left the Marines with a general discharge. Such discharges go to servicemen with satisfactory performance marked by a departure in duty performance and conduct expected of a Marine. But the damage was done, and there was no parsing of discharge papers. Wisely, Kofoed took the lesser of the two evils, and thus he avoided the notoriety of a full-blown military court martial and the possibility of criminal charges lodged against him.

Kofoed, age twenty-eight, packed his bags and disappeared quietly into the night from the military base in Yuma, Arizona, in the spring of 1985. Not even Osgood was briefed by his military superiors about the final disposition.

. . .

Upon leaving the Marines, Kofoed journeyed to California, where his brother Michael owned a thriving sportswear clothing line called Leggoons. The Leggoons sportswear apparel was in the national news a lot during the 1980s, before it had become a fad. After Michael sold Leggoons in the late 1980s, Dave Kofoed returned to his hometown of Omaha and at age thirty-two, he landed a civilian job in the Omaha Police Department, where his father, Richard, had recently retired as a high-ranking police sergeant. Kofoed's father was a member of Omaha's first K-9 unit and also became Omaha's first officer to win an award for meritorious action after he rescued someone from drowning.[3] Dave was able to sneak into the Omaha Police Department by applying for a position as an evidence technician. Evidence techs, unlike certified police officers, did not have to undergo a rigorous and intensive background check and screening. Cops must be cleared to carry a badge, possess firearms, and have the power to arrest people. If Kofoed had applied to become a police officer, there was a strong chance his problems in the Marines would have been grounds for rejecting his application. By pursuing the evidence technician job, Kofoed successfully joined Omaha's police department, and most of his colleagues had no idea of his shady past in the U.S. Marine Corps. In 1999, Douglas County Sheriff Tim Dunning hired Kofoed away from the Omaha Police Department to rebuild the county agency's antiquated crime lab. Dunning was a former Omaha street cop, who had previously worked with Kofoed and also Kofoed's father. Kofoed did not disappoint his new boss. Over the next several years, Kofoed helped crack a significant number of monumental, high-profile murder cases that gained him statewide recognition and fame.

On April 28, 2000, Amy Stahlecker had a tire blowout in a white Ford Explorer about fifteen miles from Omaha. Someone discovered Amy's body at the bottom of a bridge near the Elkhorn River, not far from where she had the flat tire. She had been raped in the middle of the night and her killer had pumped several rounds into her skull. The horrible tragedy became front-page news, but there was no immediate arrest. But by May 2, Michael Hornbacher contacted a Sheriff's deputy in neighboring Washington County, stating that his close friend had confessed to killing Stahlecker. During a subsequent interview with police, Richard K. Cook's hands and forearms showed substantial scrapes and cuts. Cook told police he fell off his bicycle. Days later, Cook, a thirty-three-year-old financial services management trainee with a wife, baby, and no criminal record, was arrested in connection with the rape and brutal murder of the nineteen-year-old college coed from Fremont, Nebraska.

Kofoed had a key role in securing Cook's conviction. Kofoed identified several fresh footprints near the muddy banks of the Elkhorn River. In the ensuing days, he visited several Omaha shoe stores. He surmised that the tennis shoe prints recovered near Stahlecker's body surely belonged to a Spalding-brand shoe. After police impounded Cook's truck as possible evidence, Kofoed detected the victim's blood inside Cook's impounded truck, but that's not all. Using his forensic chemical agents, he reportedly discovered a full-size invisible Spalding shoeprint on the exterior driver's side door of Cook's truck. The shoeprint matched the one Kofoed spotted near the site of Amy Stahlecker's body. In 2001, jurors in Douglas County swiftly returned a first-degree murder conviction. Cook received a life prison sentence. Kofoed drew lots of praise and recognition for his doggedness on the case.

A year later, another horrifying murder rocked Omaha.

. . .

On May 26, 2002, authorities recovered the body of Mindy Schrieber in the parking lot of the Ruby Tuesday restaurant where she worked as manager. Mindy had closed the restaurant the previous night. With no eyewitnesses, Douglas County Sheriff's homicide detectives were at a loss for the suspect. But that didn't slow Kofoed. He pulled consecutive double shifts for days. He noticed the victim's blue jeans contained distinct tire impressions and black markings. He also realized Mindy suffered blunt-force trauma consistent with being struck by a motor vehicle. But the make and model of the hit-and-run getaway vehicle remained a mystery, as did the killers, so Kofoed visited several Omaha auto shops and mechanics. He then went out and crawled underneath dozens of cars at local shopping malls, trying to match up an oil pan with the greasy distinct markings left on the murder victim's body. Meanwhile, the homicide detectives obtained a purported confession. Once the suspects' identities were known, Kofoed determined that the greasy oil pan from the underbelly of the suspects' Ford Escort proved to be a perfect match with the oil pan stains left on the murder victim's jeans. Kofoed's fascinating trial testimony secured the murder convictions for codefendants Luis Vargas and Victor Hernandez. Each man received a life sentence.[4]

On September 26, 2002, a hail of gunfire erupted inside a branch of the U.S. Bank 110 miles northwest of Omaha. Five dead bodies. Blood everywhere. Once news of the carnage reached Omaha, Kofoed loaded up his crime lab mobile van and drove to Norfolk, two hours away. In Norfolk, Kofoed and his CSI crew pulled double shifts for many days. They meticulously gathered up bullets, snapped photographs, and drew diagrams to record the scene. Later on, Kofoed testified he found a distinct shoe impression on top of a bank counter left by one of the killers. Ultimately, the three men responsible for the Norfolk bank slayings were apprehended, tried, and convicted. Kofoed's trial testimony in Nebraska's most deadly bank robbery and massacre helped send the killers to death row.

Accolades mounted.

Sheriff Tim Dunning bestowed Kofoed with the 2002 Civilian Employee of the Year for his dedication and outstanding performance.[5] In 2003, he rescued the small-town police department in Plattsmouth, Nebraska, as it struggled to build a murder case against a notorious confessed child killer. Kofoed's heroics on the Brendan Gonzalez case were pivotal to securing killer Ivan Henk's arrest and eventual conviction.

In 2006, once Cass County Sheriff's investigators observed the ghastly scene outside Murdock, they immediately sought Kofoed's help. Kofoed, of course, had the distinction of recovering the blood of Wayne Stock from inside the car of Will Sampson—the wrong getaway car.

That whole situation just didn't seem to pass the smell test after it became painfully obvious that Fester and Reid were the real killers and that they drove a shiny, red truck bearing Wisconsin plates to the Stock farm that Easter Sunday night back in 2006. The blood in Will's car demanded further inquiry and follow-up.

.   .   .

I remained intrigued, like other reporters covering the case, by Kofoed's mystifying discovery of Wayne Stock's blood in a Nebraska man's car that clearly had no involvement whatsoever in the Stock murders. That blood was considered a huge clue linking Matt Livers and Nick Sampson to the farmhouse murders.

But if they were not involved and the initial investigation was botched, how did the blood get there? Many respectable and decent citizens in the Murdock farming community bought into the whisper campaign led by the Cass County

Douglas County CSI Chief David Kofoed stands in the stairwell at the bloody farm-house near Murdock, Nebraska. In 2006, Kofoed produced the one and only piece of physical evidence to connect Matt Livers and Nick Sampson to the killings. (*Author's collection*)

Sheriff's Office. Law enforcement officials there continued to insist the blood-stains from Will Sampson's car actually proved the guilt of Livers and Will's younger brother, Nick. On the other hand, Cass County Prosecutor Nathan Cox was not certain what to believe. Cox, to his credit, launched his own inquiry. He spoke with investigators Schenck, Lambert, and others from the Nebraska State Patrol who had direct access in handling Will Sampson's tan Ford Contour car during the early stages of the case. Cox came away convinced that none of those police officials inadvertently transferred wet blood from the crime scene onto their uniforms and thus into Will's Ford Contour.

The mystery of the blood persisted.

By spring of 2007, a Scottsbluff, Nebraska, lawyer filed a disturbing federal lawsuit accusing the Cass County Sheriff's Office and the Nebraska State Patrol of willfully and recklessly violating Nick Sampson's rights. Plaintiff's attorney Maren Chaloupka stated that Nick was wrongfully arrested, and his civil rights continued to be violated further when Nebraska police continued to incarcerate him even though the physical evidence clearly showed the real killers were from Wisconsin. The stinging federal lawsuit also named investigators Earl Schenck, Bill Lambert, and Charlie O'Callaghan as codefendants. The Douglas County Sheriff's Office was not named as a party in the lawsuit, nor were any of its crime lab employees.

Not surprisingly, NSP and Cass County immediately circled the wagons, refusing to comment in various news media stories about the ongoing case and Nick's federal lawsuit. One law enforcement official, though, had no qualms about speaking out. Kofoed boasted in various news media interviews that his Douglas County crime lab had ultimately cracked the Murdock case. He credited his team for taking the initiative to trace the serial number on the engraved ring left on the kitchen floor of Sharmon Stock's kitchen. Kofoed pointed out that Cass County and the Nebraska State Patrol did not seem all that interested at first in tracking down the origin of the ring.

For the first time publicly, around the spring of 2007, Kofoed began to portray himself as a sympathizer for Nick Sampson and Livers, the two men wrongly accused of murdering Wayne and Sharmon Stock. Kofoed pointed out that approximately 425 separate items of physical evidence were collected and tested during the complicated forensic investigation. Most evidence was examined a minimum of two times and, in most cases, three or four times to satisfy the skeptical lead investigators from Cass County and NSP trying to link the murders to Livers and Nick Sampson, Kofoed explained. Of all those items tested, not a single item retrieved from the crime scene—including fingerprints, firearms, trace evidence, or DNA—linked Matt Livers or Nick Sampson to the Stock murders, Kofoed pointed out.

Also for the first time, Kofoed began to speak out publicly in media interviews regarding his blood harvest. He offered an alternative theory to explain how Wayne Stock's blood appeared in the wrongly suspected getaway car.[6] Unbeknownst to Kofoed, one of his longtime Douglas County evidence technicians, Darnel Kush, also had her own working theory, too.

But she wasn't talking to the press. She was talking to the police.

19

DEEP THROAT

Darnel Kush had battled and survived cancer. She was a devoted parent and dedicated public servant. She mostly worked behind the scenes as an evidence technician, gathering and processing clues from various crimes investigated mainly across metropolitan Omaha.

Kush's name and face did not appear in Omaha's newspaper or on the local television stations. She shunned the limelight. But she was proficient at her job, honest, and acted with the utmost integrity. Kush joined the Douglas County Sheriff's Office crime lab long before Dave Kofoed left the Omaha Police Department to become the county's crime lab commander in 2000. By that point, Douglas County Sheriff Tim Dunning and Kofoed agreed the county crime lab was in disarray and needed a housecleaning. According to Kofoed, some of the old-timers he inherited were unproductive. Some used to fall asleep in the office while on the clock. At other times, the group gathered outside the Sheriff's building to take prolonged smoke breaks that lasted thirty minutes or longer, often several times a day. This made it hard to get anything accomplished, Kofoed said. Within a relatively short time, Kofoed pushed many of those holdover evidence technicians into early retirement. He went out and developed a different brand of employees. He hired highly educated, highly skilled, and highly motivated CSIs, who were mostly in their mid- to late twenties. Kush, on the other hand, had a high school education. Most of them had master's degrees in chemistry and other sciences. Kofoed quickly promoted them. He paid them good wages and, in essence, he bought their loyalty. Kush, on the other hand, did not fit into Kofoed's vision of his prototype CSI. Although Kush was a soft-spoken and even-keeled crime scene technician, she was not a pushover. She strongly disagreed with how Kofoed forced many of her longtime colleagues into early retirement. At first, she and Kofoed peacefully coexisted. But within a couple of years, she landed in Kofoed's doghouse and stayed there. Gradually, he overlooked her for plum assignments. He relegated Kush to processing run-of-the-mill crimes, including auto thefts and minor burglaries. She was constantly scheduled for weekend shifts, which made it especially difficult to spend quality time with her kids. Meanwhile, Kofoed's less experienced, baby-faced CSIs were handpicked for the more interesting assignments and out-of-town professional training seminars at fancy hotels in major U.S. destinations. Kofoed also proved to be an incredible self-promoter, and a damn good one. Omaha's television stations seemed to be on his speed dial. He used some of Omaha's more gullible television news reporters and anchors to elevate him to rock-star celebrity status. It was a perfect marriage at the time. By that period, national CSI television shows were glamorized by Hollywood and becoming enormously popular across the country. Naturally, Kofoed capitalized on that golden opportunity for his own personal gain. Because most of Omaha's television news media developed a special bond with Kofoed, he tipped them off to practically every story idea he could drum up, provided it brought him and his ever-growing regional crime lab positive recognition.

Consequently, Kofoed's younger-looking team of employees developed a tight-knit bond with their boss. These naive employees adored Kofoed, which inflated his ego even more. In contrast, Kush did not hero-worship her supervisor. She saw him as a grandstander and worse. She sensed he had a dark side. She soon became curious and eager to learn more about this guy, who occasionally pulled all-nighters at work and was even known to sleep inside his office rather than return to his home in Omaha for a good night's rest.

. . .

Among other things, Kush suspected her boss was intentionally placing his own fingerprints at various local crime scenes, then pretending to find his own fingerprints on clues in order to look like a CSI super-sleuth. Kush arrived at this conclusion by determining that identical fingerprints from two unrelated crime scenes just happened to come from the same unidentified person. According to Kush, Kofoed became her obvious suspect. He just happened to process both of those crime scenes. More revealing, as an agency protocol, Kofoed required all of his CSIs to put their own fingerprints into the Automatic Fingerprint Identification System (AFIS), a fingerprint database used by law enforcement to match unknown fingerprints. Oddly, though, Kofoed's own fingerprints were no longer in the law enforcement AFIS system, Kush discovered.[1]

And there was more.

Kush suspected her boss had typed up phony commendation letters that went into his employee personnel file. One such letter praised Kofoed for assisting the Omaha Police Department in solving a particular crime. Oddly, the Omaha crime lab supervisor's first name on the commendation letter was misspelled, Kush observed. In that instant, Kush approached senior command at the Sheriff's Office. She informed Chief Deputy Sheriff Marty Bilek about the self-serving letter, but nothing came of it. Bilek told her that "He would look into the matter," Kush recalled.[2] She also discovered several birthdates on file for Kofoed. She suspected he might be trying to hide something about his past, but she was not sure what.

Her suspicions reached a new level after she established a pattern in at least three or four different murder cases in which Kofoed proclaimed he had found the blood of the murder victim inside the vehicle of the suspect. In all such cases, Kofoed had also processed the original crime scene and had unfettered access to the evidence at the crime lab he supervised.

One of those murder cases happened to be the high-profile shotgun slayings of Wayne and Sharmon Stock. Kush suspected her crime lab manager had planted the blood to frame Livers and Nick Sampson before realizing they were not the killers at all. In late 2007, Kush confided her suspicions to NSP Investigator Bill Lambert. It was somewhat ironic that Kush turned to Lambert given that he had helped obtain the false confession from Livers and now found himself embroiled in a federal lawsuit mess brought forward by a bulldog attorney representing Nick Sampson. But Kush and Lambert were professional colleagues who had previously worked together as corrections officers for the Douglas County jail. Kush considered Lambert trustworthy and an honest investigator. Lambert agreed to interview Kush at her house in Plattsmouth. There, Kush recounted her rocky and turbulent history working with Kofoed as Lambert listened intently and took copious notes. Being able to speak freely in the comfort of her own home, Kush told Lambert she was afraid of Kofoed. He was a chronic liar who could not be trusted. At the time the farmhouse slayings took place, Kush was away from work on medical leave as a result of her diagnosis of cancer. She had no direct, firsthand knowledge that her boss had planted the blood into the wrong getaway car, but she arrived at her conclusion based on a number of other factors: Kofoed's character flaws and patterns of odd on-the-job behavior, such as the identical, unidentified fingerprints in the crime scenes he processed, the phony commendation letter, and his knack for finding the blood of murder victims inside the vehicle of the obvious suspect in multiple high-profile cases.

Once Livers and Nick Sampson were both released from jail by the Cass County prosecutor, and the real killers from Wisconsin pleaded guilty, Kush concluded that Kofoed was obviously responsible for the bloodstain that mysteriously showed up in Will Sampson's car after the first CSI search of the same car turned up nothing.

Kush mentioned to Lambert that Kofoed's perplexing blood find left her greatly conflicted. On one hand, she professed a deep loyalty to Sheriff Tim Dunning and others in his administration, but she could no longer hide the fact that something was really wrong with Kofoed. He always had a tendency to save the day in high-profile murder cases. He always knew how to make friends with the right people. He was currently dating a female prosecutor in the Douglas County Attorney's Office, Kush observed. She sensed that Kofoed wanted only CSIs whom he could manipulate. Kush expressed to Lambert that no one else in the CSI unit seemed to have the courage to say what was on his or her mind or to directly question Kofoed. He was revered among his team of about a dozen full-time CSIs and had his share of admirers within the upper echelon of the Sheriff's Office administration. His immediate supervisor at the time, Capt. Dean Olson, wanted the CSI unit to succeed and no negative publicity, Kush noted. In fact, she said she had lodged a number of formal complaints up the proper chain of command over the years regarding other antics involving Kofoed, but nothing was ever done. As a result, she greatly feared retaliation. She worried she would be fired just before she reached her retirement eligibility as a crude form of retribution. Kush already had more than twenty years of service in county law enforcement, and she wanted to work for at least another five years, she told Lambert. Working for Kofoed had taken its toll. She was being treated by a psychiatrist for emotional problems and stress from her work environment, she told Lambert. She had proudly become the first member of the CSI division to achieve certification through the Intentional Association of Identification forensics organization. Yet her accomplishment only seemed to upset her boss, causing further strain in their work relationship, she confided.

After the interview ended, Lambert decided to pass along Kush's interview statement to the FBI's public corruption division in Omaha.

. . .

Around March 2008, almost two full years after the horrifying Stock murders, two powerful attorneys from Chicago, Locke Bowman and Steven Drizin, filed a federal lawsuit on behalf of Matt Livers. The suit garnered front-page headlines. It blamed egregious police misconduct for Livers's coerced false confession and his improper incarceration by Cass County Sheriff's officials. Drizin and Bowman were prominent legal minds in Illinois. Drizin served as legal services director at the prestigious Northwestern University Center for Wrongful Convictions. Bowman often represented clients in civil rights cases, former inmates who were wrongfully incarcerated because of police corruption, misconduct, or malfeasance.

People just like Matt Livers in Nebraska.

The lawsuit filed on behalf of Livers named as defendants the Cass County Sheriff's Office, lead investigator Earl Schenck Jr., Sheriff's Sgt. Sandy Weyers, plus Nebraska State Patrol investigators Bill Lambert and Charlie O'Callaghan. In a nutshell, the suit alleged: "As a result of the defendants' unconstitutional tactics, false murder charges were filed against Plaintiff, causing him to be incarcerated for over seven months, ruining Plaintiff's reputation and his relations with close family members, and producing anxiety and other psychological trauma that continues to this day."[3]

Interestingly enough, the Douglas County Sheriff's Office and Kofoed seemed to dodge another bullet. They were not named as codefendants in the civil rights lawsuit, just as they avoided the notoriety just a year earlier when Nick Sampson filed his federal civil rights suit. However, Kofoed and his crime lab were not entirely out of the woods. The Chicago lawyers noted that none of the blood belonging to murder victims Wayne and Sharmon Stock was found in Will Sampson's tan Ford Contour prior to Cass County and the State Patrol seizing control of the car three days into the case. The lawyers for Livers rolled out the following set of facts and chronology as the basis of their claim:

On April 19 and 20, 2006, Douglas County CSI Commander Kofoed oversaw a six-hour search of Will Sampson's car. No blood was recovered within the car. A week later, one of the lead investigators communicated to Kofoed that this car had to be involved. On May 8, 2006, Kofoed stated in his official CSI report that he had used a filter paper swab underneath the steering column of that car, and his swab tested positive for blood consistent with victim Wayne Stock's DNA. This "evidence" was sent to the Cass County attorney to bolster Livers's prosecution even though Will Sampson, Nick Sampson, and Matt Livers were all proven to have had no involvement, and Will's car was parked at his apartment in Lincoln and never used in the murders, which occurred some thirty miles away near Murdock. The lawsuit noted that Cass County Attorney Nathan Cox also previously stated that he did not believe the blood in the car resulted from accidental contamination. "Therefore, on information and belief, blood from the crime scene was planted in the Will Sampson automobile by one or more persons whose identity is not known to Plaintiff," the suit alleged.

Because of the obvious possibility that there had been police corruption at play here, the FBI branch in Omaha decided to take a strong interest in the Murdock case. Unknown to anybody else at that time, Kush served as the FBI's confidential informant, acting as its Deep Throat. FBI special agents began their police corruption probe by singling out Douglas County CSI forensic scientist Clelland "CL" Retelsdorf for an interview.

Retelsdorf's revelations to the FBI became a key turning point in the case.

20

SMELL TEST

The recovery of Wayne Stock's blood did not pass the smell test with the FBI.

The FBI found it suspicious that Kofoed, as head of the crime lab, would go ahead and perform a second search of Will Sampson's car several days after he had supervised a tedious and exhaustive search of the very same car that found nothing. And that Kofoed "recovered" blood underneath the dashboard—the only area of the car he supposedly checked—aroused even more suspicion. Moreover, the Cass County Sheriff's Office, the Nebraska State Patrol, and the Douglas County Sheriff's Office CSI were not making any attempt to get to the bottom of the matter. The complete lack of curiosity greatly alarmed the FBI. Its special agents knew like everybody else that Will Sampson's tan car had absolutely no involvement in the vicious murders committed by Fester and Reid of Wisconsin.

In 2008, Omaha's FBI Special Agent in Charge John Kavanagh enlisted some of his best special agents to find him some answers.

The FBI started with an obscure forensic services report filed by Clelland "CL" Retelsdorf, who processed the backseat of Will's car a full week after the first search of the car came up empty. When confronted by the FBI, however, Retelsdorf made a startling revelation. He was not alone at the time of his assignment, even though his official report indicated so. Retelsdorf confided that his supervisor, Kofoed, had also accompanied him to the Douglas County Sheriff's impound lot that afternoon on April 27, 2006. Retelsdorf assured the FBI that Kofoed found the blood in the car on that date while in Retelsdorf's presence and not on the night of May 8, 2006, as Kofoed's documented CSI report plainly showed.[1]

Retelsdorf's statement to the FBI was pivotal. At the time, it effectively removed the Cass County Sheriff's Office and the Nebraska State Patrol from any cloud of suspicion surrounding the alleged blood plant. It became obvious to the FBI that the lead homicide investigators did not tamper with the car prior to Kofoed's phony CSI report, dated May 8, 2006. When confronted by the FBI, Kofoed openly admitted his original forensic report was false. Kofoed had not in fact collected Wayne Stock's blood from the car on the evening of May 8 as he wrote in his official CSI report. Rather, he collected the blood some twelve days earlier in the company of CSI CL Retelsdorf. But Kofoed adamantly denied any wrongdoing. He tried to claim that the blood got into the car through accidental transfer, or cross-contamination. After the FBI agents repeatedly told him his story didn't pass the smell test, Kofoed demanded an attorney and cut off the interview.

And that was the last time Kofoed ever sat down and discussed the Murdock case with the FBI.

.　.　.

Several days later, Kavanagh and two special agents summoned Douglas County Sheriff Tim Dunning to their FBI headquarters for a private meeting. According to the sheriff, Kavanagh bluntly asserted he had "a dirty crime lab manager who was planting fingerprints at crime scenes." Kavanagh then displayed one of the questionable fingerprints and told Dunning, "And this is one of the prints, and I know that's his. I can see it with my naked eye."[2]

Dunning was flabbergasted. "I thought to myself, 'What a moron!' I've taken a class. You can't do that," Dunning would later testify. Dunning refused to believe the implication that he had a crook directing his crime lab. The sheriff also believed the FBI might be launching a witch hunt to discredit his popular CSI director and all of the great work accomplished by the Douglas County crime lab throughout the region. Dunning knew he needed to do something to put to rest any lingering controversy, so he decided to launch an internal affairs investigation of Kofoed.

On June 10, 2008, Kofoed surrendered his office keys and work cell phone. He was ordered to stay away from the crime lab and Sheriff's Office while the internal affairs process took place. Dunning tapped two longtime loyalists, Capt. Russ Torres and Lt. Ed Leahy, to spearhead the investigation. No outside national forensics experts were utilized for the internal affairs probe. Nobody did any independent research or analysis to verify Kofoed's claims about accidental contamination. Instead, Torres and Leahy went ahead and interviewed all of the crime lab personnel. Most of them already revered Kofoed and believed he could do no wrong.

.   .   .

An elder statesman, Don Veys served as Kofoed's steady right-hand man at the county crime lab. Veys had investigated thousands of robberies, sexual assaults, property crimes, and murders during his thirty-six-year law enforcement career in Omaha. After he retired from the Omaha Police Department, Veys reunited with Kofoed, his former colleague at OPD. During his internal affairs interview, Veys vouched for Kofoed's theory that crime scene blood was inadvertently transferred into the car. "I don't see how it couldn't [have] happened," Veys said.[3]

Forensic scientist Christine Gabig also came to Kofoed's defense. It made perfect sense for Kofoed to make a second inspection of the car, she said. After all, not even she had checked underneath the dashboard during the initial inspection, she told internal affairs. Gabig professed to being a strong supporter of Kofoed. She had worked for him the past five years, and he had hired her. When asked if she ever questioned Kofoed's integrity regarding the Stock crime scene investigation, she replied, "Absolutely not." Gabig firmly believed he did not plant the blood evidence. She insisted it made no sense for him to do that.

Bill Kaufhold, a twenty-six-year veteran, also denied having reason to question Kofoed's integrity regarding any crime scene investigation. Kaufhold raised the possibility that the blood got into the car from cross-contamination by someone at the Murdock crime scene. Kaufhold knew the farmhouse slayings were very bloody. Even though the CSIs took every precaution, one of the initial police responders may have entered the scene and inadvertently transferred some blood outside, Kaufhold advised.

Darnel Kush, the secret FBI informant, simply told Douglas County internal affairs that she had no firsthand knowledge about whether Kofoed planted evidence in the Murdock case because she was on medical leave at that time. The internal affairs investigators did not press Kush for more information surrounding Kofoed's conduct. Over a three-week period, a half a dozen other crime lab personnel were also interviewed by Leahy and Torres. Everyone pretty much shared the same opinion: their likable boss could not have engaged in forensic misconduct.

. . .

On June 30, 2008, Kofoed strutted into the Sheriff's Office accompanied by Omaha criminal defense attorney Steve Lefler. Kofoed told the two internal affairs investigators that he spent at least two full days gathering evidence at Murdock in 2006, but only recently did he learn of the FBI probe. Kofoed agreed it did not make sense for Wayne Stock's blood to suddenly appear inside a car that was no way involved in the killings. He theorized that the victim's blood came into contact with some of his crime lab's equipment that was hauled out to the crime scene. And since the issue came to light, Kofoed said he stopped using the old multiuse filter paper kits that were stacked on top of one another like Pringles potato chips. He switched over to individually wrapped single-use filter paper kits to reduce the possibility of contamination. Leahy and Torres questioned why Kofoed inexcusably let twelve days lapse from the time he produced the blood in the presence of CL Retelsdorf at the impound lot to the time he wrote his report indicating he found the blood on the night of May 8, 2006. Kofoed replied that he thought he packaged the blood in a paper bag and stored it somewhere in the crime lab's biohazard room. He just did not remember if he logged the item as police evidence. (Actually, it would be unfathomable for someone in Kofoed's position to forget to log a key piece of evidence—the only blood evidence to tie the double murder defendants directly to the crime scene.) Equally alarming, Kofoed had authored the county crime lab's written policy requiring all CSIs to file forensic reports within three days of their work. Kofoed shrugged. He was at a loss to explain why he had not reported finding Wayne Stock's blood on April 27, 2006. When asked if he planted the evidence, Kofoed roared, "No way!"

Leahy and Torres tried a different approach. They asked if Kofoed ever manufactured, concealed, falsified, removed, tampered, or withheld any evidence involved in processing Will Sampson's tan Ford Contour car.

"No!" Kofoed exclaimed. He agreed to take a lie-detector test. "I'll do fine," Kofoed promised.

At the time, Douglas County Sheriff's Deputy Brenda Wheeler was an inexperienced licensed polygraph examiner, but that's who the Sheriff's Office administration appointed to give Kofoed his lie-detector test. On July 2, 2008, Wheeler devised a standard polygraph exam consisting of several questions for Kofoed.[4]

Q: "Are you sometimes called Dave?"

A: "Yes."

Q: "Regarding planting evidence in the Stock homicides, do you intend to answer each question truthfully?"

A: "Yes."

Q: "Do you believe I will ask you only the questions we reviewed?"

A: "Yes."

Q: "Before this year, have you ever lied to protect someone else?"

A: "No."

Q: "Did you intentionally plant blood evidence in the Stock homicides?"

A: "No."

Q: "Prior to 2008, have you ever lied to protect someone who trusted you?"

A: "No."

Q: "Did you intentionally plant blood in the Stock homicides?"

A: "No."

Q: "Is there something else you are afraid I will ask you a question about?"

A: "No."

Q: "On any previous employment, have you ever lied to get out of trouble?"

A: "No."

Q: "Do you know for sure if anyone else planted evidence in the Stock homicides?"

A: "No."

Q: "Prior to 2008, have you lied on an official document?"

A: "No."

Wheeler deemed Kofoed's answers as being truthful. Another Douglas County Sheriff's Office polygraph investigator, John Pankonin, supported her findings. The final internal affairs report cleared Kofoed. He did, however, receive a minor reprimand for failing to follow his own chain of custody policies and procedures. Overall, though, Kofoed came off smelling like a rose, considering his law enforcement career was at stake. "There is no evidence to prove Kofoed planted the blood," Lieutenant Leahy stated. "Kofoed should be exonerated of this allegation, and this investigation should be closed to further investigation."

Sheriff Tim Dunning announced on July 3, 2008, that his veteran crime lab manager had been cleared of any criminal wrongdoing in connection with the Murdock case. After a four-week paid leave, Kofoed was reinstated to active duty, the sheriff announced in a press release. "I have had the utmost confidence and respect for the work of David Kofoed in the past and nothing in this investigation leads me to change that view," Dunning stated. "The polygrapher confirmed that all responses were truthful."[5]

Kofoed was eager to get back on the job and solve more major crimes.

The FBI, however, was still digging deep for answers.

21

TARNISHED

By 2009, a top-secret, federal grand jury probe consisting of sixteen citizens was reviewing the 2006 Murdock double murder case. On March 19, the target of the federal grand jury's investigation agreed to appear and testify.

"Mr. Witness, will you please state your name and spell your last name?" First Assistant U.S. Attorney William Mickle asked.

"David W. Kofoed. It's spelled K-O-F-O-E-D."

Kofoed worked for Douglas County Sheriff Tim Dunning and had managed the county crime lab for the past ten years, he explained. He also brought along a prepared statement. "Essentially, the most important thing is, I am here voluntarily," Kofoed testified. "I will answer any question that you guys ask of me—all of you. I have nothing to hide here at all." He told grand jurors he truly respected America's criminal justice system as the best in the world. He mentioned how he respected law enforcement. His late father was an Omaha police officer for twenty-eight years. "I really hope that we can find the truth here. That's all I'm trying to do," Kofoed added.[1]

Kofoed also sought to reassure grand jurors that his crime lab continued to have a top-notch reputation. "We've gotten calls from assistant U.S. attorneys for advice, even in the last month, and we've actually done some pretty good casework, specifically, for the Secret Service and ATF. So whatever the allegation is against me personally, I still have access to every bit of that lab," Kofoed testified. "I make the calls on everything that goes on there, and I feel like no one has really lost any confidence in our ability to do our job, and to be, most importantly, to be neutral in what we do."

Kofoed's testimony in the closed-door proceeding lasted about three hours. Federal Prosecutor Mickle and his boss, U.S. Attorney Joe Stecher, took turns questioning the prominent and chatty witness. Kofoed took a huge gamble by showing up. His testimony could later be used against him in a criminal court of law in the event that he was indicted.

On the witness stand, Kofoed confirmed for grand jurors that he had gone back and reprocessed Will Sampson's Ford Contour on the afternoon of April 27, 2006. The Sheriff's impound facility was six blocks away from his crime lab in northwest Omaha. Kofoed testified the request to reexamine the car came from NSP Investigator Bill Lambert during a phone call.

"Do you recall what he was asking for you to examine on that car?" asked Mickle.

"Yes," Kofoed replied. "He told me that Matt Livers had confessed and that he had thrown, or his partner in the crime had thrown the weapon in the backseat of the car, and he wanted us to go back and check the backseat to see if we could find any kind of residue or indication that the weapon had been back there."

Kofoed testified his trusted forensic scientist, CL Retelsdorf, accompanied him to the impound lot. Both CSIs arrived in separate vehicles. Kofoed signed out the car's key. At the lot, Kofoed reached into one of his forensic testing kits, he testified. He allegedly grabbed multiple Q-tip swabs and filter papers to conduct various presumptive blood tests. The filter papers resemble little disks, or communion hosts distributed at Catholic mass, Kofoed explained to grand jurors. He testified that he used some Q-tip swabs from his blood-testing kit. The black kit also contained alcohol, the chemical phenophthalein, and hydrogen peroxide.

First, Kofoed checked underneath the driver's seat, then he tested the center console, and finally, to the best of his memory, an area in the car that a pant leg might brush up against. He told the grand jurors that he performed several different chemical tests with Q-tip swabs inside the vehicle, eventually putting each of his discarded Q-tip swabs into a paper sack, which he marked with the word "trash."

Kofoed testified the first couple of tests generated the same results.

"Negative. There was no reaction," he said.

"And I presume you put that swab, then, in your paper sack, also?" asked Mickle.

"Yes, yes."

The witness later testified he conducted several more chemical tests that afternoon with the Q-tip swabs, trying to locate blood in the car.

Kofoed said, "I would say it was less than ten, yes, but it was at least five."

"Eventually, you switched to a different type of collection device, is that correct?"

Kofoed agreed. He deployed an oval piece of filter paper. After he rubbed the filter paper underneath the driver's dashboard area, the paper turned pink and showed a positive reaction for pure blood.

After claiming that he found some blood, Kofoed asked his partner Retelsdorf to test the very same area. But Retelsdorf's chemical test came back negative.

Mickle hypothesized that Kofoed's finding of the blood was merely staged.

"Mr. Retelsdorf wasn't observing you doing your activities, though, is that correct, on the 27th of April?" Mickle inquired.

"No, his concentration was basically on the backseat area."

"So he would not have the ability to put into a report what he didn't see, is that fair?"

"That's fair," Kofoed replied. "All he could do, sir, is rely on what I told him I did."

"Before you had gotten into the car, did you use an alternative light source to check the general area where you were looking?"

"I believe I used an alternative light source, yes."

"And how did that tool or equipment get to the vehicle?"

Kofoed didn't remember if he brought one along or if one was inside the crime lab van. The crime lab had two of the devices, which were essentially ultra-bright flashlights.

Kofoed also testified he put on gloves at the impound lot to prevent any potential contamination, which was a standard CSI practice.

Mickle asked, "But you didn't start your processing of the car with the gloves on, did you?"

"Yes, I did."

Mickle wondered if Kofoed normally took photographs of areas where he located some forensic evidence, like blood or other important clues.

"Yes, we would normally, if you could see the evidence. I couldn't really see anything up under there. It was dark. . . ."

Mickle switched gears.

The prosecutor was curious to know when Kofoed began to second-guess the authenticity of the blood in the car. Kofoed answered that he developed strong suspicions within a few short months of the Murdock murders.

"Again, tell us why you had those concerns," Mickle pressed.

"To me, this totally indicated that it must be contamination. We worked the crime scene for three days. The vehicle came in on the 19th [of April] and we processed the vehicle. Matt Livers lived in Lincoln. I was at his house. I examined all of his clothing. I examined his shoes. We didn't find any evidence that linked him. From Palmyra, Nebraska, where Nick Sampson lived, all that evidence came in. We didn't find anything where we should have found it, like blood on his shoes—anything that would indicate that either of the two of these gentlemen were involved with this. When I looked at all of that information, I then also looked at Will Sampson, the third party that owned this car. They didn't find anything that linked any of those folks to the crime scene. And we had evidence at the crime scene that indicated that someone else was there, somebody unknown. . . . My conclusion was that this must be some kind of contamination issue because it was one single blood sample from a third-party's car, and it didn't make any sense to me."

That afternoon, Kofoed attributed the blood foul-up to faulty crime lab equipment, namely, one of his agency's presumptive blood test kits.

"That's your plausible explanation to what happened?" inquired Mickle.

"I don't want to put the blame on us . . . that's a possibility."

"Was the kit in the car? The kit you're talking about. Was it in the car or outside of the car?"

"No, I'm positive, it wasn't in the car."

"So I'm not sure I understand how the kit could have contaminated something inside the car."

Kofoed maintained he was positive that the county's blood-test kits were brought to Murdock to test areas of the farmhouse where authorities could not tell if the specimen was rust or blood. "We had a staging area initially at the crime scene out on the back deck," Kofoed testified. "Eventually, stuff migrated inside the scene and upstairs where the two victims were. So I don't know if that happened, but that's the most likely scenario."

During a time for questions, one grand juror asked Kofoed to estimate how long the victim's blood was inside that car.

"Do you want my honest opinion about it? I don't think it was on the car at all," Kofoed responded. "I think it was on the filter paper. I think the contamination was either on the filter paper or in the kit. If you drop the lid at the scene, you're going to get, you know, small amounts of blood on the lid."

Finally, U.S. Attorney Joe Stecher asked, "In regards to the filter papers, are there any reports completed by anyone in your unit that indicates those filter paper swabs—filter paper wipes—were used at the homicide scene?"

"No," Kofoed answered.

Kofoed was free to leave.

After the target witness was excused, Stecher stressed to jurors that the car where Kofoed found the victim's blood had no link to the Murdock slayings at all.

· · ·

Five weeks later. The U.S. Attorney's Office unsealed a fourteen-page indictment handed up by the federal grand jury. Kofoed, age fifty-two, was charged with mail fraud and falsification of records, both felonies. Two misdemeanors alleged the veteran crime lab commander violated the civil rights of Matt Livers and Nick Sampson. And there was another strange twist in Kofoed's criminal prosecution. On the day of the indictment's unsealing, special Cass County Prosecutor Clarence Mock filed a felony count of tampering with evidence over at the Cass County Courthouse in Plattsmouth, Nebraska. This meant that Douglas County's embattled crime lab director faced the rare phenomenon of back-to-back criminal trials, first in federal court, then in state court. But Kofoed was eager and ready for battle. He sensed this was where things were headed. He vowed in the press to prove his innocence and continue his law enforcement career. He was allowed to remain free, pending trial. It was unprecedented for a high-profile Nebraska law enforcement leader to face a criminal indictment in connection with his duties. The charges against Kofoed greatly perturbed Sheriff Dunning. He couldn't believe it. So, for the second time in a year, the sheriff put Kofoed on paid administrative leave from his $80,000 supervisor's job.

· · ·

This time, Kofoed's CSI legacy and freedom were really on the line.

22

BLUNDER

The federal indictment against Kofoed greatly disappointed Nick Sampson's former public defender Jerry Soucie, who went so far as to predict Kofoed's acquittal months before the trial got underway.

"Kofoed has now been indicted and charged in federal and state court with allegations that can be described as 'bad note taking practices' that would call into question the 'chain of custody' of forensic evidence," Soucie stated in a letter to the federal prosecutors and other key lawyers interested in the Murdock case. "He has not been charged with planting evidence against persons he believed at the time were guilty of a brutal double murder. Both the state and federal theories of prosecution have, in effect, adopted Kofoed's defense as their theory of guilt."[1]

Defense attorney Steve Lefler certainly would portray Kofoed's actions as honest mistakes made by a busy, well-respected, decorated former Marine, who was a powerful force in the CSI division, Soucie stated. For sure, Kofoed would have a long list of exemplary character witnesses ready to stand behind him and testify on his defense. "Jurors will not like a cop that planted evidence, but they won't give a damn about misdating police reports," Soucie stated. "I can see Lefler in his opening saying, 'Ladies and gentlemen, have you ever made a mistake in balancing your check book? Well, that's what David Kofoed did, and these guys want to make that a federal crime! Give me a break!'"

Soucie ended his letter with a dead-accurate prophecy: "If the prosecution shoots low and misses, then they get nothing."

. . .

Before the federal trial, Lefler filed a motion to restrict federal prosecutors from introducing any inflammatory testimony alleging his client may have planted or manufactured blood evidence against Livers or Nick Sampson. U.S. Attorney Joe Stecher did not offer any objections. Stecher was content to convict Kofoed of committing mail fraud, civil rights violations, and falsifying public records. The federal jury trial took place at the six-story Roman L. Hruska Federal Courthouse in downtown Omaha under gorgeous blue skies in late August 2009. Kofoed wore a dark suit and swaggered into the courtroom. During breaks in testimony, the defendant gabbed and shared hearty laughs with several friends and professional colleagues on hand for emotional support. His mother, Dolores, also attended. Kofoed assured his supporters and the press that the jury would find him not guilty. Kofoed's plight was one of Nebraska's hottest stories, and gaining national attention. NBC's *Dateline* was already busy producing a two-hour news documentary about the entire Murdock case, to be broadcast by award-winning correspondent Keith Morrison.

. . .

One of the regular attendees at the back of the federal courtroom was Clarence E. Mock III. The gray-haired, bearded lawyer with glasses was responsible for bringing the felony evidence-tampering count against Kofoed in Cass County. Mock agreed to delay his prosecution of the state's case until after the federal trial was resolved. Mock was nearly as tall as the famous Illinois lawyer named Abraham Lincoln, but his frame more resembled a professional football player. Mock was in his late fifties, having been admitted to the Nebraska State Bar in 1977. He was also one of Nebraska's most respected and brilliant legal strategists. As he sat in the gallery, Mock jotted down key observations in his large yellow notepad. He paid keen attention to the jurors' faces as they watched Steve Lefler, the defendant's lawyer. Lefler, a gangly trial lawyer, was one of the most interesting personalities in Omaha's legal community. Also in his fifties, Lefler sported dark hair and dark-rimmed glasses. He was not the best criminal defense attorney money could buy around Omaha, but at times prosecutors underrated Lefler, and he rose to the occasion to achieve an acquittal in a high-profile case. He was also a likable and personable guy. He got along really well with the press. His courtroom antics conjured up images of Atticus Finch, the fictional, folk-hero lawyer in Harper Lee's Pulitzer Prize–winning novel *To Kill a Mockingbird*. In the real-life courtroom, Lefler portrayed himself as an affable country lawyer.

He often talked up the prosecutor during a trial, even though that was his client's arch nemesis. Lefler was fond of apologizing to jurors and judges in a jury trial for his own faults and shortcomings as a trial lawyer. He also liked to wear ratty gym sneakers into state court, yet he wisely did not dare to wear old tennis shoes into the immaculate federal courtroom of Senior Judge Lyle E. Strom, who was eighty-four years old at the time, yet still had a sharp legal mind. And though Lefler had limited experience representing clients in Omaha's federal criminal courts, he looked pretty comfortable and confident during Kofoed's trial.

Fortunately for Kofoed, even his capable defense lawyer did not need to bring his A-game. The U.S. Attorney's case showed serious cracks in the armor at a few days into the trial. During a break outside the jury's presence, Senior Judge Strom sternly told the prosecution how he had difficulty understanding why Kofoed was facing two misdemeanor crimes of civil rights violations. The judge noted that Livers and Sampson had both been released from custody before they were convicted of any crimes. In the end, though, the judge gave the U.S. Attorney's Office some leeway to continue with the case, but it was hardly a ringing endorsement. On one occasion during the trial, Mock summoned me into a small conference room. Mock pointed out that the jurors looked confused and bored. He sensed that the U.S. Attorney's case was not connecting with them.

.   .   .

Once the prosecution rested, Kofoed eagerly testified in his own defense. As Lefler asked the questions, Kofoed advised the jury that he simply forgot he had left the bloody filter paper to air-dry inside his county crime lab's biohazard room on April 27, 2006. According to his testimony, on the evening of May 8, 2006, nearly two weeks later, Kofoed suddenly remembered he had left it there. Of course, he never filled out the evidence log, so there was no way to prove or disprove his testimony. "I have no good excuse," Kofoed testified. "I should have signed it in. I have many administrative duties as CSI commander. I was either interrupted with a phone call or something distracted me. That's all I can tell you."[2]

Kofoed then told the jury he "was not thinking" when he wrote in his forensic report that he found the blood in the car on May 8, 2006, when in reality, he found the blood on April 27, 2006, in the presence of coworker CL Retelsdorf while both men met up at the Sheriff's impound lot.

. . .

On the witness stand, Kofoed insisted that he did not intentionally misdate his CSI report or act with any criminal intent.

"Are you a criminal, sir?" asked Lefler.

"No!"

"After you make a mistake, do you always recall having made a mistake?"

"Not if I am not aware of it," Kofoed replied.

On cross-examination, First Assistant U.S. Attorney William "Mick" Mickle tried to cast the defendant as a shadowy figure working on the dark side of law enforcement. But by the end of the trial, the prosecution's case was in bad shape. A red-faced Douglas County Sheriff Tim Dunning stormed out of the federal courthouse with his blood boiling after testifying. The longtime sheriff assured news reporters camped outside the federal courthouse building that Kofoed would be acquitted. "I was always waiting for a smoking gun to come up in his trial, but there wasn't," Dunning scoffed.

Dunning vented outrage. He accused U.S. Attorney Joe Stecher of having "something personal" against Kofoed. "This has been a witch-hunt from the very beginning," Dunning barked. "The federal government was trying to em-barrass us."[3]

Dunning's angry sound-bites made the local evening newscasts and then appeared in print for the next morning edition of the *Omaha World-Herald*. The sheriff's quotes seemed to light a fire under the federal prosecutors for the very first time in the case, even if it was too late to matter. During closing statements, Mickle displayed a giant poster board of Kofoed's original crime lab report. Mickle hoped the oversized prop would sway jurors to realize the defendant's behavior constituted four separate federal crimes. "David Kofoed lied," Mickle told jurors. "David Kofoed's cover-up in this case is criminal."

During his closing statement, Lefler characterized the federal government's case as "weak and inept." In his typical down-home folksy charm, Lefler pleaded for jurors to return a not-guilty verdict. His client badly wanted to resume his law enforcement career and help the police put the really bad people in prison. "Folks, this is not a case of planting evidence," Lefler reminded jurors. "If the government had that kind of information, they would have presented it. They want you to believe there is some evil, malicious purpose. Folks, I am embarrassed we are here. I feel bad for David Kofoed. David Kofoed is not guilty. He's an innocent man. I ask you to return the dignity back to his life."[4]

.　.　.

The jury of eight men and four women needed barely an hour to reach its unanimous verdict on September 10, 2009. Not guilty. Not guilty. Not guilty. Not guilty. Television cameras swarmed the giddy Kofoed as he left the federal courthouse in an impressive blue suit. After spending nearly five months on paid administrative leave, Kofoed assured reporters, "I will definitely be going back to work. I am positive of that." His lawyer was equally ecstatic. "I've been doing this [for] 33 years, and this is the quickest verdict I have ever been involved in," Lefler told the reporters.

Jurors told the press that the federal government did not explain its case against Kofoed very well. "We could not see any criminal intent. Generally, everything seemed like a mistake. He seemed pretty believable to us," juror Amy Niemeier commented.[5] After the acquittal, Sheriff Tim Dunning lashed out at the U.S. Attorney's Office for prosecuting his crime lab manager over what amounted to misdating a CSI report. That evening, Sheriff Dunning hastily assembled a press conference. He read a statement to the local television crews.[6] "Many of you may have noticed my anger yesterday after leaving the federal courthouse," Dunning told the media. "How do you think Dave Kofoed felt all of these months with no diversion other than to be consumed with this case, knowing that his only human error was to misdate a report after being distracted and tired? How do you think Dave Kofoed feels knowing that he now has a very large attorney bill facing him even though he is innocent? He had to protect his good name at all costs. Your integrity is everything in this business. And now he still faces Cass County and more attorney bills?" Dunning went on to complain that his Douglas County Sheriff's Office had its "good name dragged through the dirt" and had to spend thousands of dollars to pay employees who were summoned to appear at the trial as witnesses, to testify before the grand jury, or to be interviewed by the FBI. "Who repays Dave? Who repays Douglas County?" Dunning snapped.

The stinging setback for federal prosecutors left many people scratching their heads. Would Clarence Mock, the court-appointed special prosecutor, still move ahead with the evidence-tampering charge pending in Cass County?

.　.　.

In late November 2009, Ed Reinhold, assistant special agent in charge at the Omaha FBI, sent a most unusual package via Federal Express to the Serological Research Institute in California. The sealed materials shipped included rocks and can lids, toothpicks, glass, sticks, silver-colored wrappers, and other debris. These items had nothing to do with the Stock murders. They came from yet another high-profile murder case, also out of Cass County, where Kofoed had saved the day for the cops in 2003.

23

UNDERDOG

Special Prosecutor Clarence Mock went for broke. He built his entire case against Kofoed on the premise that the legendary CSI chief not only planted blood in the Murdock murders but also planted blood to frame a notorious, confessed child killer from Cass County back in 2003.

That summer, Kofoed had saved the day for the local Plattsmouth Police Department in a big way. He produced a pristine DNA blood sample of young murder victim Brendan Gonzalez from an outdoor trash bin. Kofoed's feat bordered on the miraculous because he claimed to recover Brendan's bloodstains five full months after the four-year-old boy was supposedly dumped in there. Back in 2003, nobody questioned Kofoed's discovery because killer Ivan Henk bragged to authorities in numerous confessions how he killed his son and later pleaded guilty, receiving a life sentence. However, in light of the blood evidence used to keep Nick Sampson and Matt Livers in jail for the Murdock killings, the special prosecutor found a number of peculiar and disturbing patterns.

In both Cass County murder cases:

- An outside law enforcement agency summoned Kofoed's help.
- Kofoed personally showed up at the crime scene, and blood was present.
- Kofoed's Omaha-based CSI unit collected many samples of victim blood.
- Kofoed was later notified after the prime suspect had confessed.
- Kofoed had unfettered 24/7 access to his crime lab, and he was the only supervisor in the unit.
- Kofoed produced blood under odd and suspicious circumstances

In June 2003, this trash bin was seized by Plattsmouth police from an apartment complex in a neighboring city after confessed killer Ivan Henk claimed he put his four-year-old son Brendan Gonzalez's body into the garbage bin some five months earlier. Douglas County CSI David Kofoed then claimed to find bloodstains that produced a perfect DNA profile of Brendan Gonzalez in the trash bin. Seven years later, Cass County Special Prosecutor Clarence Mock resurrected the Gonzalez case to prove how Kofoed engaged in a long-standing pattern of forensic fraud. *(Author's collection)*

to corroborate the suspect's confession and thus rescue the day for frustrated local investigators.

- Kofoed did not submit any actual debris or objects to an independent outside laboratory used to administer the DNA tests. Rather, he submitted the filter papers he allegedly used to obtain the blood specimen.
- Kofoed's filter paper samples contained perfect, complete DNA profiles of the murder victims, even though there should have been degradation.
- Kofoed worked alongside forensic scientist CL Retelsdorf.

Mock reasoned that if Kofoed had planted blood evidence against Nick Sampson and Livers when he believed in their guilt, why would the CSI chief not plant blood against confessed child killer Ivan Henk when everyone was convinced of Henk's guilt?

By early 2010, Mock asked the court to schedule a weeklong pretrial motion. He intended to show evidence suggesting that Kofoed had engaged in a pattern of forensic misconduct and that his misdeeds preceded the 2006 farmhouse slayings in Murdock. Cass County District Judge Randall Rehmeier agreed that the prosecutor's allegations warranted further scrutiny by his court. The judge scheduled a weeklong pretrial motion on the matter. Mock lined up two DNA experts from the Serological Research Institute in California to fly to Omaha to testify at Cass County's expense. Mock determined the exorbitant costs were necessary if he were to have any chance at all in securing a felony conviction and bringing Kofoed's CSI career to a halt.

.   .   .

In 2010, Assistant Plattsmouth Police Chief Brad Kreifel served as a key witness for the prosecutor at the pretrial hearing against Kofoed. Seven years earlier, Kreifel had spotted fresh bloodstains on the garage floor of Brendan Gonzalez's residence in the city of Plattsmouth. The largest blood smear was the size of a softball and had soaked into a broken recliner. At that time, Ivan Henk was immediately arrested on a pair of unrelated crimes to buy detectives more time to investigate Brendan's abduction and apparent homicide since the boy's body hadn't been located. Three months later, a dramatic and sensational outburst occurred inside the Cass County District courtroom of Judge Randall Rehmeier. Ivan Henk raised his arms into the air, shouting repeatedly, "The reason I killed Brendan Gonzalez was because he had 6-6-6 on his forehead. Brendan was the anti-Christ!"[1]

Henk, who was a cunning manipulator and pure psychopath, later told the police that he really cut off his boy's head with a serrated knife, wrapped Brendan's body in a comforter, stuffed it in a trunk, and then threw the body into a dumpster at the R Apartments, about ten miles away in the neighboring city of Bellevue.

All of the trash from the R Apartments went to the Sarpy County landfill, about thirty miles away. In the summer of 2003, law enforcement officials and hundreds of volunteers baked in the sweltering sun for weeks. They unsuccessfully sifted through mounds of trash at the landfill in search of Brendan's remains, which have never been found to this day.

Of course, Mock suspected Ivan Henk never dumped his son's body in the

Bellevue trash bin to begin with. Mock also found a number of other incriminating statements from Henk that appeared highly dubious.

"And while you believe that there are some things that Ivan Henk might have said that are truthful, you don't have any real basis to determine whether or not he actually severed his child's head, do you?" asked Mock.

"Outside his confession? No, I don't," replied Kreifel.

Henk also claimed that someone was standing on the porch at the apartment complex as he threw Brendan's body into the dumpster.

"To your knowledge, was there ever anyone produced who claimed to be a witness observing Ivan Henk near that dumpster on January 6, 2003?" inquired Mock.

Kreifel shook his head and answered no.

"I have no further questions," said the prosecutor.

.   .   .

Brian Wraxall, in his sixties, turned into the rock-star witness at the hearing. Wraxall began his work in forensic serology in the early 1960s in London at the Metropolitan Police Laboratory. He then moved to California in the 1970s to become executive director and chief forensic serologist for the private, nonprofit Serological Research Institute (SERI). Four decades later, he had testified in more than two dozen states as a nationally recognized forensic DNA expert. His impressive and impeccable résumé was ten pages long. He also had a charming and charismatic personality. After exchanging pleasantries with his witness, Mock told the noted serology expert from California to assume that Brendan's body was deposited into the trash bin back on January 6, 2003, even though Mock wasn't convinced it was ever there. Mock also told his witness to assume that the trash bin was exposed to rain, snow, and other harsh elements of extreme cold and heat during the five-month period prior to Kofoed's supposed discovery of the perfect DNA profile of Brendan Gonzalez. Wraxall then testified to his findings regarding the trash submitted to his forensic laboratory by the FBI a few months earlier. None of SERI's extensive DNA tests found any blood on those particular items, Wraxall testified. "The two scrapings that we got from the larger debris, we extracted that. It showed no DNA present," he said.[2]

To be sure, Wraxall conducted even more rigorous genetic tests. He did this because the University of Nebraska Medical Center (UNMC) in Omaha had generated a perfect DNA profile of Brendan Gonzalez from two of Kofoed's crime lab filter papers that allegedly tested the same garbage debris. SERI's powerful, high-tech laboratory testing machines barely found scant traces of human DNA from the garbage debris Kofoed removed back in June 2003, Wraxall testified.

"And you couldn't draw any kind of conclusions from it?" asked Mock.

"That's correct," Wraxall answered.

Next, Mock dimmed the courtroom lights. He showed a twenty-minute video made by Douglas County CSIs back on June 2, 2003. The footage showed Kofoed and Retelsdorf sifting through mounds of trash under the careful watch of Plattsmouth Police Chief Brian Paulsen. The video clearly showed several inches of standing rainwater and liquids at the bottom of the dumpster. Therefore, it defied scientific logic that Kofoed would have been able to produce a perfect DNA sample of Brendan's blood from this same waterlogged trash bin, which was also emptied with a mechanical lift, end over end, approximately forty times during the previous five-month period and exposed to several days of temperatures exceeding 70°F, Mock reasoned.

"Mr. Wraxall," Mock inquired, " . . . do you have an opinion to a reasonable degree of scientific certainty in the field of forensic serology whether the DNA of Brendan Gonzalez was present in the dumpster on June 2nd, 2003, in the quantity and quality found by UNMC in its testing?"

"It's my opinion that the debris in that dumpster was already degraded. Any DNA that was in there from Brendan Gonzalez was already in a degraded state before it was taken out of the dumpster, and at what time that it was taken out of the dumpster, it was already degraded," Wraxall replied.

"How likely do you think it would be that DNA would be there under the conditions that you've been made aware of?"

"I think it would be highly unlikely that it would, that you would expect to find DNA that you were able to get a full profile from."

"I don't have any further questions," the prosecutor concluded.

During cross-examination, Lefler began by complimenting the witness for letting him review SERI's serology case file as it pertained to the 2006 murders of Wayne and Sharmon Stock.

"So you're aware that Mr. Mock thinks that my client planted evidence in the Livers-Sampson case also?" Lefler began.

"Yes," Wraxall replied.

Lefler then rather foolishly asked if the passage of time would impact the recovery of Brendan's DNA from the dumpster. The answer from the serologist only deepened the doubt.

Wraxall explained, "Yes, the longer that period is between when the body was placed in there or alleged to be placed in there and the time the debris came out of it, the longer it is, the more likely it is you're going to see complete degradation."

. . .

After the prosecution rested, Lefler summoned Kofoed to the witness stand.

"Now, sir, I'm going to grab the bull by the horns. When was the first time you saw the dumpster, Mr. Kofoed?" asked Lefler.

Kofoed replied, "It would have been on June 2nd of 2003. It was in a garage in Plattsmouth. And actually to further answer your question, that's the only time I have ever seen the dumpster is that day."

Lefler asked rhetorically if Kofoed was stupid for trying to process the dumpster despite knowing it had been exposed to the elements.

"Sir, the true answer is it would be stupid not to try . . . because we don't make assumptions. Because we've been surprised all the time in many cases," answered Kofoed.

Kofoed testified that he separated the garbage items back at his Omaha crime lab, using a filter paper and distilled water or alcohol to test it against a piece of glass and a piece of cardboard.

"So I did a general swab of both. And I tested that with phenolphthalein and it was a positive reaction," he explained.

Kofoed acknowledged he did not recall anyone else being present as he conducted the lab tests for blood. "It wasn't like a two-man process. This was definitely something that somebody could do very simply by themselves, and we often do things like that."

. . .

During cross-examination, Mock wore down the defendant. Kofoed conceded he never submitted the actual bag of garbage debris collected from the dumpster for any outside DNA testing.

"There's nowhere on this report that specifically indicates that. Yes, that is true," Kofoed admitted.

"Thank you. And the Ivan Henk case was a murder case of some renown here in Cass County and the surrounding area, wasn't it?"

"Absolutely, sir."

Mock bore down and raised questions about the defendant's character. Mock told the court how Kofoed previously testified in other murder cases claiming to have a bachelor's degree in mathematics when in reality the defendant had only a bachelor's in general studies.

Kofoed was clearly agitated by the prosecutor's line of questions.

But Mock was just revving up. He directed the defendant's attention back to the murder of Brendan Gonzalez. Kofoed and Retelsdorf processed the scene in Plattsmouth back on January 7, 2003.

"Did you return to the scene on January 12?" asked Mock.

"I don't know, sir. Yes, if you're asking me. I believe I did."

. . .

In fact, the defendant's very own CSI report indicated Kofoed had gathered additional Q-tip swabs of blood from the garage floor.

This time, Kofoed showed up at the crime scene all alone. He also didn't offer a logical explanation for why he needed to harvest additional blood from the garage floor after collecting several samples just five days before.

Mock asked, "Where on the form does it reflect that there was someone there observing you?"

"It doesn't reflect that on the form at all," Kofoed replied.

"All right, well, who was the person that was there with you?"

"I don't know."

None of those additional blood samples that Kofoed collected was submitted to UNMC for immediate confirmatory DNA tests. The blood remained in the custody of the Douglas County CSI division, under Kofoed's watch, for another six months as the case against Henk progressed. The defendant, of course, could easily doctor the blood swabs when his crime lab employees were conveniently not there.

Eventually, one of Kofoed's Q-tip swabs, taken on January 7, yielded a positive presumptive for blood, but very oddly, that swab contained only a very weak positive for hemoglobin. That sample could not be amplified for any known DNA quantities.

Sure enough, that other swab of blood, taken on January 12 from virtually the same area of the concrete garage floor in Brendan's mother's house in Plattsmouth, showed a very high DNA probability that it belonged to the little boy.

"So you would have access to the DNA of Brendan Gonzalez between June 2nd and June 5th 2003?" asked Mock.

Kofoed answered, "I believe probably. Yes, I wouldn't have any doubt that I would have access to it."

"No further questions."

Lefler rose from the defense table and approached Kofoed, his longtime friend, for his chance at redirect.

"Clearly, if you're a bad guy, if you're a liar, if you're an evidence planter, you would have had access to Brendan Gonzalez's blood, correct?" Lefler inquired.

"Yes, so would everybody at CSI," replied Kofoed.

"That's what I was going to ask. Doesn't everybody have access to that?"

"Everybody's got access to the biohazard room who works in that 24/7 division," confirmed the defendant.

"Just like CL Retelsdorf would have?"

Kofoed agreed.

"And Mr. Retelsdorf was the same fellow that was with you regarding the recovery of the evidence underneath the dashboard on the Murdock [case], correct?"

"Yes, sir."

"And Mr. Retelsdorf, I think, was just brought out, he's the brother of Leigh Ann Retelsdorf, who is the district court judge [in Omaha], correct?"

"That is correct," Kofoed affirmed.

"But you're the one that's on trial here, correct?

"Yes, sir."

Lefler steered the conversation back to the afternoon of June 2, 2003, when police seized control of the dumpster.

"Now back in 2003," Lefler continued, "when Ivan Henk said he killed his son and put the body in that particular dumpster, as a professional, sir, should you not have done anything with that dumpster because seven years later a good lawyer like Clarence Mock is going to get in your face and say, 'Couldn't have got that kind of DNA?'"

"I think it would be unprofessional in any case not to follow procedures and to process evidence no matter what the difficulty," replied Kofoed.

. . .

After the weeklong hearing had ended, it remained unclear how Cass County District Judge Randall Rehmeier would rule. A favorable ruling for Mock would give him a nice boost heading into the trial. If Kofoed came out ahead, Mock would likely consider dismissing his case altogether.

24

EVIDENCE

The ruling came as a shocker.

Judge Rehmeier found clear and convincing evidence that Kofoed acted with knowledge and intent to fabricate murder victim Brendan Gonzalez's blood sample. Equally relevant, the prosecution firmly established "independent relevance" to rebut the defendant's claims of accidental or cross-contamination in the Murdock case, the judge determined.

Mock now had strong ammunition to argue that Kofoed had not just planted blood in one murder case, but in two unrelated Cass County cases.

Kofoed and his lawyer were disappointed, but still upbeat as their mid-March trial date approached. In fact, Kofoed boldly waived his right to a jury trial. He and his lawyer preferred to have Judge Randall Rehmeier decide Kofoed's fate once and for all.

The bench trial was held on the upper floor of the magnificent Cass County Courthouse in downtown Plattsmouth. The picturesque maroon brick palace was on the National Register of Historic Places. The presiding jurist, Randall Rehmeier, was not only one of Nebraska's most respected small-town legal scholars, but also a history buff. Just six years earlier, the judge oversaw a major county-funded restoration to bring the upper-level district courtroom back to its original design. For at least thirty years, many of the original courtroom relics collected dust and cobwebs in the basement of the Cass County Historical Society Museum, just a few blocks away. Rehmeier made sure the original oak-trimmed gallery posts, an ornate judge's bench, jury boxes, attorney's chairs, and wood-trimmed witness tables were restored and returned to their proper places back in his courtroom. In addition, the low-hanging courtroom ceiling was removed, revealing the original vaulted ceiling. A soothing tan carpet replaced the ugly and worn pea-green carpet.[1] The refurbished courtroom regained its historic luster. On March 15, 2010, the district courtroom served as the backdrop for one of Nebraska's most fascinating bench trials in years, *State v. Kofoed*. For the milestone occasion, the Nebraska Supreme Court granted special public access for the trial to be broadcast by the news media. Normally, cameras and digital recording devices were strictly prohibited in Nebraska's courts. In this case, it helped that the judge was both a friend and fan of the press.

As there were no eyewitnesses, Special Prosecutor Mock faced an uphill battle trying to prove beyond a reasonable doubt that Kofoed fabricated the blood evidence.

In fact, Mock's entire case rested on circumstantial evidence. Naturally, it did not help matters knowing that several Douglas County CSI employees on the prosecutor's witness list were friends and fierce loyalists of the defendant. One such person was former Douglas County CSI forensic consultant Don Veys, a former boss, mentor, and longtime friend of Kofoed.

Veys served as the first witness to testify in the criminal trial of *State v. Kofoed*. Back on the morning when the Stocks' bodies were found, Veys photographed the two bodies, the red shotgun shells, and the deer slugs used to murder the Stocks in cold blood. "I've never seen a deer slug used in a crime ever," Veys testified.[2] At the scene, he took hundreds of photos, but none of his digitized images included any Douglas County crime lab presumptive blood-testing kits, he testified.

Kofoed, of course, had staked his defense on his claim that one of his CSI kits was brought to the farmhouse and came in contact with the blood.

"When you were up on the second floor, did it appear to you to be pretty obvious what the red substances were scattered on the walls and various objects et cetera?" asked Mock.

Veys replied, "Yes, blood."

"Was there any discussion in your presence by any CSI employees to the effect that they just couldn't keep their equipment free from contamination?"

"No."

"Have you ever even heard of a circumstance in which DNA coming from kits at one crime scene has contaminated another?"

"Not that I know of," the forensic consultant answered.

Veys added that two people from the CSI division typically worked the night shift while their boss, Kofoed, worked almost all of the shifts.

"So there would be times that he would be out at the Douglas County Crime

Scene Investigations unit at nighttime, when there were not very many other employees there?"

"Yes," Veys agreed.

During cross-examination, Veys described Kofoed's work ethic as tireless, almost to a fault. Both men had previously worked together at the Omaha Police Department.

"As his supervisor, I had really a heck of a time getting him to go home. He was very detail-oriented, very singularly focused when given a task to perform. And in just about every major case situation that we were presented with at Omaha P.D., he was always one of the first on my team to go work the crime scene. Never a complaint about the work. . . ."

"Proud to work with him?" asked Lefler.

"Yes, sir."

Changing topics, Lefler asked the witness to talk about the Doje-brand of kits no longer being used by Douglas County's crime lab. Veys testified that the crime lab's former blood-test kits contained cotton swabs and filter papers that were comingled, increasing the likelihood for reverse contamination.

"They weren't individually packaged," he explained. "They were packaged as a stack of filter papers. So as you tested different items, you are touching and then touching back into the kit. So they were of no value whatsoever."

On redirect, Mock bore in on the absence of any presumptive blood-testing kits at the farmhouse in Murdock.

"You didn't see anybody at CSI handling any Doje kits at the scene, did you?" he asked.

"Not that I can recall," replied Veys.

"In fact, it didn't become known as a potential issue until questions began to be raised by the FBI and others regarding Mr. Kofoed's conduct, isn't that correct?"

"Yes."

. . .

Douglas County CSI Michelle (Steele) Potter testified how she was not aware of any internal investigation taking place in 2006 to determine whether the blood found in Will Sampson's car was caused by defective crime lab equipment.

Mock asked, "And are you aware of anyone expressing any concerns about possible contamination of any items from the Wayne Stock and Sharmon Stock crime scene during the year 2006?"

"No," Potter replied, "I'm not aware of any."

Potter, a bloodstain expert, testified it would not be normal for CSIs to re-process the same piece of evidence a second time after the first processing came up negative. Her testimony cast further doubts on her boss, the defendant.

"And why would that not be normal?" pressed the prosecutor.

"Because if you've already processed it for let's say, for blood, then I guess you wouldn't need to do it again," Potter explained.

Potter had collected four swabs off the upstairs walls of the Murdock farm-house. Although she was competent and highly skilled, even she was not per-fect. She did not realize she had left the four blood swabs inside an unsecured box back at her county's evidence storage unit.

"Apparently, I did not tape them, which is what I should have done," she said.

During cross-examination, Lefler directed his questions to the blood samples Potter left unsecured.

"I think the implication is that Mr. Kofoed might have been able to dip into that DNA that was on the swab boxes to dirty up his filter paper. I think that's the implication that eventually Mr. Mock is going to make to the judge. Would everybody at CSI have had access to those improperly packaged swabs?" asked Lefler.

"Yes, they would."

On redirect, Mock tried to set the record straight.

"Ms. Potter, did it appear to you that the defendant Mr. Kofoed is ignorant about contamination issues?"

"Is he ignorant? No."

"Do you think he would be just as committed as you are to trying to mini-mize any contamination with any equipment he uses?" asked Mock.

"Yes."

"Some witnesses have characterized him as being detail-oriented. Do you agree with that?"

"Yes," Potter agreed.

"Methodical. Would you agree with that characterization?"

"Yes."

. . .

Will Sampson had the terrible and profound misfortune of dropping off his car for an auto detailing on the very same morning the Stocks were callously murdered near Murdock. As a consequence, Cass County law enforcement officials spent months trying to link Will to the murders, but they failed miserably because two Wisconsin teenagers were responsible, and Will's car had no relevance whatsoever. Now four years later, the scales of justice had tipped the other way. The cloud of suspicion that hovered over the Sampson brothers and their cousin Matt Livers was lifted. The Cass County Sheriff's Office had been publicly ridiculed and lambasted for screwing up the initial murder case because of incompetence and shoddy work. The popular and macho CSI chief from Omaha who identified the speck of blood under the dashboard of Will's car was standing trial, facing up to five years in prison, if convicted. Co-prosecutor Adam Sipple handled the questioning of Will Sampson, the older brother of Nick Sampson.

Sipple asked if Will was involved in the deaths of Wayne and Sharmon Stock in Murdock, Nebraska.

"Absolutely not," replied Will.

"Did Matt Livers, either in the spring of 2006 or at any time prior thereto, call you periodically and ask you for favors?"

"No."

"What about Wayne Stock? Had he ever driven that car?"

"No."

"Or his wife Sharmon?"

"No."

Will testified he had not lent his car to anyone that Easter Sunday back in 2006; no one asked to borrow the car either.

That following morning, Will left his apartment earlier than usual to drop off his car at an auto-detail shop in Lincoln. Just thirty miles away, two middle-aged farmers from Will's hometown were slain during the night and the killers had fled. The timing of the two events was purely coincidental, except to the Cass County cops, who convinced themselves they were related.

.   .   .

When Will left for the detail shop on Monday morning, his car remained in the same parking stall where he had left it on Easter Sunday.

"When you got in and drove it, did you observe anything indicating to you that it had been mysteriously taken during the previous night?" asked Sipple.

"No."

"Did you observe any evidence of blood?"

"No."

"Any other ammunition of any kind?"

"No."

"Empty shotgun shells?"

"No."

"Weapons?"

"No."

"Going back to the car, when you drove it to the detail shop, did the seat appear to be in the same position that you would have normally left it in?"

"Yes."

"And the mirrors?"

"Yes."

.   .   .

Will's wife, Alynn, was also called to testify as a prosecution witness. She refuted any assertion that her husband was somehow a conspirator in the Stock slayings, as the Cass County cops had alleged. Will was fast asleep when she finally turned off the television on Easter and rolled into their bed, she testified.

"Do you have any reason to believe that between the time you went to sleep around 1 A.M. that night and when Will woke up the following morning, that he got up and left your apartment for any reason?" inquired Sipple.

"No. And our apartment door at that time would stick, so it was very loud to open and shut, so it would be pretty hard to get it open without having to slam it shut or even to open it without me hearing it."

"Did you observe anything on April 16th, Easter Sunday, 2006, indicating that Will had loaned his car to anyone to use that night?"

"No."

"Or that anyone came and took his car and committed a double homicide using it?"

"No."

.   .   .

Matthew Hale buffed, vacuumed, and shampooed vehicles at the Lincoln Auto Detail on 48th Street and Nebraska Highway 2, back in 2006. Sometimes he cleaned a Rolls Royce, a Mercedes Benz, or a Porsche. He never imagined that his mundane and ordinary cleaning of a dirty tan Ford Contour would be the subject of an intense and high-stakes Nebraska criminal courtroom drama filmed by NBC's *Dateline* some four years later.

"Do you know anybody named Nick Sampson?" asked Sipple.

Hale replied, "No, I do not."

"Or Matt Livers?"

"No, I do not."

.   .   .

Matt Hale testified he agreed to clean Will Sampson's car as a favor for Hale's brother.

Hale explained, "My brother Joe had told me that he had been given a ride to and from work and that he wanted to do something nice in return other than just pay for gas all the time."

The cleaning had been planned for three weeks, Matt Hale testified. He spoke with his boss on the Friday before Easter about cleaning the car.

The following Monday, which was April 17, Matt Hale gave Will's car a light dusting and vacuuming, called a spiff.

"While providing those services, did you observe anything unusual in the vehicle?" asked Sipple.

"No, I did not."

"Did you observe any spent shotgun shells?"

"No, I did not."

"Any other ammunition?"

"No, I did not."

"Any indication someone had had guns in the vehicle?"

"Not that I could tell."

"Or blood?"

"Nope. Didn't see no blood."

25

PHANTOM

As CSI supervisor, Kofoed hired and trained the young men and women who came to work for him. Many of the most gullible ones were about half his age. They staunchly refused to believe the allegations that their boss was a crook. This obstacle presented a significant hurdle for Special Prosecutor Clarence Mock during his prosecution of their boss.

"Obviously, I did not have any friendly witnesses," Mock told me in a June 2013 interview. "I had to be really careful with how I structured the examination and part of the questioning. I am not saying they would necessarily lie, but I was well aware that they were waiting for an opportunity to damage the prosecution's case based on their loyalty and affection toward him. They were blinded by Kofoed. They just could not believe he could do this."[1]

One of Kofoed's favorite pets around the crime lab office was forensic scientist Christine Gabig. During her trial testimony in Cass County District Court, she did everything in her power to insist that Kofoed could not have committed the evidence-tampering crime of which he was accused. Gabig left courtroom observers stunned. She wholeheartedly vouched for Kofoed's theory of accidental contamination. "All I can say is that the possibility of contamination at a crime scene is always present," Gabig testified.[2]

On cross-examination, Gabig agreed that she and Kofoed were friends. She testified that getting rid of the old set of multiuse blood-test kits at the crime lab seemed the best way to deal with the problem.

"Did you think, you know, maybe Dave did plant it?" asked Lefler.

Gabig replied, "I never thought that Dave planted evidence."

"If you had thought that Mr. Kofoed was a dirty investigator and had planted this evidence, would you have gone forward and told people about it?"

"Absolutely, I would have."

. . .

FBI Special Agent Gina Palokangas was one of the most important officials overseeing the FBI's corruption probe. She and Special Agent Michael Kelleher had interviewed Kofoed at FBI headquarters in Omaha on June 5, 2008, about the suspicious blood evidence. Kofoed did not realize at that time how much his interview with the FBI would later haunt him.

During the FBI interview, Kofoed blamed one of his crime lab kits for causing contamination.

"Did he explain to you where the kit was at the crime scene?" inquired Mock. Palokangas replied, "No."

"Did he explain to you that he ever saw anyone else using the kit?"

"No."

"Did he ever tell you that the kit was even within the Stock residence?"

"No."

"Did he tell you the kit was in the staging area?"

"No."

In late 2008, Palokangas traveled to the Cass County Sheriff's Office in downtown Plattsmouth to visit the evidence storage room. There, she came across Exhibit 208, the vials of blood evidence taken from the upstairs walls of the farmhouse by Douglas County CSI Michelle Potter.

Palokangas said, "The four swabs were in swab boxes placed in a paper bag, and what I noticed was that none of them were sealed. It did not appear that it had ever been sealed."

"Did you also view another item of evidence in this matter related to Mr. Kofoed?" asked Mock.

Palokangas confirmed that she inspected a paper bag containing murder victim Wayne Stock's blood-soaked T-shirt. The bag was originally collected the day after the murders. However, she noticed the bag had been inexplicably reopened and resealed with clear tape, marked with the initials "D.W.K."

Those initials belonged to David Wayne Kofoed.

Oddly, the resealed bag containing Wayne Stock's bloody shirt never referenced a date. Furthermore, Kofoed never filed a report stating his objective for reopening the previously sealed bloody shirt, the FBI agent testified.

Mock asked, "Did you ever get an opportunity to interview Mr. Kofoed about why his initials appeared on the bag?"

"No."

"I have no further questions."

. . .

Dave Kofoed and CL Retelsdorf were the Batman and Robin of the Douglas County CSI unit. Retelsdorf was skilled at video technology, and he considered his boss one of the all-around best when it came to investigating crime scenes. Kofoed enlisted Retelsdorf's help in most major crimes handled by the Douglas County Sheriff's Office. The duo processed the bloody scene where little Brendan Gonzalez was murdered in Plattsmouth, back in 2003. They returned together five months later to sift through the garbage bin where Kofoed allegedly recovered some bloodstains to corroborate killer Ivan Henk's latest confession.

. . .

Retelsdorf found himself in an awkward and uncomfortable position in connection with his actions during the 2006 Murdock double murder case. He considered Kofoed his mentor and the two were close friends. Retelsdorf was hardly enthused when Mock made him the prosecution's star witness against the defendant, but he also knew the stakes and repercussions for lying under oath. Retelsdorf, who was in his early thirties, steered clear of eye contact with Kofoed throughout his testimony during the trial. Judge Rehmeier listened intently as the witness recalled what he saw on the day that Kofoed emerged with the mysterious blood evidence. Retelsdorf recalled that his boss requested that he go back to the car to see if it contained any visible signs of gunshot residue. On the afternoon of April 27, 2006, Retelsdorf drove out to the county's secured impound lot a few blocks away, bringing along only a camera. Kofoed advised Retelsdorf to look for signs that Livers or Nick Sampson had tossed a shotgun into the backseat after the murders, according to Retelsdorf's testimony.

. . .

Mock wondered why Retelsdorf, a nine-year CSI veteran who had a master's degree, failed to bring along any equipment that might be useful for such an assignment.

"So did you have any kind of equipment with you in the van that would have been necessary to make that kind of scientific analysis for gunshot residue?" inquired Mock.

Retelsdorf replied, "No."

"Would gunshot oil always leave visible markings?"

"I don't know."

"Do you have any experience in that regard?"

"Specifically with gun oil, no."

Retelsdorf also didn't bring along any equipment to determine if blood was present in the backseat of Will Sampson's car.

Mock asked, "Why didn't you do that?"

"I knew the vehicle had been previously processed."

"Would you have expected to find any kind of a depression or physical indentation or any kind of other physical appearance to the backseat from a weapon being placed into the backseat?"

"Not necessarily."

Retelsdorf testified that as he fiddled around in the backseat, he noticed Kofoed came up and approached the driver's side door.

Mock inquired about the equipment that the CSI chief brought along to test the car. The prosecutor asked if Kofoed displayed an alternative light source as Kofoed had indicated in his official CSI report. Any garbage bags? Any white butcher paper for processing forensic clues?

The witness answered "No" several times.

That afternoon, Kofoed ducked underneath the driver's side dashboard and emerged with a piece of filter paper in his hand.

"Mr. Kofoed stated that he had gotten a positive presumptive for blood," recounted Retelsdorf.

Startled, Retelsdorf rushed over to take a look.

"What did he have in his hands?" asked Mock.

"A piece of filter paper."

"Did he have anything in his other hand?"

"Not that I remember."

"At that point, did you see an alternative light source anywhere near him?"

"Not that I remember."

"Did you see any trash bag?"

"Not that I remember."

"Did you see any Q-tip swabs laying in the area near the driver's side?"

"Not that I can remember."

Retelsdorf did remember Kofoed holding a filter paper that had turned pink. This signified a positive presumptive reaction for blood.

"He advised me where he had swabbed, which was underneath the steering wheel on a piece of molding that was up underneath the dash area about where a person's knees would be. And he showed me the rough area about where he had swabbed."

Mock asked, "Could you see into that area without the necessity of an alternate light source?"

"Yes."

"Why was that?

"It was in the middle of the day. The sun was up."

Retelsdorf testified that he went back to the van. He retrieved a wooden dowel similar to a standard Q-tip to attempt to find more blood in the car.

Afterward, Kofoed knelt down and showed his underling where Kofoed had allegedly found blood.

"Could you see anything visually?" asked the prosecutor.

"I don't recall seeing anything."

Retelsdorf went ahead and conducted his own chemical tests.

"Did you receive a positive reaction?" inquired Mock.

"No."

Mock continued to ask the witness even more pointed and uncomfortable questions. Retelsdorf had to admit on the witness stand that he never saw Kofoed swab the underside of the dashboard with the filter paper.

"The only thing that you know about whether he did that is what he told you?"

"That's correct," Retelsdorf admitted.

"Did this defendant tell you that he had concerns that the filter paper that he had used to swab—that he claimed to use to swab the underside of the dashboard of the Ford Contour—might have been contaminated in some fashion at some point?"

"I don't believe so."

In fact, Retelsdorf first heard about Kofoed's theory of accidental contamination only after the FBI probe was initiated, some two years after the Murdock killings occurred.

.   .   .

Kofoed's lawyer asked some rhetorical questions on cross-examination, putting the friendly witness at ease.

"Can you tell the court how stupid of a CSI person you must have been to go out to process the backseat of a car when you didn't bring material to do trace evidence collection? You didn't bring material to test for oils, and you only brought a camera. I mean, how stupid of a guy must you be, Mr. Retelsdorf?"

"I believe I had the equipment necessary to complete the request," Retelsdorf replied.

"Okay. Can I just jump to a conclusion that maybe you're better trained to determine what a CSI person needs than me or Mr. Mock?"

"I would believe so, yes."

"Let me ask you a question. I assume you like and respect Mr. Kofoed?"

"Yes."

"You think he's a good man, works hard. Does a good job for our community?"

"Yes."

"To your personal knowledge, has anyone gone to your superiors and said, 'Mr. Kofoed is a dirty cop'?"

"Not that I'm aware of, no."

"Are you telling the court that Mr. Kofoed somehow had that filter paper stuffed into his pocket and pulled it out and magically said, 'Hey I just got that.'"

"No."

. . .

Of the more than 420 pieces of evidence collected and tested by the Douglas County crime lab, only Kofoed's blood evidence find in Will Sampson's car tied Matt Livers and Nick Sampson to the Stock murders.

Yet for someone who maintained he realized relatively quickly that the blood didn't fit, Kofoed kept his feelings to himself. He never raised the issue of accidental contamination when irrefutable DNA evidence linked the killings to Fester and Reid in the summer of 2006. Even then, Kofoed remained as quiet as a mouse as Sampson and Livers remained in jail, nearing their trial dates, facing life in prison or possible death sentences.

Cass County Attorney Nathan Cox testified that Kofoed first mentioned the idea of accidental contamination during a phone call that took place about a month after Fester and Reid were given life prison sentences and the original case had concluded.

"Did the defendant explain to you how that contamination occurred?" asked Mock.

Cox replied, "No. . . . Just that he indicated, well, that's the only possible conclusion at this point is that it was by contamination."

In fact, no one else from the Douglas County CSI had ever contacted Cox suggesting the blood sample in the Ford Contour might be inaccurate because of contamination. As a result, Cox continued to rely upon the blood evidence produced by Kofoed as a key component of his case.

Said Cox, "With regard to the cases involving Matthew Livers and Nicholas Sampson, as I indicated to defense counsel at the time, there were two prongs that were really holding that case together at all, and one of those prongs was the blood evidence that was found in the Ford Contour, and so that was a significant part of the case."

The state rested. Now it was the defense's turn.

26

VERDICT

Folksy lawyer Steve Lefler tried to stir the waters of reasonable doubt in the judge's mind. He offered several alternative theories to explain the blood's recovery from the wrong getaway car. Lefler solicited the testimony of Kirby Drake, one of Sharmon Stock's brothers, who had assured Cass County investigators that the victims' nephew had to be involved in the murders.[1]

"And did you just say the name Matt Livers, sir, because you hated the guy and wanted the cops to falsely investigate him?" asked Lefler.

"No, sir," Drake replied.

On the witness stand, Drake offered some bizarre, unbelievable twists. He testified he spotted a red Dodge truck, bearing Wisconsin plates, parked outside the Bulldogs Bar & Grill in downtown Murdock on Easter Sunday afternoon, 2006.

"Are you sure you saw it?" Lefler inquired.

"I am positive."

If Drake's eyewitness account were indeed true, it meant the killings were not random at all, but surely part of the larger conspiracy that Nebraska investigators Schenck and Lambert tried to prove back in 2006.

On cross-examination, prosecutor Mock asked only one question.

"Did the pickup have a dog in the back of it?"

"Yes, it did."

"I don't have any further questions."

Mock knew that Drake's testimony was utterly preposterous and lacked any credibility. None of the bar patrons ever saw a red truck from Wisconsin parked outside the Bulldogs Bar & Grill that fateful Easter Sunday. Nobody at

Cass County District Court Judge Randall Rehmeier confers with special prosecutor Clarence Mock, at left, and criminal defense attorney Steve Lefler during Kofoed's bench trial. *(Omaha World-Herald Photo)*

the bar remembered a large panting dog, identical to one of Nick Sampson's
dogs, supposedly in the back of any truck bed, except for what was attested
to by Kirby Drake.

. . .

Judge Rehmeier blocked Kofoed's lawyer from presenting testimony related
to the Douglas County internal affairs probe that cleared Kofoed of evidence
planting back in 2008. "It's an internal investigation, not the same issues we
have before the court here," the judge announced. With little else to go on,
Lefler summoned the no-nonsense Douglas County Sheriff Tim Dunning to
testify. By this stage, Dunning's crime lab manager had spent eleven consecutive months on paid administrative leave from his $80,000 position after the
federal indictment came down, the sheriff noted.

Dunning informed the court that he had hired Kofoed around 2000.

He added, "I had high respect for him. I knew that he did a great job with
Omaha police. And I personally felt like I was stealing him from Omaha police."

"And would you like to have him back?" asked Lefler.

"Yes."

Other Nebraska officials called to testify by the defense weren't exactly helpful to Kofoed's case, however.

Nebraska State Patrol Capt. Chuck Phillips bluntly testified he had real concerns about the blood in the Ford Contour car once the two Wisconsin teenagers were arrested in the summer of 2006.

"Again, the question was how did the blood get in the car when all other physical evidence we had was lining up with Reid and Fester," recalled Phillips.

Moreover, nobody in the Douglas County CSI unit ever informed the Nebraska State Patrol investigators working on the Stock homicides that the presumptive blood-testing kits utilized at that time would create the risk of contamination during evidence processing, Phillips testified.

.   .   .

Defense witness Earl Schenck Jr. walked into the courtroom with a swagger. By 2010, Schenck's law enforcement career was on the downslide. He was one of the key defendants in the ongoing federal civil rights lawsuits filed on behalf of Livers and Nick Sampson. Cass County's lead investigator on the Stock murder cases had also been reassigned to courthouse security and prisoner transports. The Stock slayings were the first murder case he had worked on for the Cass County Sheriff's Office, Schenck testified. Incredibly, he still had not let go of his original theory that Livers and Nick Sampson helped commit the farmhouse murders, despite having no facts to back that up.

"And can you tell the court based upon your training and experience and your evaluation of all the evidence and being one of the lead investigators, is this particular case in your mind open or closed, sir?" asked Lefler.

Schenck replied, "I believe the investigation should be open, yes."

Mock managed to make Schenck's testimony useful to the state. Schenck insisted that he could not have contaminated Will Sampson's car with any of the crime-scene blood.

"I had changed clothes at least two or three times since the date we were at the crime scene," he explained. "I was wearing completely different footwear, completely different slacks, shirt, tie, and at no time did I ever come into physical contact with the vehicle."

Mock asked, "Did you place Wayne Stock's blood into the Ford Contour at any time?"

"Absolutely not."

Schenck testified that Kofoed attended many of the daily law enforcement briefings after the murders. Will Sampson's car was a key topic because it bore a general resemblance to a vehicle spotted near the crime scene by the two newspaper carriers, and Matt Livers later confessed to using Will's car in the crime, Schenck testified.

"Did the investigators suspect that blood evidence . . . from the killers of Wayne and Sharmon Stock most likely would have been transferred into the Ford Contour?"

"We believed it should be a possibility, yes, sir."

.   .   .

Shockingly, the defense rested after Schenck's testimony. Kofoed would not testify in his own defense after all. During closing arguments, Mock hammered home how Will Sampson's car "was as clean as a whistle" when it was brought to Kofoed's agency on the third day of the case. "Cross-contamination is not like a mist or a vapor that permeates around a crime scene," Mock reasoned. "That is not the way the world works. There was never any blood in that car."

During his closing, Kofoed's lawyer floated several theories to justify the bloodstains in the car. Lefler revisited the theory that Livers and Nick Sampson were really involved in the killings all along. Lefler claimed that evidence technician-turned FBI informant Darnel Kush had strong motivation and desire to plant the blood in the car to frame her boss. Kush was a highly disgruntled crime lab employee, Lefler noted. Finally, Lefler begged for the court's sympathy. The FBI had taken a good man and knocked his legs out from under him. "We're all human," Lefler pleaded. "We all make mistakes. If you err, err on the side of mercy. Give the defendant the benefit of the doubt like you are supposed to. All they have is a theory that Mr. Kofoed is a bad cop."[2]

The judge told both sides to return in four days for his verdict. Kofoed fully expected the judge to find him not guilty.

.   .   .

At least a dozen other Nebraska journalists and I gathered in the dimly lit upper hallway of the nineteenth-century Cass County Courthouse back on March 23, 2010. Most of the journalists who covered the entire trial agreed it was a coin flip on whether the judge would find the defendant guilty or innocent of evidence tampering, a felony. Kofoed's coworkers at the Douglas

County Sheriff's Office were packed in the spectator gallery. Members of the local Plattsmouth Police Department who relied on Kofoed's help during the Brendan Gonzalez murder case back in 2003 also filed into the courtroom for the verdict, including Plattsmouth Police Chief Brian Paulsen. When court resumed that Tuesday morning, the verdict from the bench did not come immediately. Instead, Cass County District Judge Randall Rehmeier spent about twenty-five minutes explaining his decision.[3] None of the trial evidence showed that Douglas County's blood-testing kits were ever used at Wayne and Sharmon Stock's farmhouse. Secondly, it didn't seem plausible for Kofoed or others in law enforcement to accidentally contaminate the car with tainted equipment or their own actions. As for other defense theories regarding the blood, absolutely no credible evidence showed that former codefendants Matt Livers and Nick Sampson had killed the Stocks, the judge announced. And finally, nothing pointed to FBI informant Darnel Kush as planting the blood to frame her boss, the judge informed everyone in the courtroom.

March 23, 2010, David Kofoed, Nebraska's celebrated CSI chief for the Douglas County Sheriff's Office in Omaha, listens as Cass County District Judge Randall Rehmeier renders his verdict at the conclusion of Kofoed's bench trial. Kofoed faced one count of tampering with physical evidence, a felony that carried a possible prison term. (*Omaha World-Herald Photo*)

Lefler sat stone-faced. Kofoed bowed his head and slumped in his chair.

Next, Rehmeier turned to Special Prosecutor Clarence Mock's case. The judge said he found "significant similarities" when analyzing Kofoed's conduct in the 2003 murder of Brendan Gonzalez and the 2006 slayings of Wayne and Sharmon Stock. The judge observed that in both of these unrelated Cass County cases, the accused suspect had confessed to police. In both cases, investigators were working to corroborate the suspect's statement. In both cases, Kofoed found victim's blood under unusual circumstances. In both cases, the DNA of the murder victim had already been collected and stored by Kofoed's crime lab.

With that, the judge pronounced Kofoed guilty of tampering with physical evidence, a Class 4 felony. The defendant could remain free, pending sentencing.

Shocked and demoralized, Kofoed barged out of the Plattsmouth courtroom. The judge had branded him a convicted felon. His law enforcement career was over. Kofoed shuffled down several flights of stairs and walked briskly out of the Cass County Courthouse under beautiful blue skies on a gorgeous spring morning. A stream of news reporters gave chase along the historic Main Street, seeking his reaction. "It is what it is," Kofoed repeated. "It's not devastating. We just move on."[4]

He hopped into a friend's car and the two sped out of town.

Back in the courthouse, Kofoed's distraught lawyer blamed himself for the stunning verdict. Lefler told reporters he should have let Kofoed testify in his own defense. Lefler also said he blundered by waiving a jury trial, instead opting for a bench trial. "I feel bad for Dave," Lefler told reporters. "I feel bad for his family, for the Douglas County Sheriff's Office CSI, for the sheriff, and for the taxpayers."

In the courthouse hallway, FBI Special Agent Robert Georgi presented Mock with a medal as a special token of gratitude. Georgi oversaw the Omaha bureau's public corruption unit. Within hours of the verdict, the Douglas County Attorney's Office issued a press statement that Kofoed had been terminated, effective immediately. Of course, no one looked more foolish as a result of the judge's verdict than longtime Douglas County Sheriff Tim Dunning. During the internal affairs probe two years earlier, the sheriff had cleared Kofoed of planting blood evidence. At that time, Dunning proclaimed that Kofoed had passed a polygraph test.

Ostracized and humiliated, Kofoed petitioned the judge for a mistrial. He claimed that Judge Rehmeier should have disclosed prior to the trial that the judge's second cousin, Charlie Rehmeier, happened to work with Kofoed at the Douglas County Sheriff's Office in Omaha. "Had that relationship been disclosed or discovered before the trial, the defendant would not have waived his right to a jury trial," Lefler stated.[5] Lefler also argued that Darnel Kush's complaints about her boss, outlined in a five-page report prepared by Bill Lambert of the Nebraska State Patrol, showed that she had clear motivation to take down her boss and plant the blood evidence in the car.

The motion for a new trial hearing turned into a spectacle for Kofoed. According to Judge Rehmeier, his second cousin testified how both of them had not even seen each other in years. The two cousins certainly never spoke about the Murdock slayings or about Kofoed's evidence-tampering case. "Last time I saw him was at a funeral in Weeping Water. My dad introduced me to him. That was at least 25 years ago," Charlie Rehmeier told the court.

When Lefler called Kush to the witness stand, she testified that Kofoed had a "sociopathic personality." She portrayed Kofoed as a chronic liar who couldn't be trusted. "He is arrogant and always lying, I do believe that, yes," Kush testified.[6]

Kush admitted under Lefler's questioning that the FBI paid her $3,000 for being a confidential informant. But she never asked for any money, nor expected it, she testified. After Kofoed's criminal indictment, he lodged a complaint with the Sheriff's Office against her, Kush testified. Fearing retaliation, she testified that she hired an attorney. "I was a little tired of him," she said.

Once the hearing ended, the judge immediately rejected Kofoed's petition for a mistrial. Kofoed barged out of the courtroom in a rage. "I'm innocent!" he shouted at the television cameras. "I'm never going to give this up. I am innocent."

Suddenly, Kofoed turned and stared at me. My coverage of the trial for the *Omaha World-Herald* had not portrayed him in the most favorable light.

"And you can go to hell!" Kofoed barked.[7]

I winced and stayed silent, realizing that he was just blowing off steam and venting his frustrations, given the circumstances.

.   .   .

Prior to the June sentencing, forensic science message boards on the Internet buzzed with reaction to the guilty verdict. Astonishingly, Kofoed joined the debate on one particular CSI message board headlined "Lab director planting evidence?"

Douglas County CSI Darnel Kush testifies at a court hearing in 2010 about how she ultimately went to the FBI with her suspicions that David Kofoed engaged in a pattern of forensic misconduct. Kush served as a confidential informant for the FBI to help build its evidence-planting case against her boss, Kofoed. *(Lincoln Journal Star Photo)*

"This has been an enormous learning experience to: first be wrongfully accused. Then cleared by an investigation which was complete and thorough in 2008. Prosecuted on four federal charges and then acquitted in less than an hour in 2009. And to be finally convicted by one man in a state bench trial in 2010. It was sort of a case of triple jeopardy: same lack of evidence, the same charges but with small legal nuances that lawyers love. There was no proof and no evidence. These experiences are an illustration of the very worst in human nature," Kofoed posted on the Internet forum.[8]

It wasn't long before Nebraska lawyer Jerry Soucie also got wind of the Internet message board chatter regarding Kofoed's case.

Soucie, too, weighed in. "In the interest of full disclosure, I was the criminal defense attorney who represented both Nick Sampson and Ivan Henk," Soucie wrote.

Soucie, in his posting, noted Kofoed's checkered past, including his history of gambling problems, his apparent misrepresentation of his college degree, and his difficulties in the Marine Corps, which led to his general discharge from the military. Soucie expressed amazement that Kofoed would use the Internet to profess his innocence.

"I am basically a statewide public defender. I have zero financial interest in Mr. Kofoed's conviction or the outcome of the pending civil rights cases," Soucie wrote. "I wish I had a book or movie deal in the works, but unfortunately, I do not. In regards to assisting the U.S. Attorney, Special Prosecutor and the civil rights attorneys, I received a witness fee from the federal court, four lunches from Mr. Mock, and a woefully inadequate number of glasses of wine from the civil plaintiff lawyers. . . ."

Soucie used the CSI forum to set the record straight with the public. He explained how Kofoed never intended to frame innocent people for murders they did not commit. "He believed just like the two lead investigators that Livers and Sampson were guilty of a brutal double murder," Soucie stated. "However, without some piece of physical evidence to corroborate Livers's confessions, Nick Sampson was going to walk. Mr. Kofoed's fabrication of the documentation and filter paper would have worked, except for the fact that it was subsequently learned in late May/early June 2006 that Reid and Fester actually did the murders. . . ."

June 1, 2010

David Wayne Kofoed, age fifty-three, wore a black suit to his sentencing. He was back inside the same Cass County courtroom, in front of the very same judge, where Nick Sampson and Matt Livers appeared more than four years before, when the Murdock murders tragically unfolded. One of Kofoed's longtime friends, retired Douglas County Sheriff's Capt. Dean Olson, showed up for the sentencing. Others felt Kofoed got his just deserts. Retired Douglas County evidence technician Tony Grazziano strutted into the Plattsmouth courtroom in a silver sport coat and dark sunglasses. His entry interrupted a pleasant and friendly conversation between Olson and Kofoed near the defense table. Grazziano, on the other hand, represented one of the old-timers who left or were forced out of the crime lab around the time of Kofoed's hiring.

Olson and Kofoed were aghast that Grazziano showed up at the sentencing. Visibly perturbed, Olson asked if Grazziano came to gloat. Grazziano just smiled and grabbed a seat toward the back of the gallery.[9] A few minutes

Douglas County CSI Director Dave Kofoed is escorted out of the Cass County Court-house after Judge Randall Rehmeier sentenced Kofoed to prison for tampering with evidence. *(Omaha World-Herald Photo)*

later, the proceedings began. Kofoed stepped forward in front of the judge's raised bench. Mock argued that a prison sentence was necessary. "I would leave it to your discretion to what you think is appropriate," Mock advised the judge.

Lefler sought probation, not prison time. Because of the felony conviction, Kofoed would never work in law enforcement again, Lefler noted.

Judge Rehmeier had the discretion to put Kofoed on probation or sentence him to a maximum of five years in prison.

Kofoed wanted to make a statement before his sentence was pronounced. "I know that you've already made a decision so anything I say now really won't affect that," Kofoed told the judge. "So what I want to say is that I do respect you very much and this court. And it's important that I say that. I think I've been a little defiant and belligerent at times, maybe outside of court, not in court, but you know, I was frustrated and I heard things that I knew were not necessarily true by witnesses and that bothered me. So if I offended you in any way, I apologize for that, all right. . . ."[10]

Next, the disgraced former CSI chief reflected on helping solve the 2003 murder of Brendan Gonzalez by Ivan Henk. He then pondered his role in the Wayne and Sharmon Stock murder case. "The two people in this case, Matt Livers and Nick Sampson, it took me a while, but . . . I didn't believe they had anything to do with it, and I did state that. . . . You know, I believe in our system. I believe that we had a unique role as forensic scientists. We're finders of fact and it's very important. And it's always been important to me to try to maintain neutrality. We become close to the police officers and prosecutors, but at the same time, I think, you know, it's been my belief that you really need to stay separate from those folks. So in that sense, I trust your judgment. I don't believe this is the last of this case for me. I want to continue on. And that's nothing personal with you. And I believe you're a fair man. And that's all I want to say."

Judge Rehmeier noted that the defendant lacked any acknowledgment of wrongdoing and had not been remorseful. Victim-impact statements submitted by Nick Sampson and Matt Livers sought incarceration.

Although Livers and Sampson were innocent, Kofoed believed they were guilty when he planted the blood evidence against them, the judge concluded. "It's clear they suffered serious harm from an emotional standpoint," Rehmeier said. In addition, Kofoed's crime was particularly egregious. His actions tarnished Nebraska's criminal justice system, the judge pointed out. Rehmeier sentenced Kofoed to a prison term of twenty months to four years. Sentences are cut in half in Nebraska, based on good behavior. Court adjourned.

The next chapter of Kofoed's life began with his prison mug shot. The Nebraska Department of Correctional Services assigned Kofoed to be inmate no. 71642. Because he had no prior criminal record, he stood a very good chance of being paroled from state custody after serving as little as ten months of incarceration.

Kofoed, though, had no interest in parole.

27

THE COP

The Lincoln Community Corrections Center sits on well-manicured grounds near a large recreational park along the southwest corner of Nebraska's capital city of Lincoln. The exterior of the state institution resembles an upscale hotel and conference center because of its large windows and sloped roof. But the inside has a definite prison feel. The building features checkpoints, video security cameras, electronic door locks, and buzzers. Guard stations are surrounded by bulletproof glass. A wall portrait honors the Nebraska governor.

The forty-thousand-square-foot building accommodates about four hundred inmates in total. Male and female inmates are kept in segregated units. The inmates can watch television, read books, or play board games in the day room. In the dormitory-style housing units, eight inmates typically live together. Floors are carpeted. There are no bars or steel cages. Inmates store their personal belongings in a large metal locker within their housing unit.

Only a tiny fraction of less than 1 percent of Nebraska's prison inmates had a prior career in law enforcement. A prisoner of Dave Kofoed's celebrity was unheard of at the Nebraska Department of Correctional Services.

When Kofoed arrived in Lincoln, he was fat, fatigued, and out of shape. He could barely jog a lap around the paved path surrounding the prison grounds. He resembled the character Uncle Fester from the 1960s sitcom *The Addams Family.*

Almost age fifty-four, he tipped the scales at 259 pounds.

But after seven months of running five miles a day and pumping iron at the medieval Weight Pile out at the prison yard, the former 1979 Mr. Midwest sported the body of a twenty-five-year-old, weighing a trim 190 pounds.

Life at the Lincoln prison consisted of a strict and regimented routine.[1] Kofoed wore standard prison clothes consisting of gray polyester pants, white tube socks, a thermal long-sleeve white shirt, and black leather boots. Five days a week, he rode a prisoner van to his regular work detail, operating a forklift at the prison distribution center. At the Central Warehouse, he unloaded wooden pallets of food, clothing, and medical supplies destined for other prisons across the state. As a prisoner, Kofoed worked about eight hours to make just $2.25 per day. Initially, state corrections put him on clerical duty at Cornhusker State Industries. This was ironic because the prison manufacturing company is best known by its acronym, CSI. On Kofoed's first day at CSI, the prisoner assigned to drive the state van glared at him. "We don't want any fucking cops on the van!" the inmate driver yelled to Kofoed and then he sped off.[2] Other issues also flared up. One day, a confrontation unfolded when Kofoed walked into the warehouse. One inmate blurted out, "Fuck you, cop!" and busted Kofoed's lip with a sucker punch. Kofoed said he grabbed the guy by his shirt with his right hand and drilled the inmate with his left fist. The guy crumpled to the floor. Kofoed didn't complain about the bare-knuckle scuffle to the prison guards. Instead, he sent a stern message with his fists. He was not an inmate to pick on. About one-third of the inmates assigned to the Lincoln Community Corrections Center were convicted of drug offenses. A small number were robbers, rapists, and killers. Consequently, other inmates didn't take a liking to Kofoed. His fellow inmates called him

In late 2010, state of Nebraska inmate Dave Kofoed reflects on his new life as a high-profile prisoner during an interview with me. A prison inmate of Kofoed's prior rank and stature in the law enforcement community was unheard of in Nebraska's penal system. *(Omaha World-Herald Photo)*

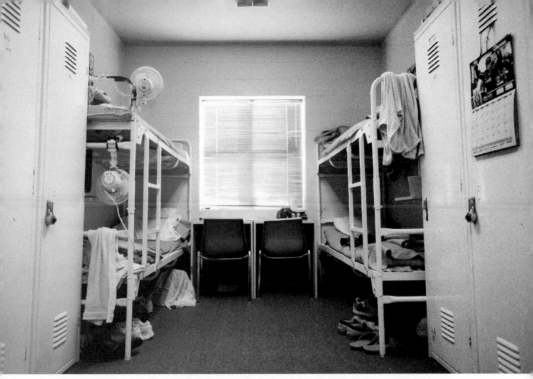

As a non-violent prisoner, Kofoed served his prison sentence at the Lincoln Community Correctional Center in Lincoln, Nebraska. Inmates there lived in dormitory-style rooms. *(Omaha World-Herald Photo)*

"The Cop" or "Copper." In the prison caste system, an evidence-planting conviction put the former legendary CSI chief on a pedestal lower than the "chimo," or child molester, Kofoed explained.

By the time I interviewed him for a January 2011 tell-all front-page story in the *Omaha World-Herald* about his prison life, a lot had changed. Foremost, Kofoed was no longer angry about my articles covering his criminal trial in Cass County. Besides dropping seventy pounds, he had undergone a true transformation after spending eight months being institutionalized. He had a scratchy beard. He knew the prison lingo. He tried not to get rolled up by the prison guards. He avoided the blind spots in the outdoor prison yard, where video surveillance cameras were not positioned. This way, inmates with violent tendencies would not subject him to a "thumping" to build stature and credibility with other prisoners.

Prison life also made for some weird reunions. Kofoed encountered a couple of convicts who remembered that he worked on their crimes while at the Omaha Police Department in the 1990s. Kofoed also boasted how he hung around with a muscular former star athlete, who had previously been shot five times. Kofoed observed how the inmate carried himself with self-respect.[3] The fallen CSI chief had two roommates at his dormitory-style prison housing unit who were also in their fifties. One was convicted of either manslaughter or motor vehicle homicide. The other was a habitual criminal. Both men kept to themselves. Younger guys in the unit had convictions of burglary and auto theft. Kofoed said he typically did not ask other inmates about their crimes. "In my case, all of them know about me," Kofoed said.

But Dave Kofoed would never be confused with Paul Newman's colorful character in the 1960s classic movie, *Cool Hand Luke*. Rather, Kofoed became a prison loner. In most institutions, inmates bond by sharing the stories of their crimes and how they got caught, but not Kofoed. He went so far as to write the Nebraska parole board, insisting he was not interested in seeking early release from custody if it meant an acknowledgment of guilt. "I was not interested in seeking parole for the simple reason that I did not commit the crime for which I was convicted," Kofoed stated. "Therefore, I have nothing to be remorseful for. . . ."

In prison, Kofoed ate his meals, jogged, and pumped iron in solitude. He skipped out on the prison's regularly scheduled activities, which included ping-pong tournaments. Other inmates did not associate with Kofoed because of the high-profile nature of his previous career in law enforcement. "Because I was law enforcement, it's like I am not one of them," Kofoed said at the time.

But he was one of them.

. . .

"One thing I keep forgetting is that I'm a convict," Kofoed realized. "We are all in here for something. I got convicted, and I am doing time." During his prison term, he began keeping a journal, entitled "Shades of Gray." He wrote the dictionary definition of "confession" as "an acknowledgment of guilt." Kofoed then wrote, "Why acknowledge guilt to another human being?" He left his answer blank.

By the middle of 2011, Kofoed had a shot at redemption. The prison moved him into a less restrictive work-release program, back in his hometown of Omaha. He became a tire mechanic at the Midwest Tire & Auto—just a few blocks from the downtown police headquarters where he began his career in police forensics some twenty years earlier.[4] On most days, Kofoed left the tire shop with sore knees, cuts, and plenty of scrapes, but few complaints. Coworkers gave him respect and the benefit of the doubt. He enjoyed the excruciating physical labor and mostly kept a low profile. When he wasn't changing tires, Kofoed lived mostly under strict house arrest. He shared an apartment with his elderly mother and had to check in every day with corrections officials from the landline phone at his apartment. He maintained slim hope that his evidence-tampering conviction would be overturned by the courts. Finally, on May 4, 2012, the Nebraska Supreme Court issued a scathing rebuke of Kofoed's appeal. His alternative blood theories of cross-contamination arose only in hindsight, when he needed to explain later evidence showing Greg Fester and Jessica Reid were the killers. "In short, he was tangled in his own web of deceit," wrote Justice William M. Connolly in the state supreme court's thirty-five-page legal opinion rejecting Kofoed's appeal. "Throughout this prosecution, Kofoed's defense strategy has been an attempt to deflect evidence of his guilt by floating theories of a mystery perpetrator or careless investigators," the justices wrote. "At the rule 404 hearing [regarding the Ivan Henk murder case], at trial, and on appeal, he has claimed that someone else could have tampered with the evidence to frame him. The irony of his defense is rich, and his theories plentiful. But there is nothing more horrible than the murder of a beautiful theory by a brutal gang of facts."[5]

Kofoed took the defeat of his appeal in stride.

Within a few short weeks, he reached his mandatory release date and couldn't wait to start granting more news media interviews with Nebraska's television stations. "When he was released from jail and ending his house arrest, he did an interview with NET," recalled Nebraska Educational Telecommunications (NET) senior producer Bill Kelly in a June 2013 interview with me. NET is Nebraska's PBS and NPR stations. "David told me that I was his only interview. This was the last time he was talking to any Omaha media. Two days later, he showed up on another Omaha television station. For whatever reason, he needed to talk about his circumstances."[6]

Prior to Kofoed's disgraceful exit from Nebraska's CSI arena, journalists benefited enormously from his open-door policy. Most longtime journalists regarded Kofoed as one of their most dependable sources. He was notorious for letting journalists visit the Sheriff's Office to show them grisly crime scene photos from active murder investigations, including unsolved crimes in which the killer hadn't been caught. In fact, shortly before Kofoed's troubles in 2008, he let me visit his office to discuss a recent unsolved murder of an eleven-year-old boy and his family's housekeeper in one of Omaha's most historic neighborhoods. He had no hesitation showing me about a dozen color photos of the gruesome crime scene. Some of those crime scene photos showed cutlery knives, taken from the kitchen, buried deep inside each of the murdered victims' necks. One was killed in the dining room. The other died in a narrow first-floor hallway. The killer caught both victims by surprise in the middle of a beautiful weekday afternoon in March 2008.

Kofoed knew it was important to forge a strong relationship with the press.

"He was a quote machine," Kelly observed. "He was a nice man to work with, always. He was a reporter's best friend and it served both he and the Douglas County Sheriff's Office well for a long time. One of the great ironies of the case is that it's the skills of his own forensics team that ends up tripping him up" by ultimately chasing down the origin of the gold ring discovered on Sharmon Stock's kitchen floor, later tracing it back to Fester and Reid, the true perpetrators.

. . .

After spending two years under the thumb of Nebraska's prison system, Kofoed and his elderly mother moved to Charlotte, North Carolina, during the late summer months of 2012. In Charlotte, Dave reunited with his youngest brother, Bart, the former National Basketball Association player turned foot soldier for Jesus Christ. Longtime serious sports fans will remember Bart Kofoed because he defied unbelievable odds by playing alongside future NBA Hall of Famers Karl Malone and John Stockton of the Utah Jazz for a few noteworthy seasons. A gritty and tenacious defender, Bart Kofoed guarded NBA stars Magic Johnson and Clyde "the Glide" Drexler during the NBA playoffs. But Bart's off-the-court troubles marred his NBA career. During a party in January 1989, he punched out Jazz teammate Bobby Hansen, breaking Hansen's cheekbone. The brawl made instant sports headlines, prompting the Jazz to waive Bart Kofoed. His journeyman career ended in 1992 after stints with the Golden State Warriors, Seattle Supersonics, and Boston Celtics. Years after basketball, Bart rejected the corporate culture and found Christ. He devoted his life to the Gospel of Matthew.[7] He joined forces with former NBA standouts David Thompson and Bobby Jones to form the 2XSalt Ministry, headquartered in Charlotte, North Carolina. This is also where Dave Kofoed went to escape Omaha.

He found his fresh start, in his mid-fifties, working at 2XSalt Ministry. Dave Kofoed mentored inner-city kids from broken homes about team building and sports fundamentals.[8] He helped Latino children play soccer. At night, he drove through some of Charlotte's most crime-infested areas to make sure the center's inner-city youth made it back home safely.

More than 1,150 miles from Omaha, Dave Kofoed was back out in society making a difference—again.

. . .

Back in Nebraska, David Kofoed's name remains a sore subject for the law enforcement and legal community. His reputation is shot. He's an outcast, sometimes mockingly referred to as Dubious Dave.

Generally speaking, most of Nebraska's police officers and evidence technicians play by the rules and don't plant evidence. These are the law enforcement types who prefer not to talk about Dave Kofoed because he epitomized all the public's worst nightmares and fears about corrupt police professionals. Kofoed proved that police corruption isn't just a big-city problem in Chicago, New York, or Los Angeles. His egregious police misconduct occurred smack-dab in the middle of America's heartland, where most people blindly trust in their police and prosecutors, presuming that all cops and CSIs are good and all people arrested for murder and crimes must certainly be guilty, if the cops are the ones saying so.

Prior to the Kofoed case, Nebraska had not encountered any CSI scandal involving forensic fraud. "It's kind of a grim satisfaction that Kofoed was exposed, and that he is not hurting anybody else," remarked former Cass County Special Prosecutor Clarence Mock when I interviewed him in June 2013. Mock added, "His case, in a way, helped cleanse the system. His conviction served as a reminder to other cops that the consequences of fabricating evidence are severe."[9]

One of the greatest lessons from the Kofoed tragedy is the need for police departments to do better background screening. His job application for a civilian position at the Omaha Police Department never raised any red flags within the upper police command staff even though issues of bad character and questionable integrity were responsible for Kofoed leaving the Marines, Mock pointed out. (Nepotism also played a factor in Kofoed's hiring. His father had been a high-ranking sergeant at the Omaha Police Department.) "Law enforcement has to be very scrupulous in screening for character traits of people who are being employed in these very vital positions," Mock told me.

"Obviously, that was not done in Kofoed's case, going well back to his career with the Omaha Police Department."

These days, dark clouds hover over practically every high-profile murder case Kofoed helped solve. In 2012, the Nebraska Supreme Court issued separate legal opinions concluding that Kofoed may have planted blood of 2003 murder victim Brendan Gonzalez and 2006 murder victim Jessica O'Grady to secure the convictions of their presumed killers. Kofoed led the O'Grady murder investigation a mere two weeks after he had just planted Wayne

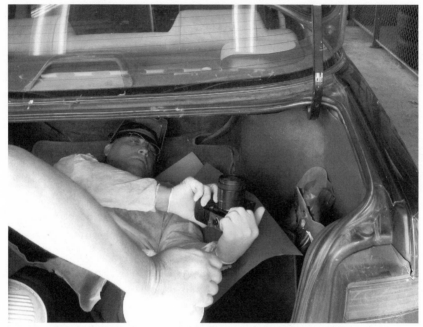

Douglas County CSI chief Dave Kofoed, shown here in May of 2006, purports to find several large bloodstains inside of the trunk of Omaha murder suspect Christopher Edwards's car. Kofoed's "blood find" occurred one day after two of Kofoed's top CSIs had conducted an extensive search of the same car and found none of Jessica O'Grady's blood. Kofoed is suspected of planting the blood, which was collected from the blood-soaked bedroom mattress of Edwards just days earlier. Edwards was ultimately arrested, and he was convicted of O'Grady's murder by a jury. *(Author's collection)*

Stock's blood into Will Sampson's car at the Sheriff's impound lot facility. Jessica O'Grady's murder marked one of Omaha's most sensational cases of the last decade.[10] O'Grady was only nineteen years old when she vanished on her way to her boyfriend's house shortly before midnight on May 10, 2006. The attractive and easygoing college student planned to tell her boyfriend, Christopher Edwards, that she was pregnant. Nearly a week later, authorities found O'Grady's blood spatter rampant throughout Edwards's bedroom, including on the headboard, nightstand, clock radio, and ceiling above his bed. Her blood saturated the underside of Edwards's mattress. There was no doubt that Edwards was the culprit, but he refused to cooperate with investigators once they found the river of blood that had soaked into his bedroom mattress. At that point, Kofoed presumed that Edwards used his Honda Accord to haul away O'Grady's body, which was missing. On the afternoon of May 17, 2006, Douglas County CSI's CL Retelsdorf and Josh Connelly processed Edwards's car, but neither reported finding any blood, according to their official forensic reports. The very next morning Kofoed orchestrated a follow-up search. At 7:30 A.M. on May 18, 2006, Kofoed summoned veteran Douglas County CSI technician Bill Kaufhold to help Kofoed reprocess the car yet again. Kaufhold even went out of his way to mention in his official CSI forensic report how Kofoed specifically instructed him to carefully concentrate on Edwards's trunk. This second time, several large and easily visible bloodstains appeared on the trunk gasket and the underside of the trunk lid. With Kaufhold standing alongside his CSI supervisor, Kofoed crawled into the trunk to snap several photos of these large bloodstains that were allegedly somehow missed the previous day by Connelly and Retelsdorf, two of the county's sharpest and most competent forensic scientists.

The bloodstains from Edwards's trunk matched O'Grady's DNA.

Other strange clues also emerged out of the Douglas County crime lab to cement the presumed killer's fate. Initially, a set of hedge-trimming shears seized from Edwards's cluttered backseat were not submitted for DNA tests. Several days later, a tiny bloodstain surfaced on the handle of the garden shears. The blood spot matched O'Grady's DNA.

Additionally, Kofoed executed another search warrant upon Edwards's bedroom. The second raid was to recover a souvenir battle sword from a closet under the theory that this sword must be the presumed murder weapon used to hack up O'Grady. Although the sword was eventually recovered at the end of the night, the object mysteriously languished in the Douglas County crime lab under Kofoed's control for another ten days before it underwent preliminary tests. CSI Christine Gabig later testified that she recovered a tiny speck of O'Grady's DNA on the tip of the sword blade. Oddly, though, the black nylon sheath that held the sword tested negative for blood.

All told, the hedge shears, the souvenir battle sword, and the prominent bloodstains discovered within the trunk of Edwards's car damned him. He was arrested the following month, even though O'Grady's body was still missing. Kofoed's heroics made him the four-star witness for the prosecution at the Edwards murder jury trial in 2007. The jury in Omaha convicted Edwards of second-degree murder even though O'Grady's body had not been found.

Back in 2007, nobody suspected that Kofoed had fabricated the evidence used against Edwards.

Five years later, the Nebraska Supreme Court felt otherwise.

"Given Kofoed's history of fabricating evidence during the same time that he was involved in investigating O'Grady's murder, we conclude that Edwards' allegations are specific enough that we cannot assume that they are not without merit," the Nebraska Supreme Court ruled in 2012.

In a June 2013 interview I conducted with Bill Kelly, the prominent senior producer for NET, he also reflected on the evidence-planting scandal.

"It's impossible not to notice that cases called into question are all high-profile, showy homicides. That's just a fact," observed Kelly, who broke into journalism in the late 1970s.

When Kofoed ran the Douglas County lab, word of mouth spread about his amazing and uncanny success in identifying latent fingerprints off handguns. However, Kofoed had a couple of stipulations if he was going to check for latent fingerprints for an outside agency. First, he needed the suspect's name; second, he requested the suspect's fingerprint card before he inspected the weapon, court records reflect. Over time, Kofoed became so good at "finding" latent prints on various firearms that some Omaha cops simply chose to bypass their own agency's crime lab. They trusted Kofoed, presuming he was a master, not a pretender.

. . .

The fallout from Kofoed's evidence-planting scandal may take many more years to wind through Nebraska's criminal justice system. Astonishingly, the prospect of any meaningful independent audit probing Kofoed's casework appears unlikely. It fell beyond the scope of the Nebraska Supreme Court's jurisdiction to appoint an independent committee to investigate the work of Kofoed and others within the Douglas County CSI unit, the court's justices ruled in 2012. Theoretically, elected officials in Douglas County could appoint an independent blue-ribbon commission, impanel a grand jury, or hire an outside team of fact-finding forensic experts to conduct a full-scale audit of Kofoed's work. But that scenario has not occurred and probably never will. There remains a huge political disincentive for Douglas County Sheriff Tim Dunning, Douglas County Attorney Don Kleine, or elected members of the Douglas County Board to reopen the Dave Kofoed can of worms by revisiting his past cases in the hopes of finding other transgressions where he abused his power.

. . .

On March 31, 2014, U.S. District Judge Joseph F. Bataillon of Omaha ordered Kofoed to pay Matt Livers and Nick Sampson a total of $6.5 million in damages, costs, and lawyer fees. In his thirteen-page ruling, the judge pointed out that Kofoed had failed to appear for his scheduled jury trial back on October 22, 2013 The case "served an important public interest in vindicating the rights of the wrongly accused and exposing public corruption and malfeasance," Jude Bataillon stated.

Kofoed's conduct was "malicious and intentional, and there have been repeated instances of the conduct," the judge stated. "Moreover, Kofoed abused a position of responsibility and trust. It is difficult for the court to quantify the extent of Kofoed's culpability in terms of moral turpitude and breach of public trust. Kofoed was convicted of manufacturing evidence and falsifying a report. He has not answered or responded to the palintiff's allegations in the case, yet he continues to deny wrongdoing and assert his innocence to the press. Further, there is evidence that Kofoed planted blood evidence in another case as well."

Although the federal court's order against Kofoed made big headlines in Nebraska, Judge Bataillon's ruling is largely symbolic.

Kofoed insists that he is broke. He does not have the ability to pay the whopping $6.5 million judgement entered against him.

Dave Kofoed may be long gone from Omaha, yet his legend in Nebraska consists of a long list of nagging, unanswered questions. He has put a burden upon the state's criminal justice system and the state's taxpayers.

In Kofoed's situation, he never took money or bribes to fix various Nebraska murder cases. There is absolutely no evidence of that.

He just wanted to be the rock star of Nebraska's CSI world—lots of fame, adulation, and numerous press clippings to puff up his enormous ego.

He fooled a lot of people along the way, yet his tumble down the CSI mountain wasn't entirely his fault.

For that, Kofoed can thank Earl Schenck Jr. and Bill Lambert, the two foolish police investigators who somehow convinced themselves that Matt Livers and Nick Sampson killed the Stocks instead of letting the real evidence unravel the murder mystery, as they should have done at the beginning.

EPILOGUE

In October 2013, Matt Livers and Nick Sampson, the two Nebraska cousins who were wrongly accused of murdering Wayne and Sharmon Stock, reached a staggering $2.6 million out-of-court settlement to resolve their federal lawsuits.

As part of that total, Cass County agreed to pay Livers and Sampson about $1.5 million. The state of Nebraska agreed to pay them $975,000. Douglas County government paid another $125,000.

"I'll never forget what happened. I kind of want to forget about it and move forward, but it's scarred me for life," Livers told me in November 2013. Livers received a payout of $1.65 million: about $1 million from Cass County, $600,000 from the Nebraska State Patrol, and $50,000 from Douglas County.

Reflecting on the case, Locke Bowman, the civil attorney for Livers, noted that none of the key investigators from the Cass County Sheriff's Office and Nebraska State Patrol were properly trained to identify the warning signs of false confessions. "This is just a horrible, horrible example of how tunnel vision can absolutely ruin an investigation," Bowman told me in November 2013. "The problem is they committed to Matt Livers on April 18 [the day after the murders]. When the police are refusing to accept the repeated denials of guilt from someone who is mentally challenged, you're crying out for a mistake. . . . It's absolutely one of the worst confessions on record. Matt answers 'Right' to all of Investigator Schenck's questions because he has no idea what he's supposed to say. . . . When the DNA results were negative on Livers and Nick Sampson, they were already down the road and not turning back then." Bowman hopes the videotaped interrogation of his client's false confession to murdering the Stocks will someday become an important training tool at law enforcement academies and police departments across the country. "This video is an instructional gold mine that should be made use of," Bowman told me. "People should look at this and discuss what went wrong and what should be done differently."

Less than a year after double murder charges against him were dismissed, Matt Livers and his sweetheart, Sarah Schneider, got married and relocated to Cypress, Texas, which is near Houston. Matt's parents, Barbara and Dave, also live nearby.

Livers said that Bowman did a fantastic job on his case. "I almost feel like we've become family after six years of working on this," Livers told me in November 2013.

He said he's also grateful to his original public defenders, Julie Bear of Plattsmouth and co-counsel Susan M. Bazis, plus forensic psychiatrist Scott Bresler and Jerry Soucie, Nick Sampson's public defender, for helping prove his innocence as he awaited his jury trial.

Since returning to Texas in 2008, Livers worked as an oil and lube technician at a car dealership in Houston. Then for much of 2013, he drove a semitrailer across the country for Schneider National trucking. His deliveries took him to Florida, Ohio, North Carolina, and South Carolina. "You could say that it's something that I can mark off my bucket list," Livers told me. "But being a truck driver, it was just too hard to be away from [my wife] Sarah and [stepson] Brandon." Livers, who is now thirty-six, said he became a tire and lube technician in November 2013 at a Walmart store in the Houston suburb of Tomball.

However, the murders have changed the course of his life. Many of his relatives back in Nebraska refuse to have anything to do with him, Livers told me. He said that they won't accept that they were absolutely wrong when they fingered him as the Stocks' killer from the very beginning of the case. "Sarah and I still wonder why they can't let it go, more or less," Livers told me. "They won't give me the time of day. Being a Christian, if I want to get to heaven, I need to forgive and forget. I've forgiven them."

Livers advised that anyone who is approached by police for questioning in a murder case should first consult with a criminal defense attorney. "My thinking was I didn't need to hire a lawyer," Livers told me. "I was there [at the Cass County Sheriff's Office] to clear my name. Sarah and my dad advised me to do that, thinking I would only be gone for a couple of hours. My God, look how that turned out for Nick [Sampson] and for me. Eight-and-a-half months later, I finally got to go home. My advice? Get a lawyer!"

Matt Livers also wants people to know that teen-age killer Jessica Reid of Wisconsin deserves some recognition for continuing to insist that he and Nick Sampson had no involvement in the farmhouse murders.

"I just thank her for being truthful," Livers told me. "She basically saved my and Nick's life. If not for Jessica staying strong, who knows how things would have turned out? It's almost scary to think about it. We could've been behind walls."

Former co-defendant Nick Sampson is twenty-nine. He and Livers have drifted apart. His civil attorney, Maren Chaloupka, blames the lead investigators and Kofoed for causing those wounds. "They blew apart a close family relationship and their lives," Chaloupka told me in November 2013.

Nick Sampson's $965,000 settlement breaks down as follows: $515,000 from Cass County, $375,000 from the state of Nebraska, and $75,000 from Douglas County, which is where Kofoed managed the crime lab. "The settlement with Cass County is not just money," Chaloupka told me.

Her client's settlement stipulated that the Cass County Sheriff's Office must implement a training program for investigators to properly identify developmentally delayed or low-functioning individuals, such as Livers, during questioning. "For five years, they have to give us a compliance report," Chaloupka told me. "We told them upfront that such a policy was going to be a deal-breaker" in order to settle the federal lawsuit.

Chaloupka said the settlements for Livers and Sampson are the highest payouts that she's aware of in the state of Nebraska regarding a law enforcement misconduct case. "The $965,000 settlement [for Nick] is basically the same thing as saying, 'We screwed up and we have to make it right,'" she said. "It's such a bizarre and tremendously life-upsetting event that's not going to go away for Nick."

Since being exonerated, Nick has achieved a General Educational Development certificate. He married his longtime sweetheart, Lori Muskat, and they moved back to Nick's hometown of Murdock. When murder charges were initially dismissed, many residents of Murdock shunned him, clinging to their belief that he and Livers were somehow involved. "I wanted to show everyone that I'm not afraid to stick around. This is my home, and I just didn't feel that I was going to tuck my tail and run or get pushed out of town. I grew up there," Sampson told me in November 2013.

These days, Nick Sampson works as a union contract laborer. Most of his jobs are larger-scale commercial construction projects across the greater Omaha metro area. He said he helped build the new Google data center in Council Bluffs, Iowa. A longtime hunting enthusiast, Nick said he volunteers as a hunter's safety instructor at a gun club in western Cass County. "I've just kind of grown up, and I am living my life the way I've always wanted to," Nick told me.

Andy Stock continues to run the farm business. A couple of years ago, Andy tore down the murder house and rebuilt a magnificent new house on the property, where he now resides with his family.

Nathan Cox, the noble small-town prosecutor who belatedly released Matt Livers and Nick Sampson from custody rather than prosecuting two innocent men for a double murder they did not commit, continues to be the Cass County attorney in Plattsmouth, Nebraska. Cox deserves a lot of credit related to the Stock case for stopping the train before it went dangerously out of control, noted lawyer Jerry Soucie, the former public defender for Nick Sampson. Soucie told me that after the arrests of Fester and Reid in Wisconsin, the Cass County Sheriff's Office pressed Cox to convene a secret grand jury to bring additional criminal indictments against Will Sampson, Tom Todd, and Ryan Paulding in Texas and possibly the wives of Livers and Nick Sampson. Instead, Cox did not bow to the pressure from the frustrated investigators, who foolishly presumed that Livers and the Sampson brothers conspired to recruit the two Wisconsin teenagers to travel to Murdock to kill the Stocks.

Randall L. Rehmeier, the pleasant, level-headed, and honorable judge who sentenced Wisconsin teenagers Greg Fester and Jessica Reid to life in prison without parole in 2007 and who was then convinced that Kofoed had tampered with evidence three years later during the historic Nebraska bench trial, announced his retirement from the bench in 2013. Rehmeier had spent twenty-five years as a judge, the last twenty as district court judge split between the two historic cities of Plattsmouth and Nebraska City. Rehmeier will certainly be remembered as one of Nebraska's most highly respected jurists.

Soucie no longer works for the Nebraska Commission on Public Advocacy. Now in his mid-sixties and nearing retirement, Soucie works in private practice and handles federal court appointments as a public defender. He is also working vigorously with Omaha attorney Brian Munnelly to overturn the 2007 murder conviction of Christopher Edwards and win a new trial date because of the blood evidence probably fabricated by Kofoed. However, the fate of the Edwards's case remains unresolved.

Clarence Mock, the special prosecutor who destroyed Kofoed's career and put the crooked CSI director in prison, remains in private practice in Nebraska. Mock splits his duties between his law offices in Omaha and the tiny town of Oakland, an hour away. According to Mock, the Kofoed trial came together after the judge made the critical pretrial ruling to let Mock show that Kofoed also likely planted blood in the 2003 murder of four-year-old Brendan Gonzalez. During the trial, Kofoed looked physically stressed and fatigued as the incriminating testimony from various witnesses buried him. "Prosecutors really love a good circumstantial evidence case," Mock told me. "The beauty in the case against Dave Kofoed is that the facts started to surround the defendant. If you close all the doors, there is really nowhere for the defendant to go."

Julie Bear, the small-town Plattsmouth public defender responsible for securing Matt Livers's release from custody, continues to work for Cass County as a public defender. Susan M. Bazis, the cocounsel for Livers, is now a Douglas County judge in Omaha.

Dr. Scott A. Bresler, the forensic psychologist who helped secure Matt Livers's freedom after eight months in jail for a double murder that he did not commit, continues to serve on the faculty at the University of Cincinnati in Ohio. Bear and Bresler cowrote a noteworthy article that was published by the National Association of Criminal Defense Lawyers (NACDL) about the Murdock case, entitled "Overshadowing Innocence: Evaluating and Challenging the False Confession."

Earl "Duke" Schenck no longer works in law enforcement. His career spiraled downward because of his mishandling of the investigation of the Stock murders. In July 2010, he was arrested for driving under the influence and two other traffic misdemeanors in western Nebraska, prompting his immediate resignation from the Cass County Sheriff's Office. A native of Ogallala, Nebraska, Schenck was convicted of the drunk-driving offense. According to his LinkedIn profile, Schenck identifies himself as a musician, singer, and songwriter who performs in the greater Omaha area. He lists himself as an entertainer, a self-employed artist, writer, and musician.

Charlie O'Callaghan, the polygraph examiner who flunked Matt Livers on the lie-detector test and insisted that Livers was the killer, continues to serve as a high-ranking Nebraska State Patrol investigator.

Bill Lambert also remains as an investigator with the Nebraska State Patrol.

Sgt. Sandy Weyers left the Cass County Sheriff's Office, but she still works for the county as its emergency management office director.

Tim Dunning, who put Kofoed in charge of his county's crime lab and then made the embarrassing mistake of clearing Kofoed of planting evidence during an internal affairs probe, remains the Douglas County sheriff in Omaha. In 2011, Dunning hired Tracey Ray, formerly of North Carolina, to replace Kofoed as his new forensic services director. Dunning has severed all ties with

Kofoed. Dunning maintains that his agency has learned its lessons from the disastrous Kofoed corruption scandal.

Darnel Kush retired as an evidence technician from Douglas County in the summer of 2013 after more than twenty-five years as a county employee. She told me that many of her coworkers in the CSI unit seemed alienated from her because she was the whistle-blower who went to the FBI with her suspicions that Kofoed planted evidence. Kush said that several of her younger coworkers who looked up to Kofoed still have a hard time accepting the fact that Kofoed is crooked and manipulative. Shortly after retiring, Kush filed a formal complaint with the U.S. Equal Employment Opportunity Commission (EEOC) against her former employer, she told me in a December 2013 interview. Her complaint alleged age discrimination and retaliation. Kush alleged that she was being treated differently than other county employees because she was the whistle-blower against Kofoed. Around June 2013, Kush, who was fifty-six at the time, said her supervisors bypassed her for a promotion in the crime lab. This came after several years of being shunned at the Sheriff's Office because of the Kofoed fallout. Disgusted, Kush notified the county of her retirement days later and then registered her formal complaint with the EEOC. Her EEOC complaint against Douglas County seeks a full retirement pension from the county and about $300,000 in lost wages. The EEOC complaint is pending in Lincoln. In 2014, Kush started a new full-time job as a drug technician for the state of Nebraska in the juvenile probation system. Kush praised FBI Special Agent Gina Palokangas and the FBI branch in Omaha for their efforts in investigating Kofoed's evidence-planting schemes after Kush's other complaints against him fell on deaf ears at the Sheriff's Office. Contacting the FBI was her last resort, Kush said. Finally, she credits Nebraska State Patrol Investigator Bill Lambert for helping to facilitate that interview through his network of contacts at the FBI.

Ivan Henk, the admitted child killer of Brendan Gonzalez, has not had any success in overturning his first-degree murder conviction. At some point, a district court judge will ultimately decide whether Kofoed's role in fabricating blood evidence against Henk warrants the dismissal of the admitted child killer's guilty plea. For now, Henk continues to serve his life sentence at the Tecumseh State Correction Institution in southeastern Nebraska. Brendan's remains have never been found.

Like Henk, convicted killer Christopher Edwards continues to serve his prison sentence at the maximum-security penitentiary in Tecumseh. Edwards, now twenty-seven, has an active appeal in front of the same Douglas

County District judge who sentenced Edwards to one hundred years to life for O'Grady's homicide. Unless his conviction is overturned, Edwards will be eligible for parole in 2056, when he is about seventy. O'Grady's body has also never been found.

Will Sampson, the owner of the car in which Kofoed claimed to have found Wayne Stock's blood, continues to live in Lincoln with his wife, Alynn. Incidentally, Will never drove the Ford Contour after Judge Rehmeier ordered Cass County Sheriff's officials to return the impounded car to Will a full year after the Stock slayings. Will noted that the car would not start and was in bad shape, so he sold it for a few hundred dollars and got a different vehicle.

Brian Wraxall, the chief forensic serologist from California who testified that it was scientifically impossible for Kofoed to produce a perfect DNA sample of murder victim Brendan Gonzalez's blood from the bottom of a dumpster five months after Henk supposedly dumped his son's body in the trash bin, died in 2012 at age sixty-eight after an illness.

Despite overseeing the botched investigation of the Wayne and Sharmon Stock murders, Cass County Sheriff Bill Brueggemann continues to hold elected office. Brueggemann has served as the sheriff since 1991.

Steve Lefler, the colorful criminal defense lawyer for Kofoed, is now semiretired and no longer practices law in Nebraska. Lefler has moved to New York, but occasionally commutes back to Omaha to visit.

Forensic scientists CL Retelsdorf and Christine Gabig, two of Kofoed's closest allies, both remain with the Douglas County CSI unit.

Lt. Jim Rohr retired as a detective from the Dodge County Sheriff's Department in Juneau, Wisconsin, after about twenty-five years of service. Today, Rohr is the police chief of Fox Lake, a small community of fifteen hundred people in central Wisconsin. Rohr received letters of commendation from his employer, Dodge County, and the Cass County Attorney's Office in Nebraska for his excellent detective work on the case that led to the arrests of Wisconsin teenagers Fester and Reid.

Murderer Greg Fester, now twenty-six, continues to serve his life prison sentence with no chance of parole at the Lincoln Correction Center, which is a maximum-security state penitentiary in Nebraska. In May 2013, Cass County District Judge Randall Rehmeier rejected Fester's post-conviction appeal. Fester claimed he was not of sound mind and on medication when he pleaded guilty to killing the Stocks in early 2007. Another Fester appeal is pending before the Nebraska Court of Appeals, but it probably won't succeed.

Jessica Reid, now twenty-four, continues to serve her life prison sentence with no chance of parole at Nebraska's only women's prison, which is in York. The women's prison houses minimum-, medium-, and maximum-security-level inmates.

Fester and Reid will probably live out the rest of their lives behind the walls of Nebraska's prison institutions. Their chances of winning a sentence commutation or parole are very slim.

They unsuccessfully appealed their sentences to the Nebraska Supreme Court on grounds that their back-to-back life prison terms for murdering Wayne and Sharmon Stock were excessive. "Contrary to Reid's arguments on appeal, the record shows that in police interviews, Reid specifically stated that she knew she had shot Wayne Stock directly above his right eye with the .410-caliber shotgun, and that she believed she had killed him before Fester shot him," the Nebraska Supreme Court stated.

Reid's diary was the most compelling evidence of her culpability and callousness, the justices noted.

Even now, people across Nebraska struggle to make sense of the awful and senseless tragedy that has defined rural Murdock. What made two teenage ghouls from Wisconsin massacre Wayne and Sharmon Stock after the pleasant, easygoing Christian couple drifted off to sleep?

The best explanation for the ruthless, cold-blooded killings came out of Fester's mouth at his presentence investigation interview in March 2007.

Commenting on the motive for the murders in rural Nebraska, Fester admitted that he and Reid "really didn't need any money. We were just there for the thrill, I guess."

Finally, one nagging issue has never been cleared up: the identity of that mystery motorist who had parked his car at the rural cemetery down the road from the Stock farmhouse on the night of their murders. The driver perhaps was a mischievous youth who went there to park with his girlfriend. He might have parked at the cemetery to indulge in marijuana or underage drinking. An even stronger scenario is that the young man parked near the cemetery because he was stealing gas. There were reports of gasoline thefts on some of the properties west of the Stock farm; one farmer heard his dog barking loudly around 3:30 A.M. At any rate, the mystery motorist's presence at the Callahan Cemetery was entirely coincidental and unrelated to the Stock murders. The newspaper carriers noticed the suspicious tan car around 4 A.M.—Fester and Reid committed the murders between 10:30 P.M. and midnight.

NOTES

1. Easter Massacres

1. Cass County Sheriff's Office investigative supplemental report CS06002033, prepared by Investigator Earl Schenck, pp. 264–66; Nebraska State Patrol Case File A2006–11055, interview of Cassondra Alexander, prepared by Investigator Chris Kober, pp. 455–56; interview of Steve Stock, Cass County Sheriff's Office investigative reports, prepared by Lt. Larry Burke, pp. 269–70.
2. The 2006 and 2007 interviews of Barbara Livers, sister of murder victim Wayne Stock, probate court files kept at Cass County Courthouse in Plattsmouth, Nebraska.
3. Nebraska State Patrol interview of Gregory D. Fester II, June 5, 2006, prepared by NSP Investigator William Lambert, pp. 731–36.
4. Dodge County (Wisconsin) Sheriff's Department report 06–4541, supplement no. 0017, interview of Jessica Reid, prepared by Det. James Rohr, p. 1232.
5. www.stockhay.com
6. Andy Stock's victim impact statement for court prior to Reid and Fester's sentencings, March 2007.
7. Discovery of Wayne and Sharmon Stock's bodies in their farmhouse on April 17, 2006: Cass County Sheriff's Office incident narrative from Deputy Virgil Poggemeyer, incident reports, pp. 7–9.

2. Legend

1. Biographical information about Douglas County Sheriff's CSI chief David Kofoed: 2008 discussions with me; Nathan Odgaard, "Lawman: Perfectionism Helps," *Omaha World-Herald,* November 20, 2000, which quotes Kofoed and Mike Stone, the former Omaha Police Department crime lab manager.
2. Self-promotion and marketing of CSI unit: Forensic Investigation: From Crime Scene to Courtroom, August 21–22, 2008, Crowne Plaza, Omaha Old Mill. Promotional marketing brochure distributed by the Douglas County Sheriff's Office, 3601 N. 156th Street, Omaha, Nebraska 68116.

3. Suspect

1. Douglas County CSI Don Veys describing the bloody carnage at the Stocks' farmhouse: Investigation Discovery cable-television true-crime series *In Cold Blood,*

the "Wayne and Sharmon Stock Case," aired November 2011.

2. David Kofoed recalling the Murdock crime scene with *Dateline NBC* host Keith Morrison: *Dateline NBC*'s two-hour special on the Murdock case, "In the Dead of Night," aired October 2010.

3. Veys's interview on Investigation Discovery's series, *In Cold Blood*, November 2011.

4. Veys's testimony, *State of Nebraska v. Kofoed*, pp. 1026–1141.

5. Veys's interview on Investigation Discovery.

6. Veys's interview on Investigation Discovery.

7. Cass County Sheriff's Sgt. Sandy Weyers's familiarity with the family of murder victim Sharmon Stock: Federal lawsuit transcripts filed in the 2007 civil rights suit brought by Nick Sampson.

8. Quotes from Kirk Drake, brother of murder victim Sharmon Stock: Investigation Discovery's *In Cold Blood* series, the "Wayne and Sharmon Stock Case."

9. Kirk Drake's interview on Investigation Discovery.

10. Background information on Wayne and Sharmon Stock's stature in the Murdock community: *Omaha World-Herald* articles, 2006–7, *Dateline NBC*'s 2010 special, "In the Dead of Night."

11. Quote from Tammy Vance, daughter of murder victims: *Dateline NBC*, "In the Dead of Night."

12. Kirk Drake's interview on Investigation Discovery.

13. Background on Cass County Investigator Earl Schenck leading the murder investigation: Sergeant Weyers for the federal civil rights lawsuits of Nick Sampson and Matt Livers.

14. Schenck family's prominence in Nebraska law enforcement: Transcripts of Kofoed's March 2010 trial; Paul Hammel, "Son of Former Sheriff Accepts Howard County's Top Law Job," *Omaha World-Herald*, September 16, 2005.

15. Schenck's documented disciplinary problems at Cass County Sheriff's Office: Court transcripts of depositions, *Sampson & Livers v. Cass County*, pp. 68–71.

16. Schenck's career as an aspiring country music singer: Social media page on www.myspace.com.

17. Transcripts of sworn deposition testimony in *Sampson v. Cass County*, p. 71.

18. The Drake family suspected Matt Livers as the killer: Cass County Sheriff's Office supplemental report, prepared by Earl Schenck, p. 47.

19. Quote attributed to Sharmon Stock in reference to her nephew Matt Livers's wish to inherit his grandmother's house: Supplemental investigative report, prepared by Sgt. Sandy Weyers, p. 21.

20. Background information on defendant Matt Livers's upbringing and mental limitations: University of Cincinnati forensic psychology assessment by Dr. Scott Bresler, November 28, 2006.

21. Information on Matt Livers's unemployment, travels to Texas preceding murders, and quotes expressing shock about the murders: Cass County Sheriff's supplemental investigative reports, prepared by Investigator Earl Schenck, pp. 47–51, 273–74.

22. Livers's quotes are also attributed to Schenck's investigative reports.

4. Mystery Car

1. Sighting of suspicious car near Callahan Cemetery on night of Stock murders: Investigative reports pertaining to interviews with Justin Hergenrader and Tamarra Jeffrey, prepared by Cass County Investigator Schenck, pp. 72–74, and prepared by Nebraska State Patrol Investigator Chris Kober, pp. 391–95.
2. Will Sampson's Ford Contour car, its delivery to an auto-detail shop on the morning of the Stock murders, Will's voluntary consent to police to search and seize his car, and multiple quotes from Will Sampson and Alynn High describing their reaction to the Stock murders and their cousin Matt Livers: Nebraska State Patrol investigative reports, submitted by Investigator Chris Kober, pp. 405–21, memo, p. 824.

5. No Luck

1. Background of Will Sampson's car search: Douglas County CSI reports for Tan Ford Contour Sedan Nebraska license plate PHM 252: pp. 1521–30, EVENT 060954: pp. 1585–91.
2. Interview of Matthew Hale at Lincoln Auto Detail: Investigative reports, prepared by Investigator Scott Haugaard, pp. 422–23.
3. Background information surrounding the origin of the Stocks' will: Cass County Sheriff's investigative report, prepared by Sergeant Weyers, p. 34.
4. Background on Livers's cooperation with investigators, driving to Omaha to furnish DNA, hair samples, and palm prints for elimination purposes: Douglas County Sheriff Property Report CCSO no. 06002033, pp. 1539–40.
5. Background on Matt Livers's employment and termination from Novartis Pharmaceutical, Lincoln, including quotes reflecting on the termination: Interview of security supervisor George Mackey by NSP Investigator William Lambert, pp. 468–71.
6. Background information on surveillance and contact of Nick Sampson during the funeral service wakes for Wayne and Sharmon Stock: Nebraska State Patrol investigative report, prepared by Investigator Chris Kober, pp. 397–98.
7. Quotes from Kirk Drake, brother of Sharmon Stock, reflecting on the community-wide funeral service: Investigation Discovery's *In Cold Blood* series, the "Wayne and Sharmon Stock case."
8. Biographical information on the lives of Wayne Stock, fifty-eight, Sharmon (Drake) Stock, fifty-five: *Lincoln Journal Star* obituaries, April 20, 2006.
9. Quotes from Murdock farmer Jim Stock, cousin of the victims, reflecting on tragedies: John Ferak, "Answers Sought in Couple's Slayings," *Omaha World-Herald,* April 18, 2006.
10. Details of the April 22, 2006, double-funeral service held at Elmwood-Murdock Community High School, including multiple quotes from the eulogy delivered by Rev. Jon Wacker: Elizabeth Ahlin, "Touching a Town in Life and Death," *Omaha World-Herald,* April 23, 2006.

6. Case Solved

1. Details surrounding the April 25–26 interrogation of Matt Livers by Cass County Investigator Earl Schenck and Nebraska State Patrol Investigator Bill Lambert,

including all quotes: Transcript of Matt Livers's interview, April 25–26, 2006, courtesy of Steven Drizin, Northwestern University, Center on Wrongful Convictions, pp. 1–362.

2. Police raid at Bulldogs Bar & Grill in downtown Murdock to arrest Nick Sampson in connection with the Stock murders, including quotes from Sampson reacting to his arrest: Cass County Sheriff's Office investigative supplemental report, prepared by Investigator Schenck, pp. 51–59; actions of Nebraska State Patrol Sergeant Doggett, pp. 373–74.

3. Background on .12-gauge shotgun recovered by Nebraska State Patrol at the residence of Nick Sampson and subsequent raids at the Lincoln apartment of Will Sampson and the Lincoln house of Matt Livers: Douglas County CSI response form SR no. B00709, pp. 1627–29; actions of Nebraska State Patrol Investigator E. Jones, pp. 378–81.

4. Quotes from Kirk Drake, reacting to news of arrests of Matt Livers and Nick Sampson: Investigation Discovery's *In Cold Blood* series: the "Wayne and Sharmon Stock Case."

5. Quotes from Cass County Sheriff Bill Brueggemann at press conference to announce the arrests of Matt Livers and Nick Sampson: Press release, "Arrests Made in Cass County Double Murder Case," April 25, 2006, distributed by Nebraska State Patrol.

7. Blood

1. Quotes from April 26, 2006, recantation made by murder defendant Livers to NSP polygraph examiner Charlie O'Callaghan: Written transcripts of Livers's videotape interview with O'Callaghan, courtesy of Jerry Soucie, public defender for Nick Sampson.

2. Background information on architecture, historical Cass County Courthouse: Archiplanet navigation, www.archiplanet.org.

3. Detailed coverage of the initial court appearances for codefendants Matt Livers and Nick Sampson, quotes from Murdock farmer Jim Stock reacting to the murder counts: John Ferak, "Heinous Crimes Bring Bail Denial," *Omaha World-Herald,* April 27, 2006.

4. Background on alibi furnished for Matt Livers by girlfriend Sarah Schneider: Nebraska State Patrol Investigator Scott Haugaard; contact with Schneider, pp. 442–43; alibi furnished by Livers's other roommate, Susan Gill, contact with Nebraska State Patrol Investigator Kober and Cass County Investigator Rex Southwick, pp. 340–42; polygraph with NSP Investigator Examiner Don Pounds, pp. 361–63.

5. Background on alibi of Nick Sampson given by roommate Lori Muskat to Cass County Sheriff's Office: Supplemental investigative report, prepared by Sergeant Weyers, pp. 279–82. Background on alibi furnished for Nick Sampson by other roommate, Ashley Hageman: Hageman interview with Nebraska State Patrol Investigator Joel Bergman, investigative reports, pp. 343–46.

6. Circumstances of Kofoed's reprocessing of Will Sampson's car: My discussion with Kofoed, October 2008; John Ferak, "Blood Doesn't Always Tell the Full Story," *Omaha World-Herald,* November 16, 2008.

7. April 27, 2006, call from NSP Investigator William Lambert to Douglas County CSI Chief Dave Kofoed to discuss Will Sampson's impounded car, quotes from

Lambert observing Kofoed's reaction to finding blood in the car: Bill of Exceptions, Case no. CR09–318, *State of NE v. David Kofoed,* Lambert testimony, direct 1924, cross 1948.

8. Odd Find

1. Discovery of engraved ring by Cass County Sheriff Lt. Larry "Ike" Burke: Cass County Sheriff supplement report, prepared by Sergeant Weyers, p. 36.
2. Background on wireless telephone search warrants obtained during Stock murder investigation by Nebraska State Patrol Investigator Charlie O'Callaghan: pp. 873–74.
3. Shotgun seized from Nick Sampson's bedroom definitively ruled out as murder weapon: Cass County Sheriff's investigative supplement report, prepared by Investigator Schenck, p. 93.

9. Ring of Truth

1. Tracking the origin of engraved ring: Nebraska State Patrol Investigative Report on Zastrow Ring, prepared by Lambert, pp. 896–904, Douglas County CSI forensic services reports, prepared by Gabig, pp. 905–10.
2. Quotes from Mary Martino, operations manager at A & A Jewelers in New York, discussing the Love Always, Cori & Ryan ring: *Dateline NBC,* "In the Dead of Night," October 2010.
3. Lambert contacts authorities in Wisconsin for their assistance in the Stock double murder case: Dodge County (Wisconsin) Sheriff's Department incident report 06–4541, prepared by Det. Mark Murphy, pp. 1184–85; Stolen Dodge Truck Report, pp. 748–52.
4. Detective Murphy interviews Cori Zastrow and her mother in Wisconsin: Dodge County (Wisconsin) Sheriff's Department incident report 06–4541, prepared by Det. Mark Murphy, pp. 911–12, 1187–90.
5. Background on the Easter Sunday 2006 theft of Ryan Krenz's truck in Wisconsin: Dodge County Sheriff Department's incident report 06–3674, prepared by Deputy Greg Weihert, pp. 1171–72.
6. Recovery of Ryan Krenz's stolen truck on April 18, 2006, in Opelousas, Louisiana: Parish of St. Landry Offense Report File no. 2006041138, complainant, Deputy J. Godchaux, pp. 753–56.
7. Incident report from Beaver Dam, Wisconsin, woman who saw two suspicious teenagers wandering near Krenz farm: Dodge County Sheriff Department, incident report 06–3674, pp. 1173–74.

10. Leopold and Loeb

1. Quotes from late Horicon Police Chief Doug Glamann discussing Fester's train-wrecked life: John Ferak, "Wisconsin Teens Took Same Turn for Worse," *Omaha World-Herald,* March 18, 2007.
2. Background on criminal histories, extensive drug abuse, and troubled lives of Gregory Fester and Jessica Reid: Arrest reports, criminal histories obtained from the Horicon Police Department, Beaver Dam Police Department, Dodge County (Wisconsin) Sheriff's Department, courtroom testimony 2006–07 in Cass County, Nebraska.

3. Quotes from Marge Mortensen, grandmother of killer Jessica Reid: John Ferak, "Wisconsin Teens Took Same Turn for Worse," *Omaha World-Herald,* March 18, 2007.

4. Information about Fester and Reid's escapades in cemeteries, break-ins at abandoned Wisconsin properties, and vandalism of a stolen van doused with gasoline: Horicon Police Department incident reports, filed by Off. Jason Roy, pp. 1366, 1378.

5. Quotes from Fester and Reid regarding their broad-daylight April 11, 2006, theft of Ned Thompson's truck in downtown Horicon: Affidavit for Search Warrant, submitted by Dodge County Det. James Rohr, pp. 257–63.

6. Details of Fester and Reid's crime spree across Wisconsin to Louisiana, bus fare back to Midwest, quotes from Reid denying involvement in the Krenz truck theft: Supplement to report no. 06–4541, prepared by Det. James Rohr, pp. 1192–95.

7. Quotes from Anthony "A. J." Wilson alerting Horicon Off. Jason Roy where to arrest Fester, details of the .410-gauge shotgun slug found in Fester's coat pocket, quotes from Fester lamenting his arrest: Supplement to report no. 06–4541, prepared by Det. James Rohr, pp. 1375–80.

8. Quotes from Reid confessing to the theft of Krenz's truck, admitting involvement in the burglaries of rural houses outside Wisconsin, confiding in another inmate that her boyfriend killed someone in a faraway state: Dodge County Sheriff Department's incident report, prepared by Det. James Rohr, pp. 1192–93.

9. Quotes from Dodge County police broadcast to several neighboring states regarding possible rural homicide case: Dodge County Sheriff Department's incident report, prepared by Det. James Rohr, p. 1180.

10. Quotes from Detective Rohr obtaining DNA samples from jail inmates Fester and Reid to compare with Nebraska murder clues: Dodge County Sheriff Department's incident report, prepared by Det. James Rohr, p. 1197.

11. DNA tests link Fester and Reid to Murdock murders, yet exclude codefendants Livers and Nick Sampson as contributors: University of Nebraska Medical Center DNA report, pp. 1458–68.

11. Wisconsin

1. Fester tells Nebraska investigators Schenck and Lambert that he purportedly met a person named Thomas from Nebraska at a drug party, confirms that he and Reid burglarized the Stock house and acted alone: June 5 interview of Gregory Fester, prepared by Lambert, pp. 731–36.

2. Quotes from Reid's interrogation in Horicon, Wisconsin, on June 5, 2006, with investigators Lambert, Schenck, and Detective Rohr: Transcripts done for Cass County Attorney, defense attorneys, pp. 1–105.

12. Diary

1. Details of shotgun shell souvenir saved by Fester and Reid from Nebraska murders, quotes from letter from Reid to Fester, and quotes from diary kept by Reid boasting of the murders: June 6, 2006, Dodge County search warrant on A. J. Wilson's house in Horicon: Dodge County Sheriff Department's investigative supplement reports, prepared by Detective Rohr, pp. 1206–9; Dodge County search warrant prepared by Rohr to obtain Fester's Trac phone from Reid's bedroom at Wilson's place, pp. 1288–95.

2. Excerpts from Reid's diary admitting she killed Wayne Stock and loved it, more quotes from her interrogation with Rohr, Schenck, and Lambert: Jessica Reid interrogation, June 7, 2006, Horicon Police Department, transcripts: pp. 1–25; Reid admits that she and Fester alone killed the Stocks, pp. 110–21.
3. Quotes from Fester's second interrogation with Nebraska cops, phony account of murder conspiracy plot, confession to killing Wayne Stock: Gregory Fester II interrogation, Dodge County Sheriff's Department, Juneau, Wisconsin, June 7, 2006, interrogation transcripts, pp. 20–37.

13. Conspiracy

1. Quotes announcing the arrests of Fester and Reid are from a press release issued June 9, 2006, by the Cass County Attorney's Office.
2. Documents indicating Reid identified Nick Sampson and another unidentified individual from Nebraska as coconspirators in the Stock murders: Affidavit for arrest warrant, State of Nebraska, County of Cass, June 6, 2006, affiant Investigator Earl D. Schenck Jr.
3. Application and Affidavit for Issuance of a Search Warrant, County Court of Cass County, Nebraska, June 8, 2006, submitted by Cass County Sheriff's Investigator Matthew Watson.
4. Background information on Tom Todd, information surrounding his polygraph test with NSP Investigator Charlie O'Callaghan, exact questions and answers, direct quotes during Todd's follow-up interrogation with Cass County Sgt. Sandy Weyers and NSP Investigator Bill Lambert: Cass County supplement report, prepared by Sergeant Weyers, pp. 241–42, NSP investigative reports submitted by O'Callaghan to Investigator Lambert, pp. 564–81.
5. Background information on Fred Wilson's interview and polygraph test with O'Callaghan: NSP reports from O'Callaghan, pp. 600–603.
6. Information surrounding Reid's admission that the .12-gauge shotgun used in the killings came from the Beaver Dam farm of Ryan Krenz, interviews with Fester's friends that proved his story about having a friend in Nebraska named Thomas was totally bogus: Dodge County (Wisconsin) Sheriff's Department incident report 06–4541, supplement no. 11, prepared by Detective Rohr, pp. 1216–21.
7. Quotes from press statement issued by Public Defender Jerry Soucie denying his client Nick Sampson ever met Fester and Reid: June 19, 2006, Statement Re: *State v. Nicholas Sampson,* Cass County District Court Case no. CR06–55.
8. Background information concerning Easter Sunday 2006 burglary and vandalism at Gary Hines's farm in rural Iowa: Investigative report on Guthrie Center, Iowa, burglary, Nebraska State Patrol, prepared by Investigator Lambert, pp. 834–65.

14. Ransom Theory

1. Background on Ryan Paulding, close friend of Matt Livers: October 2006 interviews with Soucie, plus Mansfield, Texas, Police Department Polygraph Examination Report, pp. 1148–66.
2. Direct questions and responses from Paulding's two-day July 2006 interrogation in Texas with Cass County Sergeant Weyers and NSP Investigator O'Callaghan: Videotapes of actual interviews and polygraph examinations courtesy of Locke

Bowman, Chicago attorney for Livers in his federal civil rights lawsuit against Nebraska police.
3. Excerpts from multiple jailhouse letters that murder defendant Matt Livers sent to girlfriend Sarah Schneider: Letters provided to me by Livers's parents, David and Barbara Livers, in late 2006. Information from Lori Muskat's conversations at the Cass County jail with Nick Sampson: Cass County Sheriff's supplemental reports, Nick Sampson's jail visits: pp. 218–40.

15. Tipster

1. Information on Kirby Drake's alleged sighting of Wisconsin killer Gregory Fester at the Bulldogs Bar & Grill in Murdock, Nebraska: Cass County Sheriff's Office Supplement Report CS000203, p. 100, prepared by Weyers.
2. Questions and answers from Drake's polygraph exam: Nebraska State Patrol reports, prepared by NSP polygraph examiner Charlie O'Callaghan, pp. 614–19.
3. Subsequent denials from bar patrons refuting Drake's story: Cass County supplemental report, prepared by Sergeant Weyers, pp. 100–104.
4. Quotes from Cass County Attorney Nathan Cox announcing his dismissal of murder charges against Nick Sampson on October 6, 2006: Prepared remarks given to press by Prosecutor Cox.
5. Numerous quotes from Public Defender Soucie criticizing Nebraska law enforcement for wrongly charging client Nick Sampson with the Stock murders: Press release: *State v. Nicholas Sampson,* distributed to press at 10:30 A.M., October 6, 2006, outside the Cass County Courthouse.
6. Comments from former defendant Nick Sampson to journalists proclaiming his innocence and criticizing the Cass County Sheriff's Office for arresting him in the Stock murders: John Ferak, "Freed Man Says Probe Botched," *Omaha World-Herald,* October 7, 2006.

16. Freedom

1. Details about Matt Livers's upbringing and troubles adjusting in school, work history, family relocations: Forensic Psychology Assessment, *State of Nebraska v. Matthew Livers,* executive summary, Scott A. Bresler, Ph.D., consulting forensic psychologist, University of Cincinnati Department of Psychiatry and Behavioral Neuroscience, November 28, 2006, pp. 1–10.
2. Quotes from Matt Livers's false confession mentioned in Dr. Bresler's analysis: Written and videotape transcripts of Livers's interrogation with Schenck and Lambert, conducted at Cass County Sheriff's Office, Plattsmouth, Nebraska, April 25–26, 2006.
3. Quotes from Dr. Bresler assessing Livers's diminished mental capacity: Bresler's Forensic Psychology Assessment, prepared for Cass County Public Defender Julie Bear.
4. Quotes between Cass County Attorney Nathan Cox and Cass County District Judge Randall Rehmeier: Written transcript of court hearing, Plattsmouth, Nebraska, December 5, 2006.
5. Quotes from Cass County prosecutor explaining his dismissal of murder charges against Livers: Cox's prepared statement for press, December 5, 2006.

6. Quotes from Julie Bear, Cass County public defender, reacting to the dropping of murder charges against Livers: Press release—Matthew Livers, distributed December 5, 2006.
7. Comments from Livers and his family reacting to his release after nearly eight months in custody: John Ferak, "Livers Savors Freedom," *Omaha World-Herald,* December 6, 2006.

17. Judgment

1. Quotes describing teenage killer Jessica Reid and her family upbringing: Letter from Father Val Peter, executive director emeritus, Father Flanagan's Boys' Home, to Cass County District Judge Randall L. Rehmeier, March 12, 2007.
2. Quotes from farmer Andy Stock, describing for the court how his parents' slayings terribly impacted his life: Andy Stock's March 2007 victim impact statement for court prior to Reid and Fester's sentencing.
3. Quotes describing Fester as a train wreck of a life, the horrible tragedy that ravaged the community of Murdock: Comments made by Prosecutor Nathan Cox during the March 19, 2007, sentencing hearing for Fester, published in the *Omaha World-Herald,* March 20, 2007, comments published in the Cassgram, a Cass County news service.
4. Comments from Fester and Reid apologizing for murdering the Stocks: Court transcripts of sentencing hearing before Cass County District Judge Randall Rehmeier, March 19, 2007.
5. Quotes from Jessica Reid telling a probation officer she deserved a life sentence, comments from Judge Randall Rehmeier at sentencing, quotes between Reid and Fester while committing the murders: Court documents contained within *State of Nebraska v. Reid,* no. S-07–303, and *State of Nebraska v. Fester II,* no. S-07–336.

18. Finder

1. Extensive background information on David Wayne Kofoed's career in the U.S. Marine Corps and key assignments: National Personnel Records Center, May 2009, public records request.
   Biographical information about David Kofoed, including his transformation of the Douglas County crime lab into a full-service regional crime lab: 2008 discussions with me; John Ferak, "Blood Doesn't Always Tell the Full Story," *Omaha World-Herald,* November 16, 2008.
2. Background on Kofoed's abrupt departure from the U.S. Marine Corps as a result of a gambling problem: Federal Bureau of Investigation report of interview of Jerry Osgood, Canby, Oregon, by FBI Special Agent Michael F. Kelleher Jr., Omaha, Nebraska, April 2009.
3. Background information on the late Richard Jerome Kofoed: December 2010 interviews with Dave Kofoed along with funeral program given to me by Dave Kofoed.
4. Background information on 2000 homicide of Amy Stahlecker, 2002 murder of Mindy Schrieber, and 2002 Norfolk, Nebraska, bank slayings of five individuals: "Crime Scene to Courtroom" seminars presented by Kofoed, August 21–22, 2008; John Ferak, "Kofoed Case Threatens to Reopen Painful Wounds," *Omaha World-Herald,* May 23, 2009; my numerous discussions with Kofoed, 2008–12.

5. Information concerning Kofoed's awards and accolades: Photocopies I made from trial transcripts of various Omaha murder trials that required Kofoed's testimony.

6. Kofoed makes his first announcement that the blood in Will's car may have gotten there through inadvertent transfer or accidental contamination: Two-page CSI summary sent to me concluding that Matt Livers and Nick Sampson had no role in the Stock killings, April 2007.

19. Deep Throat

1. Background information on Douglas County CSI Technician Darnell Kush's career and her problems with Kofoed: Numerous conversations she had with me, 2010, 2011, and 2012.

2. Details of Kush's secret meeting with NSP Investigator Bill Lambert on October 30, 2007, that first suggested Kofoed planted blood evidence: Investigative Notes, compiled by Lambert, pp. 3–6.

3. Quotes cited in federal lawsuit brought on behalf of Matt Livers by Chicago attorneys Locke Bowman and Steven Drizin: John Ferak, "Man Exonerated in Cass County Killings Files Suit," *Omaha World-Herald,* March 12, 2008.

20. Smell Test

1. Background information surrounding Douglas County CSI Clelland "CL" Retelsdorf's revelation that Kofoed found blood in Will's car on April 27, not May 8, is reflected in Retelsdorf's sworn testimony at Kofoed's criminal trial in Cass County, Nebraska, March 2010, pp. 1627–1734.

2. Quotes from Douglas County Sheriff Tim Dunning's terse conversation with FBI Special Agent in Charge John Kavanagh, who suggested that Dunning employed a crooked CSI chief: Dunning's sworn testimony at Kofoed's criminal trial in Cass County, Nebraska, pp. 2064–82.

3. Comments about the blood found in Will's car and about Kofoed from Douglas County CSIs Don Veys, Christine Gabig, Bill Kaufhold, Darnel Kush, Dave Kofoed, etc., are all contained within Internal Affairs reports generated by Douglas County Sheriff's officials Ed Leahy and Russell Torres, including Leahy's conclusion that Kofoed did not plant blood in the Murdock killings: Kofoed Documents Internal Affairs Reports, Polygraph Documents, submitted by Leahy, completed July 10, 2008, pp. 1–15; Kofoed's Internal Affairs report of his interview with Leahy and Torres, Internal Affairs no. 1947, June 30, 2008, pp. 1–28.

4. Kofoed's polygraph test questions: Douglas County Sheriff's Internal Affairs Report, submitted by Douglas County Sheriff's Deputy Brenda Wheeler, July 2, 2008, pp. 1–4.

5. Quotes from Sheriff Tim Dunning welcoming Kofoed's reinstatement after Internal Affairs probe exonerated Kofoed: Media release, Douglas County Sheriff, Nebraska, July 3, 2008.

21. Tarnished

1. Questions and answers of Kofoed's sworn testimony and questioning from U.S. Attorney Joseph Stecher and First Assistant U.S. District Attorney William

Mickle: In the United States District Court of Nebraska in the Matter of: A Grand Jury Investigation, Testimony of David Kofoed, March 19, 2009, pp. 1–142.

22. Blunder

1. Quotes from Jerry Soucie predicting a not-guilty verdict in Kofoed's upcoming federal trial: April 27, 2009, letter sent by Soucie to Cass County Attorney, Special Cass County Attorney, Nebraska Attorney General's Office, Douglas County Attorney, and the U.S. Attorney's Office, Re: *State v. Ivan Henk, State of Nebraska v. David Kofoed,* and *United States v. David Kofoed.*
2. Quotes from Kofoed answering questions from Defense Attorney Steve Lefler on September 8, 2009, during his federal jury trial in Omaha: John Ferak, "Kofoed Testifies in His Own Defense," *Omaha World-Herald,* September 9, 2009.
3. Quotes from Sheriff Tim Dunning criticizing the federal government's case against Kofoed: John Ferak, "Dunning Rips Case Against Kofoed," *Omaha World-Herald,* September 10, 2009.
4. Quotes from First Assistant U.S. Attorney William Mickle and Defense Attorney Steve Lefler: John Ferak, "Prosecutor's Closing Argument: Kofoed Lied," *Omaha World-Herald,* September 10, 2009.
5. Quotes from Kofoed, Lefler, and juror Amy Niemeier reacting to Kofoed's acquittal of four federal crimes: John Ferak, "Kofoed Juror Cites Weak Case," *Omaha World-Herald,* September 11, 2009.
6. Court Deposition Exhibit 350, p. 49, submitted by the plaintiff's attorney Maren Chaloupka in *Sampson v. Cass County.*

23. Underdog

1. Background on Kofoed's assistance in the January 6, 2003, murder of Plattsmouth child Brendan Gonzalez, details of Ivan Henk's dramatic confession to the killing in the Cass County District Courtroom on April 29, 2003, and Henk's direct quotes claiming he murdered his four-year-old son because Brendan was the anti-Christ: Bill of Exceptions, 404 pretrial evidence hearing in Cass County District Court, testimony from Plattsmouth Police Assist. Chief Brad Kreifel, actual pp. 107–13.
2. Questioning and sworn testimony at Kofoed's 404 evidence hearing from witness Kreifel, Brian Wraxall, executive director and chief forensic serologist at Serological Research Institute in California, and defendant Kofoed regarding his recovery of murder victim Brendan Gonzalez's blood in the January 6, 2003, murder committed by Ivan Henk: 404 Evidence Hearing, Cass County District Court March 2010; court transcripts of Kreifel, pp: 107–26; Wraxall, pp. 504–71; Kofoed, pp. 717–839.

24. Evidence

1. Background information on the restoration of the historic Cass County District Courtroom: John Ferak, "Cass County Courtroom Taking a Step Back to Its Former Glory," *Omaha World-Herald,* March 21, 2004.
2. Questioning and sworn testimony from prosecution witnesses Don Veys, Michelle

(Steele) Potter, William "Will" Sampson, Alynn (High) Sampson, and Matthew Hale: Bill of Exceptions, *State of Nebraska v. Defendant David W. Kofoed,* Case no. 09-CR-40 in the District Court of Cass County, Nebraska, proceedings before Honorable Randall L. Rehmeier, Plattsmouth, Nebraska, March 2010: Veys's testimony, pp. 1026–1141; Potter: pp. 1142–1200; Will Sampson: pp. 1380–1421; Alynn Sampson: pp. 1422–31; Matthew Hale: pp. 1432–41.

25. Phantom

1. Special Prosecutor Clarence Mock reflecting on his strategy heading into the bench trial against Kofoed: My interview with Mock, June 2013.
2. Questioning and sworn testimony from witnesses called for prosecution: Christine Gabig, Gina Palokangas, Clelland "CL" Retelsdorf, and Nathan Cox: Bill of Exceptions, *State of Nebraska v. Defendant David W. Kofoed,* Case no. 09-CR-40, March 2010: Gabig's testimony: pp. 1443–1626; Retelsdorf: pp. 1627–1734; Palokangas: pp. 1817–1923; Cox: pp. 1975–2010.

26. Verdict

1. Questioning and testimony from witnesses called for defendant: Kirby Drake, Tim Dunning, Charles Phillips, and Earl Schenck: Bill of Exceptions, *State of Nebraska v. Defendant David W. Kofoed,* Case no. 09-CR-40, March 2010: Drake: pp. 2038–44; Dunning: pp. 2064–82; Phillips: pp. 2083–96; Schenck: pp. 2097–2124.
2. Quotes from closing arguments made by Special Prosecutor Clarence Mock and Defense Attorney Steve Lefler: John Ferak, "Trial Ends Without Testimony from Defendant David Kofoed," *Omaha World-Herald,* March 20, 2010.
3. Background on Cass County District Judge Randall Rehmeier's verdict of Kofoed's guilt: *State of Nebraska, Appellee, v. David W. Kofoed, Appellant.* Filed May 4, 2012, no. S-10–613, pp. 767–801.
4. Kofoed, Mock, and Lefler's reaction to guilty verdict: John Ferak, "Guilty of Tampering," *Omaha World-Herald,* March 23, 2010.
5. Motion for mistrial petition submitted by Defense Attorney Steve Lefler with the Cass County District Court, April 2010.
6. Sworn testimony from Douglas County Sheriff's Patrol Deputy Charles Rehmeier and Douglas County CSI Technician Darnel Kush: Cass County District Court hearing, April 21, 2010: Bill of Exceptions, *State of Nebraska v. David Wayne Kofoed,* Case no. CR-0940: Rehmeier: pp. 2242–47; Kush: pp. 2248–72.
7. Quotes from Kofoed after the judge rejected his petition for a new trial: John Ferak, "Kofoed Is Denied New Trial," *Omaha World-Herald,* April 22, 2010. Kofoed's quotes when he turned to me and told me to go hell were not published in the *Omaha World-Herald* but were captured on video and aired by various Omaha television stations.
8. Numerous quotes and comments from Kofoed and Public Defender Jerry Soucie discussing Kofoed's past gambling problems, his departure from the Marine Corps, and evidence-planting conviction are posted on the Web site: www.clpex. com, Detail Chat Board: Complete Latent Print Examination, under the topic: "Lab Director Planting Evidence?" Kofoed's comments used for this book were

posted on the Internet by dkofoed on April 28, 2010. Soucie's comments used for the book were posted online as DefAtty on May 1, 2010.

9. I witnessed the exchange between retired Douglas County Sheriff's Capt. Dean Olson and retired CSI Technician Tony Grazziano in the Cass County District Courtroom on the afternoon of June 1, 2010, just minutes before Kofoed's criminal sentencing.

10. Numerous quotes offered at the Kofoed sentencing from Special Prosecutor Clarence Mock, Defense Attorney Steve Lefler, Kofoed, and Cass County District Judge Randall Rehmeier: Bill of Exceptions, sentencing transcripts of June 1, 2010, Cass County Courthouse, pp. 2321–33.

27. The Cop

1. Numerous quotes and details about Kofoed's prison life were included in: John Ferak, "Hard Reality for Kofoed: I'm a Convict," *Omaha World-Herald,* January 23, 2011.

2. Kofoed's quotes reflecting on his problems with other inmates came from my interviews with him in late 2010 and early 2011.

3. Kofoed provided me with numerous journal entries and letters describing his daily life as a former CSI chief turned prisoner.

4. Details about Kofoed's work-release job at an Omaha tire shop: My discussion with him, May 2012.

5. Nebraska Supreme Court ruling denying Kofoed's appeal of his conviction: *State v. Kofoed,* filed May 4, 2012, no. S-10–613, cite as 283 Neb. 767, pp. 767–801.

6. Reflections and quotes of Kofoed's constant yearning for attention and affirmation through the Omaha and Lincoln news media: My interview with Bill Kelly, senior producer, Nebraska Educational Telecommunications (NET), June 2013.

7. See www.2xsalt.com, the Web site pertaining to Bart Kofoed's sports ministry program.

8. Kofoed's August 2012 relocation to Charlotte, North Carolina: Kofoed's discussions with me in January 2013.

9. Quotes pertaining to the aftermath and legacy of Kofoed's conviction and prison term for planting blood in multiple Nebraska murder cases: My interview with Clarence Mock, special prosecutor, June 2013.

10. Details surrounding the May 2006 murder of Omaha college student Jessica O'Grady, allegations that Kofoed planted blood in the car of suspect Christopher Edwards to secure his arrest and conviction, and the Nebraska Supreme Court's decision not to impanel an independent committee to conduct an extensive review of Kofoed's misconduct while running the Douglas County crime lab: *State v. Edwards,* cite as 284 Neb. 382, pp. 383–413, ruling by the Nebraska Supreme Court, amended verified motion for post-conviction relief, DOC 170 no. 122, *State of Nebraska v. Christopher Edwards,* submitted by Attorney Brian S. Munnelly: John Ferak, and Paul Hammel, "Court Rejects Broad Review of Kofoed But Grants Hearing for Edwards," *Omaha World-Herald,* September 28, 2012.

INDEX

alibis: Livers's, 59, 131; Nick Sampson's, 59, 120; Todd's, 101–2; Will Sampson's, 183

ammunition, in Stock murders: not found in Sampson's car, 183–84; Reid saving shell from murder weapon, 89, *90;* retrieval of shells from crime scene, 15, *17;* retrieval of shells from Krenz family's gun, 102; shell casing proving two guns used, 124; use of deer slugs, 17, 179

arrests: of Livers and Sampson as police mistakes, 116, 130; Livers's, 38; Nick Sampson's, 51–52, 120; no evidence for Will Sampson's, 52; press conference to announce, 52–53, *53;* Reid and Fester's, 77–78, 98

attorneys, 82, 101, 215; public defenders, 58–59, 218. *See also specific individuals*

bail, denied for Livers and Sampson, 58

Baird, Roger, 104

Bazis, Susan, 129, 215, 218

Bear, Julie, 129–30, 218; on effects of false accusations against Livers, 130–31; as public defender for Livers, 58, 124, 215

Beaver Dam, Wisconsin, 69–72

Berkey, Trudy, 118

Bilek, Marty, 149

blood: found in Krenz truck, 97; Kofoed's pattern of finding in suspects' cars, 149–50, 210–11; in Livers's confession, 50, 59; prosecution not allowed to accuse Kofoed of planting, 165; Reid trying to clean up, 78, 84; on Reid's clothes, 86, 103; on ring found at crime scene, 84; Todd's clothes tested for, 101–2, 116; unsecured storage of, 181, 186; Will Sampson's residence searched for, 60

blood, found in Will Sampson's car, 35, 143–45, 195; cross-contamination

theory ridiculed, 195, 207; CSIs defending theory of accidental transfer, 155, 185; Kofoed denying planting, 156–57; Kofoed finding, 60–61, 153–54, 160–61; Kofoed "finding," 59–61, 143, 160–61; Kofoed "forgetting" to log, 156, 166–67; Kofoed misdating report on date of discovery of, 153–54, 164, 166–68; Kofoed's theory on source of, 146, 156, 161–62, 189, 190, 207; Kush's theory on source of, 146, 150; not noticed in Sampson's car, 182–83, 184; as only evidence against Nick Sampson, 114, 190; possibility of accidental transfer of, 155, 179–80, 189, 194; thought to be planted, 151–52. *See also* evidence tampering

blood spatter, at Stock murder scene, 5, 15

Bohaty, Mark, 64

Bowman, Locke, 151, 214–15

Bresler, Scott A., 215; Livers's psychological profile by, 125–28; on phenomenon of false confessions, 130, 218

Brueggemann, Bill, 21, *53,* 220

Bulldogs Bar & Grill: Kirby Drake's story of seeing Fester in, 117–18; Sampson working at, 31, 117–19, 123

Burke, Larry "Ike," 37, 62; Schenck put in charge of Stock murders by, 20, 22

car, Krenz's truck: stolen, 70–71, 76, 82–83; used as getaway vehicle, *99*

car, Will Sampson's: driven by no one else, 31, 33, 182–83; dropped off for detailing after murders, 30–31, 33, 36, 181–84; never driven again, 220; police focused on, 194; Reid denying knowledge of, 85; search for link to Livers, 29–30; search of, 33–34, 60, 187–88; searched for evidence, 60; suspected of

car, Will Sampson's (*cont.*)
being getaway vehicle, 30–31, 33, 50; suspiciousness of Kofoed reexamining, 153, 160, 181, 188; tests on, 34–35, *36,* 187–89. *See also* blood, found in Will Sampson's car

cars: Fester and Reid stealing, 74–75, 77–78, 80; Nick Sampson's and Livers's seized for testing, 52; report of one parked in cemetery near Stocks', 27–28

cars, getaway, 104; Krenz's truck as, *99;* in Livers's confession, 50; report of one speeding away from murder scene, 28–29, 195

cars, Kofoed finding blood in Edwards's, *210,* 210–11

Cass County Courthouse, 57, 178–79

Cass County Jail, Livers and Sampson in, 55, 103, 112–14

Cass County, settling Livers's and Sampson's lawsuits, 214, 216

Cass County Sheriff's Office, 9, 11; arrests of Livers and Sampson as mistake by, 116, 130; assumptions about Stocks' killer, 16–17; cleared of planting blood in Sampson's car, 154; conspiracy theory of, 99–100, 102, 106, 111–12, 114, 116–18, 122–23, 192, 195–96, 217; Cox and, 119, 217; evidence storage at, 186; incompetence of Stock murders investigation, 121–22, 151, 153, 181–82; Kofoed's CSIs and, 13, 17; lack of experience with homicide, 20; Livers's lawsuit against, 151; receiving tip about speeding car, 27–29; Sampson's disdain for, 123; Sampson's lawsuit against, 145, 216; Soucie's criticism of, 121–22; trying to link Will Sampson to Stock murders, 181–82; unwilling to give up on guilt of Livers and Sampson, 99, 103, 124, 132. *See also* Schenck, Earl D., Jr.

cemeteries: Fester and Reid's fascination with, 74; getaway car in, 27, 50

Chaloupka, Maren, 145, 216

civil rights: Kofoed charged with violation of, 163, 165–66; Livers and Sampson suing for violation of, 145, 151, 163, 194

clothes: blood on Reid's, 86, 103; no blood on Livers's, 59–60; Todd's tested for blood, 101–2, 116

confession, Fester's, 77–78, 81, 90

confession, Henk's, 170, 172–73

confession, Livers's, 48–51, 109, 160; coer-cive interrogation leading to, 126–29; Cox admitting falsity of, 130; diagram of Stock house to illustrate, 55–56; errors in, 124; Kofoed's discovery of blood corroborating, 171; lack of evidence supporting, 59; Lambert and Schenck grilling Reid about, 94, 96; Lambert and Schenck unwilling give up on, 80–82; motive for, 112, 127; as only evidence against Sampson, 120–21; police plan to get, 45–47; recanting, 56–57, 128–29; victims' families told of, 52

confession, Reid's, 78, 84, 221

confessions: false, 130, 214; Kofoed "discovering" blood evidence to corroborate, 171, 197, 200

Connelly, Josh, 210

Connolly, William M., 207

Cook, Richard K., 142, 213

Cox, Nathan, *119;* admitting falsity of Livers's confession, 129–30; on charges and possible sentences, 58; dropping charges against Livers, 129, 132; dropping charges against Nick Sampson, 119–20; on effects of Stock murders, 134–35; relying on blood found in Sampson's car to build case, 114, 190–91; resisting pressure to continue prosecution of Livers and Sampson, 132, 217; Schenck and, 21–22; on sentences for Reid and Fester, 133, 137; Soucie giving information to, 103–4; on source of blood in Sampson's car, 145, 152, 190

crime scene, processing of Stocks' home as, 9, *10,* 11

Dateline, documentary about Murdock case on, 165

Davis, Rhonda, 73, 77

death sentence: Livers threatened with, 46, 48; Reid threatened with, 84–86

DNA, 79, 100; contradictions to discovery in Gonzalez boy's blood, 173–75; found on marijuana pipe, 11, 65; found on ring, 65, 83; linking Fester and Reid to murder scene, 83, 124; linking Reid and Fester to murder scene, 79, 103; Livers giving sample of, 25, 38; not linking Livers or Sampson to crime scene, 65

Douglas County, settling Livers's and Sampson's lawsuits, 214, 216

Dodge County Sheriff's Office (Wisconsin), 69–71, 98–99

Douglas County crime lab: Dunning hiring Kofoed to rebuild, 141, 147–48, 200; good reputation of, 13, 159; internal affairs investigation of Kofoed in, 155, 193; Kofoed in charge of, 12–13, 200; Kofoed terminated by, 197; Kush filing complaint against, 219; no audit of Kofoed's other casework by, 212; not named in lawsuits, 145, 151; possibility of cross-contamination by blood and, 153, 179–80, 196; pressured by Cass County police, 59–60; role in Stock murders investigation, 38, 62, 97; support for Kofoed in, 155, 179–81, 185, 187; tests of Will Sampson's car by, 34–35; waiting for verdict on evidence tampering, 195–96

Drake family, 138; fingering Livers, 22–24, 127, 215; Livers and, 52, 56; prominence of, 19, 22

Drake, Kirby, 23, 117–19, 192–93

Drake, Kirk, 19–20, 23, 41

Drizin, Steven, 130, 151

drugs, 24, 101; Fester and Reid using, 72–76, 78, 83; Sampson brothers' use of, 25, 32, 45

Dunning, Tim, 13, 150; continuing as Douglas County Sheriff, 218–19; internal investigation of Kofoed under, 154–55, 158; Kofoed hired by, 141, 147; Kofoed terminated by, 197; on Kofoed's work, 143, 212; supporting Kofoed, 163, 167–68, 193–94

Edwards, Christopher: continued incarceration of, 217, 219–20; Kofoed finding blood evidence against, 210, 210–11

Elmwood, Nebraska, 37

evidence tampering, Kofoed's trial for: effects of scandal and, 209–13; importance of ruling on Kofoed's pattern of forensic misconduct on, 177, 217–18; Kirby Drake's story of seeing Fester in Bulldogs Bar & Grill in, 192–93; Kofoed expecting acquittal, 178, 195; Kofoed petitioning for mistrial on, 197–98; Kofoed's appeal overruled, 207; Rehmeier explaining verdict on, 196–97; Retelsdorf testifying about Kofoed discovering blood in Sampson's car, 187–89; ruling about Kofoed's pattern of forensic misconduct preceding, 172–77

extradition, of Reid and Fester, 97–98

FBI, 197; Kofoed's interview with, 186; Kush and corruption division of, 150, 219; Kush as secret informant for, 152, 198; reexamining another Kofoed case, 168–69

Fester, Greg, 79, 111, 133; admitting murders, 90, 132; appeals by, 219–20; arrest of, 77, 98; background of, 72–73; confessing to breaking into Stock home, 81; confessing to car thefts, 77–78, 80; discrepancies between stories of and Livers's confession, 124–25; extradition of, 97–98; false stories told by, 91, 116–17; implicating Will Sampson and Tom Todd as accomplices, 90–91, 116–17; in Kirby Drake's story, 118; lack of acquaintances in Nebraska, 101, 102, 103; on motive for Stock murders, 221; murder weapon destroyed by, 95; in police conspiracy theory, 99–100, 106; Reid and, 73–74, 82, 90, 92; Reid blaming murders on, 92, 96, 103; Reid denying accomplices besides, 96–99, 117; Reid telling about murder by, 78, 84, 103; Reid's letter to, 89, 90, 92–93; on the run, 74–77, 82–83; sentence of, 135, 220–21; statement before sentencing, 135

Fester, Greg, Sr., 75–76, 135

fingerprints: Livers giving, 25, 38; Reid worried about leaving, 78, 84; suspicions about Kofoed's uncanny successes with, 148–50, 154, 212; Todd giving, 100

Gabig, Christine, 35, 211; continuing as CSI, 220; defending Kofoed, 155, 185; investigating ring found at crime scene, 66–67

Georgi, Robert, 197

Gill, Susan, 24, 59

Glamann, Doug, 72

Godchaux, Josh, 71

Gonzalez, Brendan, 20, 143; body never found, 172, 219; Kofoed suspected of planting blood evidence in case of, 173–76, 178, 197, 209; Kofoed's discovery of blood of, 170–72, 171, 187

grand jury, investigating Stock murders, 159–63

Grazziano, Tony, 200–201

gunshot residue, 60

Hageman, Ashley, 59

Hale, Joseph, 31, 33, 184

Hale, Matthew, 36, 183–84
Hansen, Bobby, 208
Haugaard, Scott, 35–36, 40–41
Henk, Ivan, 20, 143, 170–72, 177, 219
Hergenrader, Justin, 27–29
Hernandez, Victor, 143
High, Alynn, 30–31, 33, 183
Hines, Gary, 104–6
Hines, Leland, 105–6
Horicon, Wisconsin, 72–76
Hornbacher, Michael, 142

initial hearings, for Livers and Sampson, 57–58
Iowa, vandalism of and thefts from home in, 104–6

Jeffrey, Tamarra, 27–29

Kaufhold, Bill, 62–63, 155, 211
Kavanagh, John, 153–54
Kehl, Betty, 71
Kelly, Bill, 207–8, 212
kidnapping, Paulding's story of Livers's plan for, 109, 116
Kleine, Don, 212
Kofoed, Bart, 208
Kofoed, David Wayne, *144,* 151, 164; appeal rejected, 207; background of, 139–41, 200, 209; convicted of evidence tampering, *196,* 197; on CSI message board, 198–200; CSIs under, 66, 147, 150, 185, 187; "discovery" of Brendan Gonzalez's blood, 170–71, *171,* 187; Dunning's support for, 154, 193–94; FBI investigation of, 168–69, 186; federal trial of, 165–66, 168; "finding" blood in Edwards's car, *210,* 210–11; "finding" blood in Will Sampson's car, 59–61, 143, 160–61; finishing sentence with house arrest, 206–8; "forgetting" to log blood found in Sampson's car, 156, 166–67; found to have fabricated Gonzalez blood sample, 173–76, 178, 217–18; at grand jury probe of Stock murders, 159–63; incarceration of, 202–8, *204;* internal affairs investigation of, 154–56, 158, 193; Kush accused of framing, 195–96, 198; Kush testifying against, *199;* Kush's complaints about, 148–50; misdating report on blood in Sampson's car, 154, 164, 166–68; motives of, 213; no audit of other casework by, 212; not admit-

ting guilt, 202, 206; not testifying in evidence tampering trial, 195, 197; pattern of forensic misconduct by, 149–50, 154, 165, 170, 172, 217–18; petitioning for mistrial, 197–98; polygraph of, 156–58, 197; post-incarceration life, 208; relations with press, 205, 207–8; reputation of, 12–13, 17, 59–60, 141–43; self-promotion by, 13, 145, 148–49; sentencing of, 200–202, *201;* state and federal charges against, 163–64; statement before sentencing, 201–2; suspiciousness of reexamination of Sampson's car by, 153, 160, 181, 188; taint on other murder cases, 209; taking over Stock murder scene, 14–15; terminated by Dunning, 197; testimony at federal trial, 166–67; testimony in pretrial proceedings about pattern of forensic misconduct, 175; tests of Will Sampson's car under, 34–35, *36;* theory on source of blood in Sampson's car, 146, 189; uncanny successes of, 149–50, 197, 212; used as example of police corruption, 209; victim-impact statements before sentencing of, 202; waiving jury trial, 178, 197–98. *See also* Douglas County crime lab; evidence tampering, Kofoed's trial for
Kofoed, Dolores, 165, 208
Kofoed, Richard Jerome, 139, 141, 159
Kreifel, Brad, 172–73
Krenz, Ryan, 79, 106; gun stolen from home of, 96, 102; murder weapons found in truck of, 93; Reid and Fester confessing to stealing truck of, 80, *82,* 82–83; ring found at crime scene given to, 69–71; truck in Drake's story of seeing Fester in Murdock Grill, 117–18, 192–93; truck used as getaway vehicle, *99*
Kush, Darnel: accused of framing Kofoed, 195–96, 198; at Douglas County crime lab, 147–48, 150, 219; as informant for FBI, 152, 198; suspicions about Kofoed, 146, 148–50, 155; testifying against Kofoed, *199*

Lambert, Bill, 39; continuing in law enforcement, 218; expecting evidence from Will Sampson's car, 34–35, 36–37, 61; getting Livers to confess, 45–47, 126–29; incompetent investigation by, 213; interrogating Fester, 80–82, 91; interrogating Livers, 23–25, 44, 47–48; interrogating Reid, 82–85, 92–97; investigating ring found at crime scene, 64–65, 69; investigating vandalism of and thefts from home in Iowa, 104–6; investigating Will Sampson, 30–33; Kofoed reexamining Sampson's car for, 61, 160; Kush sharing suspicions about Kofoed with, 149–50, 219; Livers's confession and, 48–51, 54–57, 94, 96; named in lawsuits, 145, 151; pressing Fester and Reid for accomplices' names, 84–85, 90–91; unwilling to give up on guilt of Livers and Sampson, 80–82, 99

lawsuits, Livers's and Sampson's, 145; requiring police training on low-functioning individuals, 216; Schenck named in, 151, 194; settlements of, 214, 216

Leahy, Ed, 154–58

Lefler, Steve: defending Kofoed at federal trial, 180, 189–90, *193,* 197; defense of Kofoed, 164–67, 195; and Kofoed petitioning for mistrial, 197–98; at Kofoed's conviction of evidence tampering, *196,* 197; on Kofoed's sentence, 201; post-trial life, 220; at pretrial proceedings about Kofoed's pattern of forensic misconduct, 174–75, 177; representing Kofoed in internal affairs investigation, 156; weakness of evidence tampering defense case, 192–95

Lincoln Community Corrections Center, Kofoed incarcerated at, 202–6, *205*

Livers, Barbara, 19, 125, 131, 215

Livers, Dave, 56–57, 126, 131, 215

Livers, Kenneth, 32

Livers, Matthew David, 22, *38;* alibi of, 59, 131; arrest of, 38; blood in Sampson's car used as evidence against, 144–45, 190–91; in Cass County Sheriff's conspiracy theory, 106–7, 132, 195–96; charges against dropped, 129–30, 132, 217; cooperating with investigation, 38, 44–46, 53–55; defense of, 58, 95, 124, 215; finding religion in jail, 109, 113; incarceration of, 55, 109, 112–14, 131; initial hearing for, 57–58; jobs of, 37, 39, 126–28, 215; Kofoed playing sympathizer of, 145–46, 162; lack of evidence against, 29, 64, 184; lawsuit by, 151, 214; likelihood of false confession by, 130, 214; mental limitations of, 23–24, 125–28, 214; motives attributed

to, 26, 37, 109; Nick Sampson and, 41, 114–15, 122; Paulding and, 63, 107–9, 111; polygraph of, 45–47, 127; post-trial life, 215; praising Reid for continuing to deny his presence at crime scene, 215; psychological profile of, 125–27; reaction to Stock murders, 24–26, 44; Reid denying knowledge of, 85–87, 93–94, 215; Schenck and Lambert unwilling to give up on guilt of, 80, 99, 103, 124, 132, 194, 217; Schenck and Lambert's interrogation of, 23–25, 45–48; at Stocks' service, 41, 43; threatened with death sentence, 46, 48; Todd denying contact with, 100–101; treated as prime suspect, 43, 52; trial scheduled for, 120; victim-impact statement before Kofoed's sentencing, 202; Will Sampson and, 30, 32. *See also* confession, Livers's

Mackey, George, 39

marijuana pipe, found outside Stocks' home, *10,* 11, 23, 83; DNA on, 65, 79; linked to Reid and Fester, 76, 124; in Livers's confession, 54, 57, 124

Martino, Mary, 66–68

Mayfield, Chad, 9

McHugh, Brian, 37

memorial service, for Stocks, 39, 41–43

Mickle, William "Mick," 159–60, 167

Mock, Clarence E., III, 217–18; benefits of prosecuting Kofoed, 197, 209; on Kofoed's pattern of forensic misconduct, 172–73, 175–76, 197; on Kofoed's sentence, 201; at Kofoed's trial for evidence tampering, 179–81, 185–89, 192–93, *193,* 195; prosecuting Kofoed for evidence tampering, 163, 165, 170, 179

Morrison, Keith, 165

Mortensen, Marge, 73

motives, Kofoed's, 213

motives, for Stock murders, 53; attributed to killers, 17–18, 32; attributed to Matt Livers, 24, 26, 37; curiosity about Livers's, 58–59; lack of, 100, 122; in Livers's confession, 50; no signs of robbery, 37, 62; Reid and Fester's, 221

Munnelly, Brian, 217

murders, Stocks': Livers's reaction to, 44

murder weapons, in Stock murders, 4–5, 11, 102, 111; Kofoed reexamining Sampson's car for evidence of, 160; Reid and Fester admitting disposing of, 95, 125;

murder weapons (*cont.*)
Reid and Fester's stories on sources of, 91, 93, 96, 102, 124; Reid's claims about, 92–93, 97; Retelsdorf looking for evidence of, 187–88; Rohr's investigation of, 122–23; Sampson's shotgun proved not to be, 52, *64*, 124; two guns used as, 124. *See also* ammunition

Murdock, Nebraska, 91; effects of Stock murders on, 132–34; Nick Sampson returning to, 216; Reid not aware of being in, 84–85, 117; Stocks as pillars of, 43; Stocks' murders in, 1, 41

Murphy, Mark, 69–70

Muskat, Lori, 41, 59, 114; marriage of, 115, 216; at Sampson's release, 120, 123

Nebraska: Fester's lack of friends in, 102–3; no previous CSI scandals in, 209; settling Livers's and Sampson's lawsuits, 214, 216

Nebraska State Patrol: blood in Sampson's car and, 153–54, 194; named in lawsuits, 145, 151, 214; role in investigation of Stocks' murders, 14, 17, 39, 79, 119; searching Will Sampson's car and apartment, 33–34; Soucie's criticism of, 121–22. *See also* Lambert, Bill

Nebraska Supreme Court: Fester and Reid appealing sentences to, 221; not auditing Kofoed's casework, 212; rejecting Kofoed's appeal, 207; on suspicion of Kofoed planting blood evidence in murder cases, 209–11

Niemeier, Amy, 168

O'Callaghan, Charlie, 106; anger at Livers recanting confession, 56–57; continuing in law enforcement, 218; interpretations of polygraphs, 45–47, 101–2, 118; intimidating Paulding, 106–8, 112; Livers's polygraph by, 45–47; named in lawsuits, 145, 151; second polygraph by, 55–56

O'Grady, Jessica: Edwards convicted of murdering, 219–20; Kofoed suspected of planting blood evidence of, 209–11

Olsen, Thomas, 136

Olson, Dean, 150, 200

Omaha Police Department, Kofoed joining as evidence tech, 141

Osgood, Jerry, 140

Palm, Colin, *119*, 129

palm prints, 38, 100

Palokangas, Gina, 186, 219

Pankonin, John, 157

parole: Kofoed not interested in, 202, 206; unlikely for Fester and Reid, 221

Paulding, Patrick "Ryan," 24, 63; Livers's friendship with, 107, 126; in police conspiracy theory, 111–12, 114, 217; polygraphs of, 108–10; shown crime scene photos, 110–11; story of Livers's plan for kidnapping Stocks, 109, 116; story of Livers's plan to kill Stocks, 111, 114; told he failed polygraph, 108–9

personality: Kofoed's, 140, 148, 150, 180–81, 190, 198, 209; Livers's, 32, 39, 108, 127, 128; Will Sampson's, 33

Peter, Val J., 132–33

Phillips, Chuck, 194

phone records: Livers's, 45, 56; Paulding's, 63; Reid's, 103; showing Livers's and Sampson's lack of contact, 122, 125; Todd's, 101, 116

photographs: Kofoed showing reporters crime scene, 207–8; of Livers's hands, arms, face, 38; of Will Sampson's car, 35

Plattsmouth Police Department, 196. *See also* Gonzalez, Brendan

Plzak, John, 75

Poggemeyer, Virgil, 9

police: false confessions and, 59–60, 126–29, 214; Livers's security work leading to trust in, 128; need for background checks for, 209; preferring to use Kofoed for forensic work, 212; Wisconsin's asking for news of unsolved homicides, 78. *See also* Cass County Sheriff's Office; Nebraska State Patrol

police corruption: FBI investigating, 152; Kofoed used as example of, 209

polygraphs: false interpretations of, 46–47, 101; Kirby Drake's, 118; Kofoed's, 156–58, 197; Livers's, 45–46, 55–56, 127; Paulding's, 108–10; Todd's, 101; Wilson's, 102

Potter, Michelle, 15, 180–81, 186

press: arrests of Livers and Sampson announced to, 52–53, *53;* coverage of initial hearings for Livers and Sampson, 57–59; coverage of Kofoed's federal trial, 165, 168; coverage of Kofoed's trial for evidence tampering, 179, 195–96; Kofoed talking to, 145, 146; on Kofoed's conviction, 197–98; Kofoed's relations with, 148, 207–8; on Livers and Sampson, 103, 122, 131; told about Reid and Fester, 98

Rehmeier, Charlie, 197–98
Rehmeier, Randall, 114, 119; dismissing
    charges against Livers, 129; explaining
    verdict on evidence tampering charge,
    196–97; Fester's sentence by, 135; im-
    portance of ruling on Kofoed's pattern
    of forensic misconduct, 177, 217–18; on
    Kofoed's pattern of forensic miscon-
    duct, 172, 178; Kofoed's sentence by,
    201–2; Kofoed's trial for evidence tam-
    pering under, 178, 193, 195; overseeing
    restoration of Cass County Courthouse,
    178–79; post-trial life, 217; Reid's sen-
    tencing by, 132–33, 137–38; rejecting
    Fester's appeal, 220; rejecting Kofoed's
    petition for mistrial, 197–98
Reid, Jessica, 63, 136; arrests of, 77–78,
    98; charged with bail jumping, 87–88;
    confessions of, 82–83, 103, 132;
    continued incarceration of, 220–21;
    denying accomplices besides Fester,
    84, 93–94, 96–99, 117, 215; denying
    knowing Livers, 85–87, 215; denying
    murders, 84–85; diary entry on murder
    of Wayne Stock, 89, 92–93, 137, 221;
    discrepancies between stories of and
    Livers's confession, 124–25; extradition
    of, 97–98; Fester and, 73–74, 80–81,
    90, 92–93; implicating Sampson, 99,
    114; mementos saved by, 89, 90, 92; in
    police conspiracy theory, 99–101, 103,
    106, 111; police intimidation of, 84–86,
    92–97; Rohr and, 79, 95, 102–3; on
    the run, 74–77, 82–83; sentencing of,
    132–33, 137–38, 220–21; statement
    before sentencing, 136–37; stealing
    cars, 74–75, 82–83; stories on Stock
    murders, 83, 95–97, 103; telling about
    Fester committing murder, 78, 84
Reinhold, Ed, 168–69
Retelsdorf, Clelland "CL," 15, 187, 211; con-
    tinuing as CSI, 220; on Kofoed discov-
    ering blood in Sampson's car, 152–53,
    187–89; Kofoed discovering blood in
    Sampson's car with, 156, 160–61, 166;
    with Kofoed on two suspicious cases,
    171, 175, 177
revenge, as motive attributed to Stocks'
    killer, 17
ring, found at crime scene, 62, 63, 67; as
    breakthrough in case, 121, 145; DNA on,
    79, 83; investigation of, 64–67; Reid
    and, 83, 87; traced to Cori and Ryan,
    69–71, 79

robbery, lack of, 9, 17, 37, 62, 137
Rohr, Jim, 71; as mediator at Reid's inter-
    rogation, 87, 92, 94, 103; post-trial
    life, 220; questioning Reid and Fester,
    77–79; Reid charged with bail jumping
    by, 87–88; verifying Reid's statements,
    102, 122–23
Roy, Jason, 77

Sampson, Crystal, 120
Sampson, Nick, 25, 39, 56, 121; alibi of,
    59, 120; arrest of, 51–52; blood in Will
    Sampson's car as evidence against,
    144–45, 190–91, 200; charges against
    dropped, 119–20, 122, 217; defense of,
    58–59, 95; initial hearing for, 57–59;
    job at Bulldogs Bar & Grill, 31, 117–19,
    122–23; Kofoed playing sympathizer of,
    145–46, 162; lack of evidence against,
    31, 64, 114, 120–22; lawsuit by, 145,
    216; Livers implicating in confession,
    45, 50–51, 53–56; in Paulding's story,
    111; in police conspiracy theory, 80,
    106, 195–96; police unwilling to give up
    on guilt of, 99, 103, 194, 217; post-trial
    life, 216; Reid denying knowledge of,
    85, 93–94; Reid naming as accomplice,
    86–87, 99; search for evidence against,
    30, 52–54, 100, 184, 200; settlements
    of lawsuit by, 214, 216; shotgun of, 52,
    64, 124; Soucie and, 114; at Stocks' ser-
    vice, 40–41; victim-impact statement
    before Kofoed's sentencing, 202
Sampson, William "Will," 25, 120; distant
    relationship with Stocks, 31–32; Fester
    claiming as accomplice, 90–91; not
    linked to Stock murders, 117, 182–83;
    in police conspiracy theory, 99–100,
    217; post-trial life, 220; Reid denying
    knowledge of, 85, 93–94; Schenck and
    Lambert interviewing, 30–32; search of
    car and apartment, 33–34, 52. See also
    car, Will Sampson's
Scalora, Mario, 129
Schattschneider, Craig, 75
Schenck, Earl D., Jr., 25; conspiracy theory
    of, 80, 95; disappointed by lack of
    evidence from Will Sampson's car, 34,
    36–37; focusing on Livers as suspect, 24,
    26, 29–30; interrogating Fester, 80–82,
    81; interrogating Livers, 23–25, 47–48;
    interrogating Reid, 82–85, 92–97; in-
    vestigating Will Sampson, 30–33; law
    enforcement background of, 20–21;

Schenck, Earl D., Jr. (*cont.*)
leading Livers to false confession, 48–
51, 214; Livers's confession and, 29–30,
45–47, 51, 53–54, 57, 80–82; music
aspirations of, 20–22, 218; named in
lawsuits, 145, 151, 194; Nick Sampson
arrested by, 51–52; picking Livers up,
44; post-trial life, 218; pressing Reid
and Fester for accomplices' names,
84–85, 90–91; Stock murders' investigation under, 9, 11, 20, 213; trying to
find evidence against Sampson, 29–30,
53–54; unwilling to give up on guilt of
Livers and Sampson, 80–82, 99, 194.
See also Cass County Sheriff's Office
Schneider, Sarah, 24–25, 131; interviewed
for Livers's psychological profile, 125; as
Livers's alibi, 59; Livers's relationship
with, 112–13, 126–27; post-trial life, 215
Schrieber, Mindy, 142–43
Sipple, Adam, 182–84
Smith, Gary, 34
Soucie, Jerry, *121,* 164; asserting Sampson's
innocence, 103–4, 114, 120–22; assigned
as public defender for Sampson, 58–59;
on CSI message board, 199–200; post-
trial life, 217; praise for, 130, 215; on
Sampson's release, 120–22, 217
Southwick, Rex, 9, 11
Stahlecker, Amy, 141–42
Standefer, Ralph, 108–10
State v. Kofoed. See evidence tampering,
Kofoed's trial for
Stecher, Joe, 159–60, 165, 167
Steele, Michelle. *See* Potter, Michelle
Steinheider, John, 58
Stock, Andy, 1; in business with father, 1,
6–7, 15, 217; discovery of parents' murders, 6–8; inheritance of, 37, 42–43; at
initial hearings for Livers and Sampson,
57–58; as last person to see parents, 42;
replacing parents' house, 217; satisfac-
tion with Reid and Fester's sentences,
138; victim's statement about parents'
murders, 133
Stock, Cassondra, 1
Stock family, 52, 63; accusations against
Livers, 127, 130–31, 215; Matt Livers as
black sheep of, 23–24, 48
Stock home, *16–18;* Andy tearing down
and replacing, 217; car reported speeding away from, 27–29; CSIs processing as crime scene, 14–17, 62; Fester

confessing to breaking into, 81; Livers
drawing diagram of, 55–56; murder-
ers' access to, 3, 15–17, *17,* 54, 96; not
robbed, 9, *18, 137*
Stock, Jim, 42, 59
Stock, Lorene, 22–23, 25–26, 43
Stock murders, 1–6, 9–11, 14; assumptions
about, 16–17; bloodiness of scene, *5,*
7–8, 14; discrepancies between facts of
and Livers's confession, 124; effects of,
132–34, 137, 215–16; Fester's stories
about, 91, 116–17; grand jury probe of
handling of, 159–63; incompetent investigation of, 213; Livers getting details
of, 56–57; Matt Livers's reactions to,
24–26; motives proposed for, 32; police
conspiracy theory on, 80, 95, 99–100,
106, 111–12, 116–18, 122–23, 192, 195–
96, 217; Reid's stories about, 84–85, 86,
92, 96–97; similarities of blood evidence
to Gonzalez case, 170–72, 197; victims'
statements by family, 132–33
Stock, Sharmon Drake, *40;* family of, 19–
20; memorial service for, 39, 41–43;
murder of, 1–6, 9–11, 14; nephew's
feud with, 22–23; Paulding's story of
Livers's plan for kidnapping, 109, 116;
popularity of, 19–20, 24, 39, 42–43;
Reid and Fester blaming one another
for shooting, 90, 103; Sampson's relationship with, 31–32; son's discovery of
murder of, 6–8; wealth of, 37, 48. *See*
also Stock murders
Stock, Steven, 37, 42, 57–58
Stock, Tammy. *See* Vance, Tammy Stock
Stock, Wayne, 19, *40;* blood found under
dash of Will Sampson's car (*See under*
blood); business of, 15, 42–43; family of, 19–20, 42; Fester admitting to
shooting, 90; Kofoed opening bag with
bloody shirt of, 186; Livers and, 22–23,
109; memorial service for, 39, 41–43;
Paulding's story of Livers's plan for kidnapping, 109, 116; popularity of, 19–20,
24, 39, 42–43; Reid admitting to shooting, 103; Reid's diary entry on murder
of, 89, 92–93; Sampsons' relationship
with, 25, 31–32; son's discovery of murder of, 6–8; wealth of, 37, 48. *See also*
Stock murders
Stock, Willard, 22–23, 43
Stoler, Alan, 135
Stone, Mike, 12

Strom, Lyle E., 166
suicide, ruled out, 9

Thomas (Fester's mysterious acquaintance in Nebraska), 80–81, 91, 102–3
Todd, Tom, 80; Fester fingering as accomplice, 90–91; lack of evidence against, 101, 116; in police conspiracy theory, 99–100, 102, 217
Torres, Russ, 154–58
truck-driving school, Livers's plan to attend, 55, 109
2XSalt Ministry, Kofoed working with, 208

Vance, Tammy Stock, 20, 37, 42
Vargas, Luis, 143
Veys, Don: Kofoed and, 155, 179–80; at Stock murder scene, 15–17
Vidrine, Mary and Francis, 76

Wacker, Jon, 43
Walmart, ring from crime scene traced to, 68–69
Watson, Matthew, 99–100, 118
wealth, Stocks', 1–2, 32
weapons: Kofoed's uncanny successes finding fingerprints on, 212; Nick Sampson's shotgun, 52, *64;* not found in

Livers's house, 52; shotgun and ammunition stolen from Hines's home, 105; Todd denying firing, 101; Will Sampson not owning, 32. *See also* murder weapons, in Stock murders
Wendel, Jonathan, 80, 101–2
Weyers, Sandy, 19, 37, 62, 151; interrogating Paulding, 106–8, 110–12; leaving law enforcement, 218; Schenck and, 20–21; Stocks' murders and, 9, 11; trying to prove conspiracy theory, 100–101, 106, 118
Wheeler, Brenda, 156–57
Williams, Mark, 35
Wilson, Anthony "A. J.," 77; Reid living with, 87–88; Reid's belongings taken from house, 88–89, *90*
Wilson, Fred, 100–102
Wisconsin: Paulding denying knowing anyone in/from, 109–10; Sampson's lack of contact with anyone in, 122; Todd denying knowledge of, 101
Wraxall, Brian, 173–75, 220
wristwatch, stolen from Hines's home, 105–6

Zastrow, Cori, 69, 79
Zastrow, Louise, 79